Britain's Withdrawal from East of Suez

The Politics of Retrenchment

Jeffrey Pickering
Associate Professor of Political Science
Kansas State University
Manhattan
Kansas

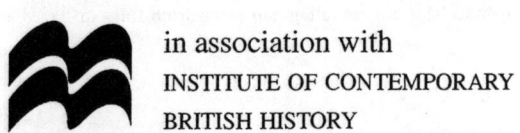

in association with
INSTITUTE OF CONTEMPORARY
BRITISH HISTORY

First published in Great Britain 1998 by
MACMILLAN PRESS LTD
Houndmills, Basingstoke, Hampshire RG21 6XS and London
Companies and representatives throughout the world

A catalogue record for this book is available from the British Library.

ISBN 0–333–69526–7

 First published in the United States of America 1998 by
ST. MARTIN'S PRESS, INC.,
Scholarly and Reference Division,
175 Fifth Avenue, New York, N.Y. 10010

ISBN 0–312–21436–7

Library of Congress Cataloging-in-Publication Data
Pickering, Jeffrey, 1967–
Britain's withdrawal from east of Suez : the politics of
retrenchment / Jeffrey Pickering.
p.   cm. — (Contemporary history in context)
Includes bibliographical references (p.   ) and index.
ISBN 0–312–21436–7 (cloth)
1. Asia—Foreign relations—Great Britain. 2. Great Britain-
-Foreign relations—Asia. 3. Great Britain—Foreign
relations—1945– 4. Great Britain—Colonies—History.
5. Decolonization. I. Title. II. Series: Contemporary history in
context series.
DS33.4.G7P53 1998
327.4105—dc21   98–4957
                                                                         CIP

© Jeffrey Pickering 1998

All rights reserved. No reproduction, copy or transmission of this publication may be made without written permission.

No paragraph of this publication may be reproduced, copied or transmitted save with written permission or in accordance with the provisions of the Copyright, Designs and Patents Act 1988, or under the terms of any licence permitting limited copying issued by the Copyright Licensing Agency, 90 Tottenham Court Road, London W1P 9HE.

Any person who does any unauthorised act in relation to this publication may be liable to criminal prosecution and civil claims for damages.

The author has asserted his right to be identified as the author of this work in accordance with the Copyright, Designs and Patents Act 1988.

This book is printed on paper suitable for recycling and made from fully managed and sustained forest sources.

10 9 8 7 6 5 4 3 2 1
07 06 05 04 03 02 01 00 99 98

Printed and bound in Great Britain by
Antony Rowe Ltd, Chippenham, Wiltshire

For Kay, who taught me to swim

Contents

General Editor's Preface		ix
Acknowledgements		xi
1	Introduction: Perspectives on the Withdrawal from World Power	1
2	Decline and the Politics of Retrenchment	18
3	The Return to Normalcy: Postwar British Strategy	43
4	Holding Course: The Labour Government of 1945–51 and the Struggle over Strategy	60
5	Reappraisal: The Suez Crisis and its Aftermath, 1957–60	88
6	Setting the Stage: Longer-Term Implications of Suez	118
7	Relinquishing World Power: Britain's Financial Crises of 1966–7	150
8	Conclusions: Politics, History, and the East of Suez Decision	177
Notes		194
Index		224

General Editor's Preface

In the aftermath of the Second World War successive British governments found themselves trying to juggle three major defense commitments. To the defense of empire through the long-established network of Mediterranean and east of Suez bases was added the burden of the British Army of the Rhine (BAOR) and of maintaining British influence in the councils of the world through possession of a nuclear deterrent. To British planners of the 1940s and early 1950s the former was vital to preserve the commodity trading interests of the Sterling Area and particularly the flow of oil from the Middle East. But the commitment involved in the BAOR or nuclear weapons was no less important. However, all were costly. The British had repeated rows with the Germans over stationing costs in the 1950s, and were not above threatening to scale back their commitment significantly to try to get their way with Chancellor Adenauer. The merits of the expensive effort to maintain the nuclear deterrent were also questioned, particularly in the Labour Party. After the cancellation of Blue Streak in 1960 had signalled the end of a fully independent nuclear deterrent the party leadership broadly concluded that the effort to maintain a nuclear capability should be abandoned. Instead, as Harold Wilson told the House of Commons on 31 January 1963,

> Our conventional troops are stretched out dangerously as a tenuous red line all over the world. Their security and their contribution to our still scattered defence should count more in the final reckoning than nuclear prestige... We can, with our limited resources, either pay for the pretence of the nuclear deterrent or honour our commitments in NATO and elsewhere. But we cannot do both.

His inclination, as this speech made clear, was to sacrifice the nuclear of the three defense commitments. However, instead, his first government was to see the abandonment of the historic east of Suez commitment. The desire to maintain an out-of-area capacity remained after the withdrawal was announced in 1968, but the ability to exercise this was greatly reduced.

There was, however, as Jeffery Pickering shows, nothing inevitable about this decision. Too many of the studies on the east of Suez decision have presented it simply in whiggish fashion as the culmination of some ineluctable process of progressive financial restraint. But, as Pickering points out, economic overstretch was a constant, dating back to well before 1939, indeed, was a problem wrestled with by the Cabinet committee on estimates in 1908. Nor did it necessarily point only to retrenchment east of Suez, rather than, for instance, on the nuclear front. In themselves economic factors, therefore, are not sufficient to explain why the decision to retrench was taken then, or in that way. Instead, economic factors can be seen as engines driving ever more creative attempts at stretching limited resources: defense agreements after colonial departure; the thinning out of bases; the miracles of improvization during confrontation in 1963–6. Meanwhile, whatever the murmurings on the backbenches, the consensus within the policy-making elites in officialdom and both parties was to maintain the east of Suez role. In the end this consensus was to fracture sufficiently, and it was the east of Suez commitment, of Britain's three major defense commitments, that was dropped.

The aim of the *Contemporary History in Context* series is to critically reappraise our understanding of the recent past. This book draws upon new research both to address the historical record and to engage with the theoretical literature on foreign policy decision-making in government. In the process, by interweaving domestic political with external and economic factors, Pickering provides a more sophisticated explanation than any hitherto of how the British decision to withdraw from the east of Suez bases came to be taken.

Peter Catterall
London

Acknowledgements

I have benefited from the insight and the assistance of many in writing this book. James Christoph, William Thompson, and Norman Furniss supported this project from its earliest stages and have provided invaluable advice along the way. They also read the entire manuscript, in one version or another, as did Robert A. Baumann, Peter Catterall, Jeffrey Hart, and John Lovell. I want to thank them for their useful suggestions. Needless to say, I alone am responsible for any inadequacies which remain.

Valuable counsel has also been offered over recent years by Joel Glassman, Frederic Pearson, David B. Robertson, and J. Martin Rochester. Peter Catterall has been a wonderful series editor, providing every manner of assistance and advice. Michael Dockrill, Saki Dockrill, and Michael Kandiah deserve much thanks as well, for they were extremely generous and helpful while I researched parts of this book in Britain. I would also like to express my appreciation to those participants who were kind enough to discuss the events with me, particularly Sir Frank Cooper, Sir Patrick Nairne, and J.K. Wright.

Of course, much thanks must go to my family, especially John D. Pickering, Susan Pickering, and Jane Pickering, whose love and encouragement have sustained me in this as in so many endeavors. My mother, Susan, deserves special mention, for she has often had more faith in my writing than I have. Finally, it is to my wife, Rachel, that I owe the deepest debt of gratitude, for putting her career on hold and allowing me the time and solitude to complete this book.

1 Introduction: Perspectives on the Withdrawal from World Power

For over two decades after the Second World War, Britain maintained a great chain of fueling stations, air-bases, and military outposts stretching eastward from the Suez Canal through the Indian Ocean and on to Hong Kong in the Far East. Commonly termed the east of Suez role, this chain was considered vital for the nation's material welfare and an essential underpinning of the country's greatness. By the late 1960s British policymakers had decided to abandon this role and all that it symbolized to the British. In hindsight, the reasons they did so seem transparent. The country's relative economic and military capabilities eroded throughout the twentieth century and, hence, withdrawal can be interpreted as part of the linear progression of British decline. Given changes in the international political environment and Britain's dwindling international influence, the contraction of British power appears natural and perhaps even unavoidable. Yet, rarely is the intersection between historical inevitability and a critical policy decision so clear-cut. Numerous policy options remained open to decision-makers at this time, and the decision to retrench would remain controversial for many years afterward. Britain's withdrawal from east of Suez commitments is thus a more complex tale than is commonly appreciated. This book analyzes the domestic and international factors that intertwined to convince British policymakers to take this decision and, in the process, dramatically influence the future of British foreign policy.

While one goal is to provide a more exhaustive explanation of the British retreat from east of Suez, this work is motivated by more than historical curiosity. It also provides insight into the more general political phenomenon: the process of retrenchment or of withdrawing from an overseas military role. As might be expected, this process can have major global ramifications. When a declining power departs from its strategic positions overseas, it can have an immense impact on the stability of the regions concerned, even the entire globe. The retreat from overseas power may also, of course, have significant political and economic repercussions in the retrenching state. If nothing else, such a transition will likely be a tremendous psychological rite of passage for a people weaned on the privileges that international might can bestow.

This topic also has much contemporary relevance. In the United States, for example, questions are increasingly raised over whether that country should maintain, or indeed is capable of maintaining, far-flung military commitments.[1] Although US retrenchment is unlikely in the foreseeable future, merely raising the possibility underscores the significant role that a major power's overseas military network may play in shaping global affairs, and the potentially wide-ranging consequences of its abandonment. If such a withdrawal were to take place, even if paced slowly, the after-effects would substantial. Diplomatic, economic, and strategic reverberations would be felt across the globe, and the entire architecture of world politics would be radically transformed. The purpose of this work is not to detail what such reverberations might be, for they will vary greatly depending on international circumstances. Rather, it is to delineate the factors that can compel the leaders of a powerful nation to take this dramatic step. In other words, it explains the influences that can convince policymakers to relinquish something which surely has enormous symbolic importance at home and strategic importance abroad – the nation's overseas military network.

Of course, what holds true for post-1945 Britain may not hold true for other nations at other times. Yet it should be remembered that Britain possessed the most extensive overseas military network the world had ever seen throughout the nineteenth and the first half of the twentieth centuries. There is little question that Britannia truly did rule the waves for over a century and a half, controlling key strategic waterways and littorals throughout the world. No other country derived such immense benefits from its overseas role as Britain did at this time, and perhaps none ever has. No other power wielded the same amount of global influence. And undergirding it all was a sprawling chain of naval stations and military complexes, the barbicans of world power. Given Britain's relatively recent departure from this network of military outposts and the vast scale of the nation's overseas commitments in comparison to all prior examples, an understanding of the British case should allow us to see the essential elements of the retrenchment process in action. By doing so, it will provide insight into other examples of the phenomenon, particularly contemporary examples. At the least, we may conclude that any grand theory of the causes of retrenchment in the contemporary world must, at a minimum, fit the British case.

In the pages that follow, Britain's post-1945 east of Suez role is described and the explanations for retrenchment currently found in the international relations literature are summarized. Outlining the network of military outposts that Britain retained after the Second World War provides a more concrete image of the phenomenon examined, while also underscoring the vast scale of the change under study. Reviewing recent perspectives on the significance of great powers' military networks abroad provides the initial building blocks for this analysis.

THE EAST OF SUEZ NETWORK

Britain's military role abroad after 1945 lay along the central artery of European trade established from the late fourteenth century, from the Red Sea and the Persian Gulf into the Indian Ocean and on to China.[2] In the old world, empires had risen to glory and collapsed into ashes along this 'trans-Suez' arc. Later, the riches of the Far East were opened up to the West along this oceanic route, and it was here that the European powers first established dominance of the seas.[3] More importantly for this study, the trade and later military networks that the British established provided a crucial underpinning for the country's growth as a world power from the late seventeenth century.[4] As such, Britain's role in this area became, in many ways, interwoven with the fabric of the nation. Well into the twentieth century, a presence east of Suez was thought to be crucial for the nation's security and its vitality. It should not be surprising, then, that British statesmen would only reluctantly abandon the military network east of Suez.

Before the Second World War, the hub of Britain's military presence abroad had been India. In the trite jargon of strategic commentators of the 1930s, its was the 'keystone of the imperial arch'.[5] India was not only geographically central to Britain's military network extending across the Indian Ocean, it was the focal point of communications and administration, a massive supply center, a place for acclimatizing troops, and, most importantly, it was the home of the mighty Indian Army. For all intents and purposes, the Indian Army was the strategic reserve for the British Empire in the East. In 1914, for example, its strength of 160 000 fighting troops was one-half of Britain's peacetime worldwide military strength.[6]

Yet, Indian independence and the loss of what had been the undergirding of empire, the Indian Army, in 1947, did not mark the end of Britain's international ambitions. A dense, but thinning, network of British fueling stations, air-bases, and military complexes continued to straddle the Indian Ocean after 1945. After the departure from the Indian subcontinent, the three key nodes on the east of Suez network became the Suez base in the Middle East, Singapore in the Far East, and the Trincomalee naval station in Ceylon as a midway point. When Britain was forced from its Middle Eastern and Indian Ocean strongholds in the wake of the Suez crisis in 1956, British military planners simply adapted the groundplan, with Aden and the Maldive Islands soon established as the first two nodes in the network. Of course, the chain consisted of dozens of smaller outposts as well – in the Persian Gulf, Hong Kong, Borneo, Kenya, and Indian Ocean islands such as Diego Garcia and the Seychelles. Overall, the east of Suez network after 1945 was a vast, sprawling, interconnected chain of bases which policymakers felt to be necessary to safeguard British interests in the postwar world.

It must be emphasized that after the loss of the nation's most prized imperial possession, India, these interests were principally strategic and economic, not colonial.[7] In essence, Britain's time-honored system of imperial defense was refashioned to fit the Cold War context in the late 1940s. The network of bases in the Indian Ocean area was considered a valuable bulwark against Soviet expansion into the Middle East and Africa as well as being a potential launching pad to attack more peripheral, and seemingly more vulnerable, areas of the Soviet Union during a global war.[8] Yet, its utility in the struggle against communism was not this network of bases' chief strategic purpose.

As DeWitt Armstrong explains, postwar statesmen continued to feel that 'Britain's foremost vital national interest [was] to keep the sea communications of the island with the supplying regions of the world continuously open.'[9] Conscious of the central role that overseas commerce played in the nation's past economic success, Britain's postwar policymakers felt that without access to food, raw materials, and oil from abroad, the British economy would grind to a halt. Supporting this belief was Britain's dependence on oil from the Middle East, which is illustrated in the import figures for 1949–50. In that year, Britain imported £22.1 million worth of crude petroleum from Kuwait and Bahrain, £25.4 million from Saudi Arabia, Iraq, and Iran, and only £8.4 million from the rest of the world.[10]

Thus, the country was dependent upon imports for its economic survival, and sea power, buttressed by a chain of strategic outposts, had historically kept the waterways of the world open for Britain. Even when defense strategists began to consider using air power instead of the navy to safeguard the lines of communication flowing eastward, a network of bases was thought to be necessary for much the same reason as it was for the fleet – for supplies, repair, and increased mobility. As Phillip Darby observes, 'The instrument of power might change then, but it was the principle that the lines of communication must be defended which mattered and this was seen to rest firmly on the maintenance of the great chain of bases.'[11]

Nor did the advent of nuclear weapons alter British decision-makers' calculations on the value of east of Suez bases. It became accepted wisdom in Britain's foreign policy establishment in the 1950s and 1960s that in the event of a devastating nuclear strike on the British Isles, the country would retaliate using conventional and nuclear arsenals located at sea and on its overseas bases. The possibilities held by such 'broken-back' nuclear warfare seemed to enhance the country's deterrent capability substantially.[12] Thus, instead of underscoring the limitations of fixed bases abroad, the dawn of the nuclear age bestowed overseas positions with a new prominence.

There was a further, less tangible, reason why British arms remained scattered across the Middle and the Far East. The network of bases spanning the Indian Ocean held a great deal of historical and emotional significance for the public and policymakers alike. It was, at once, the core and the broader symbol of the country's 'world role.'[13] What is more, Britain's position as a world power was commonly perceived to rest upon this role. For possession of a mighty chain of bases was not only crucial for the country strategically and economically, it also seemed to grant Britain a significant, at times even a decisive, voice in world affairs. Thus, much more than military complexes and dockyards lay along the lines of communication flowing across the Indian Ocean.[14] The country also had a considerable psychological investment in this string of outposts, and the underbrace it was perceived to provide for the country's great power status. Given the broader meaning commonly attached to the east of Suez network during this period, this network will often be referred to as Britain's global or world role in the pages that follow.[15]

In sum, then, post-1945 British policymakers felt that a military presence in the Indian Ocean area was vitally important for the country's welfare. Over the course of the postwar era, however, Britain's global role showed increasing signs of strain. As the economic and military foundations of British power slowly crumbled, questions about the sagacity of supporting an extensive overseas military role became increasingly common and forceful. Consequently, this analysis of Britain's east of Suez role essentially focuses on the tension which arises between relative decline and the continuing desire for world status. Contemporary international relations literature tends to focus on the causes of such tension as well as its consequences, both strategic and economic. In contrast, this study concentrates on the principal remedy for this strain by looking at the factors that convince leaders to abandon overseas commitments. As the next section reveals, recent literature on the great powers offers little insight into the process of retrenchment.

OVEREXTENSION AND RETRENCHMENT

The overseas military roles assumed by great powers have been a topic of particular interest to international relations scholars. Yet, the literature tends to emphasize the perils facing nation-states with extensive military networks abroad. As Paul Kennedy has perhaps most convincingly demonstrated, the leaders of great powers often tend to take on overseas commitments which exceed the state's economic and military capacities.[16] Worse still, they have had a tendency to cling to such commitments tenaciously even as the tide of history turns against the nation and other actors begin to surpass it in conventional measures of power. This situation has been termed the dilemma of overextension, and historically great powers have rarely been able to escape it.[17]

Primarily because of its assumed consequences, overextension is the principal focus of recent literature on the great powers and their overseas positions. There are obvious strategic dangers when a state attempts to uphold far-flung commitments which are beyond its capabilities. Adversaries can take advantage of thin spots in the overextended state's strategic network, and military setbacks abroad demonstrate more than overstretch. They also reveal the overextended country's military and economic weakness and undermine its international standing.

Introduction

Perhaps even more important in the longer term, overextension is thought to have deleterious consequences for a nation's economy. Building on the work of Robert Gilpin, among others, Paul Kennedy argues that if a

> nation overextends itself geographically and strategically; if, even at a less imperial level, it chooses to devote a large proportion of its total income to 'protection,' leaving less for 'productive investment,' it is likely to find its economic output slowing down, with dire implications for its long-term capacity to maintain both its citizens' consumption demands and its international position.[18]

William R. Thompson and Gary Zuk underscore the latter point, pithily outlining the wider implications of what they call the 'territorial trap' of excessive and overly costly strategic commitments (in other words, overextension):

> The historical evidence suggests that it is at least highly probable that [a great power's] global network will become encrusted with the barnacles of unproductive commitments. As in the case of barnacle-encrusted hulls, the outcome is a sluggish vehicle which no longer performs as originally intended nor as well as it might. To continue the metaphor, the captains and crews of sleeker, less burdened vehicles are encouraged to challenge the ponderous leader and give race. The dynamics of the 'territorial trap' thereby contribute to the perpetuation of the cyclical sequence of the rise and decline of world leadership.[19]

It is such wider ramifications for a state's global standing which make overextension an intriguing puzzle in the contemporary study of international politics. This is particularly so since many observers feel that throughout the 1990s the United States has shown signs of economic strain induced by the tremendous political, economic, and military burdens the country carried during the Cold War.[20]

There is little question that Britain suffered from geographic and strategic overextension throughout much of the twentieth century. In fact, Kennedy argues that Britain's numerous overseas military responsibilities, from patrolling the slave trade in Africa, collecting debts in Latin America, and maintaining a vast string of military outposts worldwide, began to outstrip the country's military capabilities as early as 1856, at the end of the Crimean War.[21] As C.J. Bartlett notes, the First Sea Lord fretted at this time: 'The undeniable fact is that we are doing or endeavouring to do much more than our force is sufficient for. It is fortunate that the world is not larger, for there is no other limit to the service of the fleets.'[22] Complaints such as this were not unusual as the nineteenth century wore on. Rather, the First Sea Lord's trepidation is in many ways representative of growing concern within the British military over the scope of Britain's defense commitments and the armed forces' subsequent overstretch.

The international strategic landscape would only become more crowded in the late nineteenth and early twentieth centuries as rival states industrialized. Germany, Japan, France, and the United States began to build substantial naval fleets at this time, both to symbolize their newfound might and to reap the benefits from overseas trade which Britain had monopolized for so long. Yet, Britain expanded even further as its relative economic and military position in the world waned. In fact, the British Empire reached its territorial zenith not in the mid-nineteenth century, at the pinnacle of Britain's relative power, but in 1933, just as the sun was about to set on Britain's global pre-eminence.[23] Not surprisingly, then, British policymakers became increasingly preoccupied with the yawning gap that existed between the country's vast array of overseas commitments and its economic and military capabilities in the first half of the twentieth century.[24] In 1920, for example, General Sir Harry Wilson, who represented the General Staff, warned the Cabinet:

> I would respectfully urge [that] our policy [be] brought into some relation with [the] military forces available to it. At present this is far from the case... I cannot too strongly press on the Government the danger, the extreme danger, of His Majesty's Army being spread all over the world, strong nowhere, weak everywhere, and with no reserve to save a dangerous situation or avert a coming danger.[25]

Despite repeated warnings such as that by General Wilson and the specter of rapid rearmament in Germany, Japan, and Italy, the British rearmed only reluctantly during the interwar period while clinging stubbornly to their overseas possessions. Even as German troops swept across Central Europe in the late 1930s, the British government refused to abandon its outposts in the periphery and concentrate its forces on protecting the homeland.[26]

Britain's international position was only undermined further in the Second World War. Victory in 1945 was in many ways illusory, and was in no way synonymous with the preservation of British power.[27] For, in securing victory, Britain had stretched its productive capacities to its limits, running down gold and dollar reserves, exhausting industrial machinery, and selling off one-third of the nation's overseas assets, which had long been essential for the balance of payments. Britain emerged from the Second World War economically devastated, going from the world's second largest creditor nation in 1939 to its largest debtor in 1945. Moreover, it was clearly in the political shadow of the world's two new superpowers, the US and the USSR.[28] Yet, despite evident political and economic decline and concern about overextension stretching back nearly a century, the country's overseas military network was reassembled in essentially its pre-war form soon after hostilities were terminated. By August 1945, all of the possessions lost in the war were back in British hands. British troops, airbases, and naval stations sprawled across North Africa, the Middle East, and Southeast Asia. Consequently, a widening breach between the country's overseas commitments and its economic and military capabilities was a defining feature of British defence policy after 1945.[29] As early as 1948, for example, Field Marshall Montgomery, Commander of the Imperial General Staff, would inform the Minister of Defence: 'I had been forty years in the army and never had I known the services reduced to such a perilous condition in relation to their commitments. I said we had sunk to the lowest depths.'[30]

This long history of overextension can be partly explained by the tendency of both British policymakers and the general populace to take the country's military positions abroad for granted, assuming that British arms and production will invariably be strong enough to uphold such a role. Sociologists might term this tendency a cultural 'hangover,' since the legacy of the country's past glory undoubtedly weighed heavily upon British policymakers after 1945. A deeply ingrained maritime tradition also played a role in the continuation of the east of Suez role, as did overextension itself, for the pitting of 'short bayonets against long odds' occurred so frequently in British imperial history that it seemed to become something of a national tradition.[31]

It is at this point, during the post-1945 period, that this analysis of Britain's overseas military role begins. Neither the extent of Britain's overextension nor the economic and strategic consequences of such overstretch are measured. These considerations have been studied extensively elsewhere.[32] Rather, this work analyzes the reasons why British leaders eventually decided to rectify the imbalance between the nation's power and its policy by withdrawing from the east of Suez role. In a sense, it might be said that it is an analysis of the factors which cured the cultural 'hangover' in post-1945 Britain.

Of course, a nation may suffer from strategic overstretch even after it has abandoned its military positions overseas, particularly if it assumes heavy defense burdens in its immediate neighborhood. But withdrawal from such a network is perhaps the most decisive step leaders can take to bring the nation's power and its policy into closer correlation. More importantly, the abandonment of a global military network carries tremendous symbolic importance. It denotes, in many ways, the transition away from world power.

There is little doubt that this transition was one of the most momentous episodes in twentieth-century British foreign policy. The decision to withdraw from the nation's overseas military network, commonly called the east of Suez decision, discarded centuries of history. Although Britain retained scattered possessions around the world after retrenchment, such as British Honduras, the Falkland Islands, and Hong Kong, it no longer had a fixed network of strategic outposts designed solely for the purpose of extending British influence. It is also true that the country would continue to send forces to distant parts of the globe such as the Falklands or Kuwait after it had withdrawn from east of Suez bases, but such actions were spasmodic and limited in scope. Both the permanent facilities undergirding Britain's capacity for global reach and the desire to possess such a capacity disappeared with the decision to abandon the east of Suez network. With them the country's ability to wield either continuous or decisive influence in a region outside of its own evaporated. After the east of Suez decision in 1968, Britain became foremost a European, and not a global, actor.[33]

Such a transition is a defining moment for any declining country, a moment this study labels retrenchment. Although the term retrenchment has a broader, pre-existing definition which would allow it to describe any limited withdrawal from overseas positions, it is given a more specific operational definition in this work. Retrenchment denotes the complete abandonment of an overseas military role based upon a network of strategic commitments and outposts. And, as such, it should be considered to be very different from the numerous and sometimes significant restructurings of policy which are designed to perpetuate an overseas presence.

British policymakers, for example, attempted to streamline east of Suez commitments almost continuously after 1945, decreasing the number of men and volume of material which were assumed necessary to safeguard the country's interests in the area. The scope of the overseas military role also gradually narrowed. Yet, these adjustments were intended to correct flaws which hampered Britain's ability to carry out its global responsibilities. They did not alter the basic principles underlying post-1945 British foreign policy. Most importantly, these policy changes did not transform the ingrained belief among both policymakers and the general public that a permanent overseas military role was intrinsically valuable and that it somehow enhanced the nation's international standing.[34]

Thus, there is a fundamental difference between the numerous modifications to Britain's military network abroad over the course of the twentieth century and the east of Suez decision: the aim of policy alterations before 1968 was to strengthen or at least prolong the life of Britain's east of Suez military role, whereas the only purpose of retrenchment was to dismantle it. The differentiation of these two types of policy change draws upon the work of Charles Hermann and Richard Rose, who provide useful typologies that distinguish minor policy changes, such as adjustments in the means used to implement a policy or in a policy's scope, from more meaningful changes which alter the state's basic goals.[35] In the text which follows, the term retrenchment will be used interchangeably with that of the east of Suez decision, for both signify the abandonment of a nation's permanent overseas military role and, in a sense, global power.

Surprisingly, although a great deal of attention has been given to the phenomenon of strategic overstretch, an analytical framework explaining why leaders would choose to abandon a military network abroad has not been advanced. The variables which lead statesmen to maintain defense commitments long after the economic and military means to support them have dwindled away have, on the other hand, been thoroughly analyzed. Among the considerations said to produce overextension are: the poor quality of information given to decision-makers, which leads to faulty calculations of the state's power;[36] societal groups which penetrate the decision-making structure and push for expansion;[37] the competition among overseas bureaucracies and their drive for departmental aggrandizement;[38] the attempt to balance rival powers;[39] the existence of a 'strategic culture' which espouses the benefits of extensive overseas commitments, a culture created at an earlier period by overzealous national elites who were attempting to gain support for expansion;[40] the tendency for elites in declining states to seek strength and credibility in the periphery to compensate for weakness in the core;[41] and the existence of a dominant 'model' in international politics, based upon the state which has made the greatest gains in contemporary world affairs, which suggests that the maintenance of extensive overseas commitments is a wise policy course.[42]

It might be expected that considerable insight into the retrenchment process could be gained by examining the causes of overextension. After all, overextension and retrenchment are in many ways intertwined phenomena, each being conceptually at least the reverse of the other. And, ultimately, the political pillars supporting overextension would have to give way before there could be any substantial withdrawal from overseas positions. Yet, this is not the case. As plausible as each of the explanations listed is for overextension, none offers a great deal of insight into Britain's postwar retrenchment.

Any contention that poor information caused British leaders to overestimate their country's economic and military capacities, thus leading to strategic overstretch, for example, is inaccurate. As the following chapters demonstrate, British decision-makers had a very solid grasp of their country's relative economic and military decline. Thus, an improvement in the quality of the information given to policymakers did not contribute to their decision to abandon the east of Suez commitments. The role of domestic pressure groups can be considered negligible in this decision as well. Britain's foreign policy apparatus has been remarkably insular over the postwar era.[43] As a result, the likelihood that societal pressure groups could have compelled British decision-makers either to hold on to overseas commitments or to abandon them is remote at best. If anything, Britain's economic elite, which had long-standing and usually profitable ties to the Empire/Commonwealth, would more likely be expected to resist retrenchment than to advocate it.[44]

The influence of advocacy groups within the state, however, was quite different. Overseas bureaucracies, such as the Foreign Office, the Commonwealth Relations Office, the Colonial Office, and the armed service departments, had important interests served by a military presence east of Suez. Not only did the stabilizing role that the British military played in the region help to lubricate diplomatic relations in the area, it also worked to expand the overseas departments' power in Whitehall. As might be expected, then, these departments played a prominent role in the perpetuation of Britain's military role abroad after 1945, in part because any diminution of the overseas role would reduce their budgets and their influence. The potency of the overseas departments is thus important in the east of Suez decision, but only in a negative sense. Reformers would have to overcome bureaucratic resistance before there could be any substantial revision of Britain's overseas commitments.

Another explanation given for overextension, power balancing among the great powers, adds to our understanding of why Britain's overseas military role persisted in the post-1945 era. There is little doubt that British decision-makers felt that military installations east of Suez provided a bulwark against Soviet aggression in the Middle and the Far East.[45] Moreover, unlike Europe and East Asia, the east of Suez network lay in a relatively placid niche in the global competition between the superpowers. Except in crises such as the Suez episode in 1956, superpower activity in the Indian Ocean area was limited in the first two and a half decades after 1945.

Yet, while the global balance of power adds to our understanding of why Britain's overseas military role endured in the age of the superpowers, it does not provide much insight into why British decision-makers chose to abandon this role. The need to provide a buffer against potential Soviet aggression remained as essential in 1968, when the decision to retrench was made, as it had been in the preceding two decades. It was in this year, after all, that the Soviet Union invaded Czechoslovakia. Tensions between the East and the West had not yet eased as they would in the 1970s with détente. And even in the 1970s, as Soviet–US rivalry began to cool down, British and American policy pundits continued to be troubled by the strategic void left in the Indian Ocean area after Britain's departure.[46] The need for a western presence in the region obviously had not diminished, and the continuing strategic void is one indication that neither the Soviet Union nor the United States had successfully replaced Britain in the area. Thus, the global environment which both justified and allowed for Britain's east of Suez role was still present in 1968.

Another variable which is supposed to buttress overextension – what Charles Kupchan has termed a 'strategic culture' – clearly contributed to the maintenance of Britain's world role after 1945.[47] A strategic culture, again, is said to be present in a nation when the virtues of military ventures and positions abroad are exalted, particularly among the political elite. In post-1945 Britain, this culture centered on the overriding goal of preserving Britain's greatness.[48] And since the overseas military network was assumed to undergird the country's great power status, the permanence of this network was accepted as an article of faith by successive postwar governments. Such ingrained beliefs figured into the east of Suez decision because they obviously would have to be discarded, or at least worn down, before the decision to retrench could be taken.

Overextension has also been blamed on the tendency of statesmen in declining nations to compensate for weakness in the core by emphasizing the nation's military role on the periphery. In a sense, the east of Suez role, along with other symbols of power such as the nuclear deterrent and sterling's parity with the dollar, did help to keep Britain at the top table of international diplomacy in an era when Britain's relative economic and military capabilities were rapidly dwindling.[49] It was, as was just noted, considered an integral component of the nation's great power position. The emphasis given to the nation's role on the periphery is thus, in this case at least, intertwined with a strategic culture which stressed the necessity of an overseas military role. As with such a strategic culture, decision-makers' perceptions of the peripheral role would have to be altered before any dramatic transformation would be expected in the nation's military presence abroad. In other words, decision-makers would have to conclude that, contrary to past experience, the nation's role on the periphery no longer worked to buttress its international prestige, and may have even contributed to a perception of weakness, both at home and abroad.

Part of the explanation for why the overseas military role might be considered a liability where it used to be a strength lies in what Richard Rosecrance calls 'models' in world politics.[50] 'Models' are specific nation-states which, because of the international policies they choose to pursue, are uniquely successful in the world arena. Before the First World War, ambitious leaders sought to emulate the British model, which was based on the wealth extracted from colonies and a global trading network. In the 1930s, the model of Fascist Italy influenced revisionist leaders in both Berlin and Tokyo. A strong, military-oriented regime created an appealing alternative to the social divisions which seemed endemic to European democracies and the US. According to Rosecrance, after a brief flirtation with the Russian model which promised rapid development and greater social equality, the predominant model in the post-1945 international system has been that of Japan and its export-led growth. If nations tend to draw policy lessons from 'models' during different time periods, then perhaps the Japanese and also German models of extremely low military spending and an emphasis on productive investment and economic growth convinced British decision-makers to discard the east of Suez role. If policymakers did, in fact, choose to emulate the Japanese 'model,' the country's extensive overseas military network must have been seen as a drain on the economy which served to lessen Britain's perceived strength in the world.

There is evidence that British leaders looked enviously to Germany's economic success and its limited military responsibilities in the late 1950s and 1960s. There is less proof that they similarly admired Japan, for the dynamism of the Japanese economy was not yet fully appreciated during this period.[51] Nonetheless, this study demonstrates that the decision to withdraw from the east of Suez role did not occur simply because leaders changed their minds about the requisites of world power, and subsequently decided to throw their weight behind a political formula, successful elsewhere, of limited military spending and economic growth. The factors involved in retrenchment are much more complex than is allowed by such an idea-driven explanation. In fact, it does not appear that British statesmen were persuaded by the Japanese 'model' even after the nation disengaged from east of Suez commitments. In the over two and a half decades since Britain abandoned its overseas military role, British military spending as a percentage of GNP has consistently ranked third among industrialized nations, below the US and the Soviet Union, but well above Japan, Germany, and even France.[52]

None of the factors assumed to be important in the maintenance of an overseas military role, then, offers a particularly compelling explanation, either alone or in combination, for Britain's withdrawal from east of Suez commitments. They can be anticipated to have limited utility in explaining other examples of retrenchment as well. It is true that bureaucratic resistance and ingrained assumptions about the intrinsic value of an overseas military role must be overcome before retrenchment can occur. But knowing this does not give us any indication of the types of variables which are important in surmounting such obstacles to change. Thus, we are left with an incomplete explanation of the process of retrenchment when examining the literature's current focus on the causes of overextension.

The most common explanation given for why a nation's leaders would choose to relinquish a military network overseas is one of the principal causes of overextension, relative economic decline. As has already been noted, overextension is often the result of statesmen's tendency to maintain overseas outposts even as the resources needed to uphold them dwindle away.[53] But while economic decline may cause the problem of strategic overstretch, it is also presumed to resolve it. It is, in fact, usually assumed that spiralling relative decline drives the retrenchment process, compelling leaders to come to terms with the imbalance between the state's power and its policies by abandoning overseas responsibilities. Economic decline thus is thought to act as the invisible hand does in classical liberal economic theory, producing harmony among the various economic and social components of society. In this case, the result is greater consonance between the state's capabilities and its defence commitments. It is perhaps the widespread acceptance that an invisible mechanism is at work in the process of economic decline, forcing leaders to ratchet their international ambitions consistently downward, which explains the paucity of research on the factors which can convince leaders to abandon strategic networks abroad.[54]

Not surprisingly, then, the conventional explanation for the east of Suez decision is that Britain eventually came to a point where it simply no longer had the economic capacity to maintain an overseas military network. For example, Phillip Darby, the historian of Britain's east of Suez policy, concludes: 'In the evolution of the [east of Suez role] the relationship between ends and means was often blurred, but in the last resort the means determined the ends... ultimately lack of resources rather than intellectual rejection ensured its abandonment.'[55] Thus, according to this customary view of the east of Suez decision, economic pressures constrained British decision-makers, eventually leaving them no alternative but to abandon the nation's overseas military role.

This standard explanation of the east of Suez decision is insufficient. While obviously important, Britain's relative economic decline and related short-term economic pressures do not provide a satisfactory explanation for the withdrawal from global power. The decision to abandon the country's overseas military network was political as well as economic.[56] Cabinet shifts, alterations in the machinery of government, and policy calculation played an equally important, and perhaps even a more important, role in the east of Suez decision than economic exigency.

In summary, then, most recent literature on the overseas commitments that great powers tend to acquire emphasizes their intractable character. Once nation-states undertake strategic commitments abroad, their leaders tend to cling tenaciously to them even after the initial reasons for acquiring them have evaporated, and the state's global economic and political standing has waned. The potential hazards that may befall overextended states have been extensively documented, as have the causes of overextension. But the factors which can cause leaders to abandon an overseas military role, thereby taking a decisive step toward bringing the state's power and its policy into closer harmony, have not been thoroughly analyzed. And although overextension and retrenchment are in many ways interrelated phenomena, an understanding of the causes of strategic overstretch offers little insight into the factors which can cause decision-makers to abandon a world role. Focusing on Britain's decision to abandon its commitments east of Suez, this study explicates the types of variables which can be expected to lead decision-makers to abandon an overseas military network, be it a strategic or an imperial network. In other words, taking the contingencies of time and place into consideration, as always, the analytical framework used to bring understanding to Britain's east of Suez decision is generalizable to other cases of retrenchment.

As has been highlighted, the transition away from global power can be a momentous one for considerations of international security, depending, of course, on the global political circumstances of the time. But, perhaps even more importantly, it is also a pivotal, perhaps even a defining, episode for the retrenching nation. When British statesmen decided to abandon the east of Suez network in 1968, they were, as Philip Morgan puts it, 'making a public statement that the last pretense of being a world power was being stripped away.'[57] Policymakers, if not perhaps all of the general public, had finally accepted the fact that overseas bases did not automatically confer great power status upon Britain. In the words of Richard Crossman, a member of Cabinet when the decision was made, British statesmen were finally 'breaking through the status barrier,' by laying down the old symbols of empire, wealth, and overseas military might.[58]

2 Decline and the Politics of Retrenchment

Post-1945 British foreign policy is typically thought to be characterized by a single linear trend of decline. Paul Kennedy summarizes this standard perspective when he states that after 1945, 'step by step the British retreated – or rather stumbled – back to their island base, whence they had emerged some two or more centuries earlier to dominate a great part of the globe and its oceans.'[1] According to this conventional view of postwar British foreign policy, economic decline has placed British leaders in a policy straitjacket which constrains policy choice and, in essence, dictates policy.[2] In fact, the emphasis given to the country's relative decline over the past 50 years is so prevalent that some even claim that decline is approaching the status of an overarching paradigm in the study of British foreign policy.[3]

Economic factors are certainly considered the central cause of British policymakers' decision to withdraw from the east of Suez commitments. Michael Dockrill, for example, maintains that the decision to 'abandon Britain's pretensions east of Suez was one clear case where the pressure of economic circumstances forced Britain into a sudden change of course.'[4] Keith Hartley similarly states that 'economic factors, especially balance of payments, were dominant' in the decision to withdraw from east of Suez.[5] The consensus among policymakers and officials is much the same – that the country's relative economic decline and the harsh realities of Britain's economic situation left no alternative but to abandon world power.[6] For example, when recalling the east of Suez decision, one senior mandarin in the Ministry of Defence concludes that 'policy only changes when someone turns off the money tap.'[7] Yet, although the 'money tap' was indeed important, Britain's economic problems alone do not provide a sufficient explanation of the decision to withdraw from the east of Suez network.

Important qualifications must be added to the supposed effects that relative economic decline and changes in the balance of world power had on Britain's overseas role. There is little doubt that the relative decline of Britain's economic and military power after 1945 was an evident and profoundly important fact for postwar British decision-makers. The emergence of the Soviet Union's dominating power in Europe compelled British leaders to enter into a peacetime alliance and to commit to a permanent military presence on the European continent. The world's two new superpowers, the United States and the Soviet Union, made clear that they abhorred Britain's postwar colonial ambitions, and Britain's military positions in the Indian Ocean were thought to be imperialist in intent long after the country's colonial empire began to fade. In addition, the creation of the United Nations marked a shift in world opinion in favor of advancing colonial territories to independence and limiting European intervention in the affairs of developing nations. Perhaps most importantly, Europe's era of global primacy had drawn to a close, as was made abundantly clear by Japan's humbling defeat of the European colonial powers in Asia and the rise of the new superpowers. It appeared that European states would never again play a decisive role in shaping the parameters of international affairs, particularly through military operations overseas. In fact, some have argued that after 1942 Britain quickly declined into client-state, or even protectorate, status in the age of the *pax Americana*.[8]

Amid such marked change in international politics, the contraction of Britain's overseas role appears natural and perhaps even unavoidable. With Britain clearly relegated to the periphery of world power, it is not all that surprising that the country began gradually to retreat from commitments and interests abroad. Dependence on the American nuclear umbrella underscored the fact that, whatever her past glory, Britain would never again enjoy pre-eminence on the world stage, as she had until perhaps 1939.[9] If one accepts the view that relative decline eventually compelled British leaders to abandon overseas commitments, then a succession of foreign policy crises, such as the Suez crisis in 1956, was all that was required to force British statesmen to accept their sinking status in the world.

As this summary of the international circumstances that British decision-makers faced in the postwar period demonstrates, the rapid decline of Britain's international power and influence after 1945 is an irrefutable fact. Yet, although British leaders tended to have an accurate grasp of the extent of their nation's international decline, it is much less clear that they recognized the implications for Britain's global ambitions during the first two postwar decades. In addition, the international environment was not as hostile during this period as is sometimes suggested. Despite its anti-imperialistic rhetoric, the US government's approach toward Britain's overseas possessions was typically supportive, and its role as the guarantor of European security (through the North Atlantic Treaty Organization) provided Britain with greater security than it had enjoyed in the 1930s. Moreover, the superpowers were not willing to, or indeed capable of, rapidly expanding their influence to all corners of the globe. For a long period, a large and strategically important sphere remained where Britain was the only active major power. Additionally, although Britain was dwarfed in economic and military capacity by the two superpowers, the country remained, for well over a decade after 1945, the world's third power, much more powerful than any other middle-ranking country.

This context helps to explain British leaders' often criticized reluctance to grasp the extent of their nation's decline and to discard obsolete images of British world power.[10] It also suggests that international pressures rarely provided transparent guidelines for British policymakers. If relative economic decline and related international circumstances placed seemingly ever-increasing constraints on British policy, they also provided ample room for a continued world presence. Even as Britain began to slip from third power status in the late 1950s, and the colonial empire was winding away in the early 1960s, important cultural, economic, and strategic reasons for maintaining an overseas military role remained. At no point in the first two and a half decades after the war was it obvious to British decision-makers that Britain's relative economic weakness clearly outweighed the multiple reasons for staying east of Suez. In sum, then, it seems that the connection between relative economic decline, diminishing world status, and Britain's withdrawal from its overseas military network has to be more carefully drawn.[11]

Conventional interpretations of British foreign policy, and of the east of Suez decision in particular, are characteristic of a growing trend in political and historical inquiry: to treat economic issues as the central dynamic variable driving international change, leaving everything else as constant, and by implication, secondary causes. Among others, scholars such as Robert Gilpin and Paul Kennedy have brought renewed attention to the material underpinnings of state strength.[12] As both these scholars have shown, once the economic foundations which buttress international power begin to crumble, the state's international status and its international ambitions will, over the long run, crumble as well.

It is difficult to argue with the assertion that there is, in Kennedy's words, 'a very significant correlation over the longer term between productive and revenue-raising capacities on the one hand and military strength on the other...' and that '...there is a very clear connection in the long run between an individual Great Power's rise and fall and its growth and decline as an important military power (or world empire).'[13] If it has been true historically that as a state's relative economic clout dwindles, it will eventually be forced to abandon its international ambitions, this still begs vital questions such as when retrenchment will take place and how. For example, certain British statesmen were, it seems, aware of their nation's declining productive capacity in comparison to industrial newcomers such as Germany, France, and the United States as early as the 1870s.[14] But the country's relative economic and military power eroded slowly for nearly a century, with, of course, the brief hiatuses provided by victory in the two world wars in the first half of this century, before decision-makers concluded that the country could no longer support a permanent overseas military role. It would seem, then, that relative economic decline does not, in and of itself, provide a sufficient explanation of Britain's withdrawal from its world role. Britain's dwindling economic and military power in the world should be considered, as it is in this study, an important context for the decision to withdraw from overseas commitments, but not an all-encompassing explanation.

There is little question that the economically-driven research which currently pervades the study of British foreign policy, and much of the international relations literature on the rise and decline of great powers, is characterized by considerable insight. Nevertheless, arguments which focus exclusively on the economic determinants of foreign policy behavior sacrifice depth of research on the altar of breadth. And, in so doing, they undervalue the critical role that historical antecedents and political considerations can play in episodes of dramatic policy change, such as Britain's withdrawal from the east of Suez role.

To provide a thorough and reliable explanation of the east of Suez decision, political variables must be retrieved from their current relegated position as static, background considerations and placed at the center of analysis. This study demonstrates that historical and political considerations are as important as, if not more important than, economic hardship in explaining British policymakers' decision to withdraw from their overseas military network in 1968. And, the political and historical variables which allow one to grasp the east of Suez decision will also provide considerable insight into other examples of major powers choosing to abandon global networks.

The remainder of this chapter outlines the approach taken in this study. Discussion begins with the analytical framework employed to provide a more comprehensive explanation of the east of Suez decision. Descriptions of the specific explanatory variables and decision-making episodes analyzed are then provided. As will be seen, this study is a longitudinal comparison of important transition periods in Britain's post-1945 foreign policy.

AN ALTERNATIVE FRAMEWORK

A troika of variables is necessary for understanding the east of Suez decision and, furthermore, this troika can be expected to be at work in other cases where great powers choose to abandon overseas military networks. The three variables hypothesized to drive the retrenchment process are relative economic decline, crises in foreign policy or in the economy, and the domestic coalition-building process. The last variable is perhaps the most important. It seems logical that before a dramatic reversal of policy can be taken on an issue as vital as the east of Suez role, a winning coalition must be constructed in key British policymaking institutions. In other words, a policy change as momentous as Britain's withdrawal from its permanent overseas military role, a role laden with political and emotional baggage, must of necessity entail some form of domestic political shift. And coalitional politics, or more specifically the process of crafting a winning coalition, is the framework needed to comprehend the interaction between domestic and international variables in the east of Suez decision.[15]

It is necessary to look at the construction of winning coalitions when analyzing major shifts in British foreign policy because a single actor has rarely been able to dominate the decision-making process in Britain, a feature common across many, perhaps even most, foreign policy decision-making arenas. A winning coalition can be defined as any alliance of domestic and international actors which is sufficient to dominate the policy process and to promote policy change.[16] The size and the type of winning coalition needed to underpin policy change depends on the political institutions and policymaking processes in the country in question.

In the British case, a winning coalition need only be built within the Cabinet for a major reversal of policy to occur. While most diplomacy is carried out on lower levels, typically in the Foreign Office, essential decisions require Cabinet action. In taking such action, the Cabinet faces little in the way of constraints, largely because tight party discipline provides policymakers with a solid parliamentary underpinning. As numerous critics have emphasized, the British state is remarkably insular with regard to foreign policy formulation. Societal groups and public opinion have made only a limited impression on the architects of British foreign policy in the postwar period.[17] As a result, David Vital's assertion nearly three decades ago that 'the making of foreign policy in Britain is the business of the executive and for almost all practical purposes the executive is unfettered in this function' remains true to this day.[18]

Despite the simplicity of the British decision-making arena, the construction of a winning coalition on an issue as vital as the east of Suez role is still a complex process. Figure 2.1 illustrates how this study unravels the elaborate knot of variables involved. The framework presented builds upon Bruce Russett's triangular schema of the pressures and constraints that executives face when making foreign policy.[19] He contends, along with many others, that these pressures can be usefully categorized into three levels of analysis: societal, state, and system. In Russett's formulation, influences from these three levels are located on different corners of a triangle, providing an uncomplicated conceptualization of various policymaking pressures. The specific factors listed at the corners of Figure 2.1 are those that could potentially influence the coalition-building process in the British setting, particularly in a major shift in policy such as the abandonment of the east of Suez network. These influences, which can also be thought of as quasi-independent explanatory variables, will be detailed below. More noticeable than the edges of the triangle, though, are two dimensions which have been added to Russett's model.

The first rests within the triangle. Essential to understanding the construction of a winning coalition in British foreign policy is a variable which is both mercurial and ever-present: Cabinet politics. Since the Cabinet sits at the heart of the policy process, with all major policy decisions flowing up and through it, or at least through a partial Cabinet of concerned ministers, shifts in the balance of Cabinet authority are inexorably intertwined with the process of creating a winning coalition. Furthermore, while the political maneuvering which takes place in the British Cabinet system is in many ways shaped by the unique structure of that body, such politicking is present in all political systems. Thus, the inclusion of Cabinet politics in this framework formalizes an aspect of the foreign policy process that

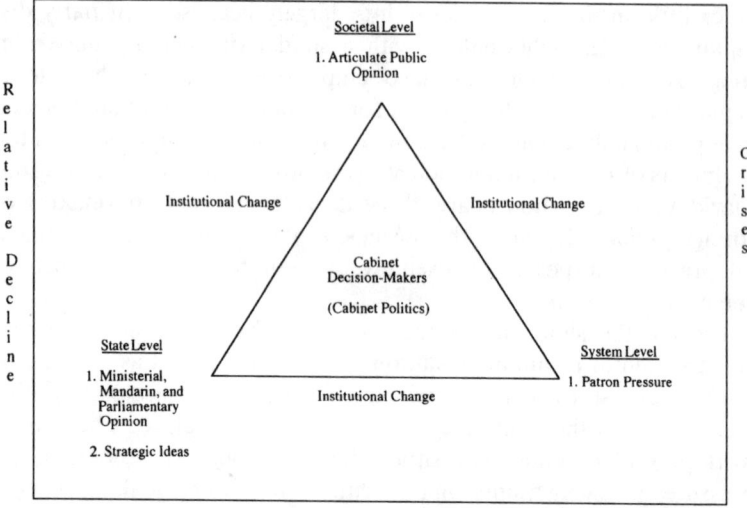

Figure 2.1 Potential Influences in the East of Suez Winning Coalition

remains implicit in Russett's schema and many other conceptualizations: that political plotting, strategy, and bargaining – in other words, politics – can play an important role in foreign policy change.[20]

The second dimension added to Russett's framework is unique to declining powers. It is hypothesized that declining states tend to face relatively consistent pressures from the international system, which are illustrated in Figure 2.1 by the box surrounding the triangle. On one side of the box is relative decline itself, and leaders' perceptions of such decline. On the other side are the foreign policy and economic crises which are often a consequence of decline. In the British case, these crises were so frequent that they can be characterized as practically a constant in postwar British political life. At the least, one would have difficulty characterizing Britain's post-1945 foreign policy crises as departures from the norm. As has been mentioned, these two pressures, decline and crises, are key variables hypothesized to drive the retrenchment process in post-1945 Britain. They are, in fact, customarily assumed responsible for the east of Suez decision. Yet, decline and crises differ conceptually from the pressures within the box in Figure 2.1. In contrast to the other pressures which shaped the coalition-building process, their presence was nearly continual and their significance extended well beyond the single issue of overseas military bases. Perhaps the clearest differentiation of the explanatory variables resting outside the box in Figure 2.1 and those resting inside can be found in Arthur Stinchcombe's distinction between 'constant causes' and 'historic causes.'[21]

A constant cause is one that affects policymakers year after year. It is a long-term, perhaps even permanent, phenomenon which has deep social and political consequences for the polity. The outcome produced by such a variable is relatively continuous. Britain's relative economic and political decline can be considered a constant cause for British retrenchment, constraining policymakers' options year in and year out for nearly a century. Until the decision to retrench was taken in 1968, the outcome was consistent: limited, piecemeal withdrawal from Britain's overseas commitments and the scaling down of the forces deployed to manage the commitments that remained.[22] Britain's series of foreign policy crises after 1945 can best be considered a relatively constant cause as well, for reasons already discussed.

Historic causes are relatively abrupt political events which open or foreclose options for policymakers, and which are important primarily for the policy issue under study. The variables arrayed around the triangle in Figure 2.1 can be characterized as historic causes, as can the somewhat capricious variable of Cabinet politics. Although these explanatory variables will be outlined below, the example of strategic ideas provides a good illustration of their relatively limited scope. The creation of new strategic doctrines concerning Britain's overseas military network in the 1940s and 1950s would have altered the climate of ideas that decision-makers operated within from that point on, but their importance would have evaporated after the decision to abandon the network was taken in 1968. Since it is improbable that these ideas would have had significant ramifications in other policy arenas, their impact on the policy debate would be brief and relatively limited in comparison to the constant cause of relative economic decline. The other variables associated with the triangle in Figure 2.1 institutional change, elite opinion, and external diplomatic pressure – have a similar ability to transform the political dynamics of a specific policy area.[23] One final note needs to be added with regard to nomenclature. In the remainder of this study, what Stinchcombe calls 'historic causes' will be labelled 'bounded causes,' since the term historic lends a degree of gravity to this type of explanatory variable which may not always be appropriate.

Explained in a slightly different way, the variables to the left and the right of the box in Figure 2.1 can be considered the underlying causes of British retrenchment. After all, if their country had not suffered from a decline in relative economic and military capacity over the course of the twentieth century, British policymakers would have had little or no reason to contemplate abandoning the country's overseas military network. Beyond this, there is little doubt that international pressures related to relative economic decline reverberated within the British political arena, playing an important role in the eventual creation of a winning coalition on the east of Suez issue. Clear evidence of decline and a series of crises could be expected to transform the agenda of British foreign policy, bringing to the forefront questions about reducing overseas responsibilities and eventual withdrawal.

But it cannot be assumed that such consistent international pressures, often labelled structural pressures, alone tipped the balance in Cabinet in favor of retrenchment. As has been increasingly recognized in the international relations literature, foreign policy is the result of the interaction between domestic and international politics.[24] External hammer blows such as the almost continual crises Britain faced in the postwar period must be interpreted by relevant political actors, and policy alternatives have to be formulated, before change occurs. Since such interpretation takes place within domestic political institutions, it should not be surprising that the process of adapting to external pressures is inherently a political process.

Of course, while categorizing decline and crises differently from other explanatory variables is a useful analytical exercise which helps to clarify the process of retrenchment, the real world of the policymaker is often more complex. Consistent structural pressures such as relative decline and related crises often seem to interact and even to be intertwined with political variables at different levels of analysis. One central task, then, is to determine which variables worked in combination with these two structural pressures to produce a winning coalition favoring retrenchment. As has been intimated, the variables arrayed within the box in Figure 2.1 will guide us in this endeavor.

These variables seem numerous, perhaps to the point of being unwieldy, when grouped by levels of analysis, as in Figure 2.1. But there are essentially only four explanatory variables arranged around the corners and sides of the triangle and one situated inside it. First is pressure from a more powerful international actor, or in other words, patron pressure. Second is elite opinion, which is divided among the preferences of the articulate public at the societal level and ministerial, mandarin, and parliamentary views at the state level. Third is changing strategic ideas, which in this case refers to the alteration of strategic assumptions. The evolution of strategic ideas involves the interplay of both state and societal actors, such as commentators knowledgeable in military strategy. Yet, since the only policy-relevant reformulation of strategy takes place at the state level, this variable is listed on the lower left corner of Figure 2.1. The fourth variable, institutional change, is situated along the triangle's sides. Institutional change is differentiated from the other variables encircling the triangle because it is less a specific pressure on decision-makers than an alteration of the political playing field. Changes in the institutional structure of the state affect the way that other explanatory variables, both actors and ideas, impact the policymaking process. Thus, alterations in the policymaking terrain can, in a sense, be considered both an explanatory variable in itself and a mediating variable which works to shape the pattern of political battles. There is a fifth variable inside the box in Figure 2.1 which can also be characterized as a bounded cause: Cabinet politics, which has been described above.

For obvious reasons, leaders' perceptions of decline and the crises which beset their country are an important theme running throughout this work. But emphasis is not placed upon the consistent structural pressures outside of the box in Figure 2.1. Analytic focus is instead placed on the interaction of the political variables ringing and inside the triangle. This study determines which of these pressures were necessary to shape a winning coalition favoring retrenchment, along, of course, with more constant structural pressures. The following section describes the variables associated with the triangle in Figure 2.1 in greater detail. First, however, it is necessary to provide a more complete description of the Cabinet system, since it rests at the heart of the coalition-building process in the British political system.

CONSTRUCTING A WINNING COALITION IN BRITISH FOREIGN POLICY

The logical starting point for an analysis of the domestic factors which undergird major foreign policy change in Britain is the pliable structure of the British Cabinet. Within this system, a good deal of attention must of necessity be placed upon the Prime Minister, who is often able to take the lead on international issues. This can be partially explained by the fact that the Cabinet system is, as William Wallace notes, 'less a machine than a network of well-understood procedures.'[25] Consequently, while the British foreign policy apparatus is highly centralized, it is also unusually informal. It operates through convention and practice, and the Prime Minister is central in determining exactly how this malleable system functions. He (or she) determines the Cabinet's political agenda, the structure of Cabinet committees, who sits on them, and, remarkably, which administrative departments will exist and what functions they are assigned.[26] As a result, the nature of Cabinet government inevitably alters with each Prime Minister. To understand how British foreign policy is made during any given period, one must first consider *whose* Cabinet is being studied.[27]

Although his role is pivotal, the Prime Minister's transcendence in the Cabinet is far from assured. Much depends on the political standing of his ministers, their domestic constituencies, and ultimately, the collection of personalities sitting around the Cabinet table.[28] If he establishes authority over his Cabinet, the Prime Minister can narrow the range of policy options open by simply vetoing certain courses of action. For instance, Harold Wilson's success in keeping devaluation off the political agenda from 1964 to 1967, despite the support such a policy course had in his Cabinet, has been well documented.[29] If the Prime Minister, on the other hand, considers his role to be that of a manager and a coordinator rather than a policy initiator, he may have little impact on policy. In this regard, Clement Attlee, the country's undemonstrative Prime Minister during the first postwar Labour government from 1945 to 1951, is often thought to have been overshadowed by his outgoing Foreign Secretary, Ernest Bevin, in matters of both international and domestic policy.[30]

The balance of authority in Cabinet thus rests upon a delicate equilibrium of factors such as political power, personality, and external pressures.[31] Yet, even a subtle tilt in authority between reform-minded and status quo ministers has the potential to produce a new winning coalition on a foreign policy issue, such as the east of Suez role. Consequently, Cabinet politics, a somewhat unpredictable variable which is always near the center of British policymaking process, must be a central component of this analysis.

Even though Britain's Cabinet machinery and its foreign policy apparatus are rather impermeable structures, the Cabinet is plainly not a sealed unit. Influences other than leaders' perceptions of relative decline and political maneuvering within Cabinet have the potential to facilitate the creation of a winning coalition on an issue such as the withdrawal from east of Suez. And, hence, we must look beyond the political executive to the boundaries of the triangle in Figure 2.1. Although bounded causes similar to Cabinet politics, the four factors arrayed there are also different. These four variables add specificity and depth to our framework of the coalition-building process on the east of Suez issue. Whereas the politics of personality and power in the Cabinet tend to be inconsistent, varying greatly depending upon the specific mix of political players involved, the following explanatory variables are generalizable to other periods and to other nations. It is for this reason that Cabinet politics is situated within the triangle in Figure 2.1 while the other bounded causes rest outside.

The second potential influence on the process of building a winning coalition examined, then, is an external factor, and hence it is situated at the lower right corner of the triangle in Figure 2.1. It is conceivable that diplomatic pressure from a state more powerful than Britain might have helped to convince leaders to withdraw from the east of Suez role. Since Britain was not compelled to abandon its global role when another actor threatened to use force or actually used force, it can be expected that a closely allied state would have the greatest ability to exert influence over British decision-makers. In other words, British leaders chose to adjust to a more limited, regional role; they were not forced to take this course of action. And in a decision of such magnitude, counsel or even pressure from one's enemies or from loosely associated states was likely to have little sway in British policy-making circles.

In this regard, no diplomatic ties carried greater value for postwar British statesmen than those with the United States.[32] In fact, it is not an exaggeration to characterize transatlantic ties after 1945 as a patron–client diplomatic relationship.[33] British policymakers from all shades of the political spectrum recognized America's global pre-eminence after the Second World War, and the image of a declining Britain benevolently passing the mantle of world leadership over to the United States during the war was widely accepted in the British foreign policy establishment.[34] Harold Macmillan echoed a sentiment common among the country's policymaking elite when he alleged that post-1945 Britain was playing the calming, educating role of the Greeks to America's impetuous and somewhat barbarous new Rome.[35] And although it was an unequal partnership, Macmillan's characterization of the Anglo-American alliance illustrates that it was not a dependent relationship. As in all patron–client connections, ties with the client hold some value for the patron, and hence both sides possess some degree of leverage over the policies of the other.[36] What is of interest here, though, is the sway that American administrations had in the formulation of British foreign policy after 1945. In particular, it must be determined if signals or the use of political and economic sticks or carrots from Washington helped to bolster reformers in postwar British Cabinets, thereby facilitating the construction of a winning coalition favoring retrenchment from the east of Suez role.

External variables other than this patron–client relationship are, of course, relevant. Yet, they did not have the same potential to influence the coalition-building process on the east of Suez decision. Consequently, these external pressures are treated as contextual considerations, albeit sometimes important contextual considerations. The rise of potent anti-British sentiments throughout much of the Indian Ocean area is a prominent example. Such nationalist pressures led to the abandonment of individual bases, and hence help to explain Britain's gradual retreat from the region. Nonetheless, since many governments in the region remained on friendly terms with Britain and preferred the maintenance of British arms in the area, it would be a vast oversimplification to claim that the British were swept from the east of Suez area by nationalist forces.[37] More to the point, with numerous supporters remaining in the region, it is unlikely that nationalist tensions were uppermost in policymakers' minds when the decision to retrench was taken. Britain's relations with such supportive governments, like Australia, New Zealand, Singapore, and the Persian Gulf sheikdoms, all of which had strong historical ties with Britain, are further external influences included in the narrative. But, again, during much of this period the preferences of these governments were not likely to carry as much weight in British policy-making circles as views expressed from Washington. Moreover, these closely allied states benefited from Britain's military presence in the region and thus would not be expected to lobby for retrenchment. Also noteworthy are Britain's continental neighbors, whose remarkably successful experiment in regional integration would in time offer a legitimate alternative to overseas military power for British decision-makers. The effect that European integration had on British leaders' conception of the east of Suez role is considered in the chapters which follow. Yet, as indicated from its exclusion from Figure 2.1, it is speculated that when British decision-makers seriously pondered retrenchment this external influence was a secondary concern. It was not as prominent as either patron–client ties with the US or internal influences.

Decline and the Politics of Retrenchment

Turning to such internal factors, the image that policymakers had of the overseas military network and what it meant for Britain, both in terms of global strategy and in a more general way for the country's prestige, was important in the eventual decision to retrench. Such images are listed on the lower left corner of the triangle in Figure 2.1. They can be termed strategic assumptions, or widely accepted beliefs about specific components of a state's overseas strategy.[38] Or, in Charles Kupchan's terminology, discussed above, such images may be thought of as issue-specific elements within the broader strategic culture that exists in a nation.[39] Strategic assumptions are a combination of values (such as peace and security) and presumptions about the means necessary to achieve them and, not surprisingly, they are a crucial undergirding for any state's global strategy. More importantly for our purposes, the durability of strategic assumptions can be important in the domestic coalition-building process. For the greatest potential for creating a new winning coalition exists when relatively stable assumptions begin to be questioned.[40]

It is useful to concentrate on one key strategic assumption in postwar British military strategy, an assumption which buttressed almost every aspect of the country's overseas policy. This is the idea, ingrained within both the foreign policy establishment and the public, that an inexorable link existed between Britain's military network overseas and the country's wealth and security, and ultimately, its greatness.[41] The vital importance of the country's overseas possessions and trading links had been a long running theme in British history. The country's rise to world power since the late seventeenth century had, after all, been built upon the mutually beneficial relationship between industry and overseas trade on the one hand, and naval mastery and a strategic chain of bases abroad on the other.[42] This quadrangle of forces would preserve Britain's auspicious position in world affairs for over two centuries. It should not be surprising, then, that over time British statesmen came to believe that the country's network of bases abroad was inherently valuable, rather than an apparatus which had been used to further the nation's commercial and strategic interests. DeWitt Armstrong observes that long after 1945 a 'firm belief' persisted within Britain's foreign policy establishment that:

> Britain would always be able to control her destiny because of the great power that resided in the chain of strategic bases stretching across much of the world. The capture of some in World War II and

the loss of others since... have only lowered the amount of power visualized, not the fact that power is believed to repose innately in a chain of bases.[43]

The erosion of such deeply ingrained beliefs about the bases east of Suez would naturally be a slow process. The overseas role, and the bases abroad, had been for centuries intertwined with British national identity and assumed to be crucial for the national welfare. Yet, before policymakers could contemplate abandoning the east of Suez network, these long-standing assumptions would have to give way. At the very least, it would seem that some alteration in this strategic assumption would be necessary before a winning coalition favoring retrenchment could be fashioned in the Cabinet.

Yet, the abandonment of the assumption that British bases were a necessary and vital component of British foreign policy could only open the door, so to speak, for policymakers to change their views on the world role. It would provide the opportunity for change. To understand the east of Suez decision, we must also grasp when the positions of different policy-relevant groups altered and how they influenced the coalition-building process.[44] To do this, the four groups, or really layers, of elite opinion which are the most identifiable and influential in the British foreign policy process are analyzed.[45] Attitudes among ministers, mandarins, Members of Parliament (MPs), and the articulate public are studied.

Not surprisingly given its relatively insular structure, scholars often identify Britain's foreign policy apparatus as an arena dominated by an elite.[46] An elite can be defined as the occupants of top positions within political, diplomatic, bureaucratic, and military hierarchies, and groups outside such official posts who have the potential to influence the policymaking process, such as journalists and legislators. In classical elite theory, this elite is thought to be relatively cohesive because of the linkages which exist between institutional hierarchies.[47] Yet, although a good deal of consensus exists among the British foreign policy elite, because of similarities in educational backgrounds and close social networks, it cannot be characterized as strictly unified.[48] There is ample evidence that bureaucrats, politicians, and commentators have bitter disagreements over foreign policy. By analyzing four different layers of elite opinion, one recognizes that the British policymaking elite is differentiated, and that influences outside of Whitehall such as the media can help to shape the parameters of decision-making.

Of these four layers of opinion, the relevance of ministerial attitudes toward the world role should be obvious, since alterations in ministerial preferences will inevitably be tied up with Cabinet politics, and hence the coalition-building process. Given the influence that they wield in the British foreign policy process, changes in mandarin attitudes are significant for much the same reason. As has been well-documented, during the decades following the Second World War, senior civil servants often employed their considerable 'administrative' resources in efforts to determine the contours of policy.[49]

In Parliament, the ruling party's backbenchers typically have the greatest ability to influence the Cabinet and, by extension, policy.[50] The government depends on its backbench supporters to remain in power, and hence it cannot afford to run roughshod over them. Usually, though, outside of minor revolts, backbench support is willingly given to the government because MPs would prefer to see their party govern rather than the opposition. Also, rebellious backbenchers run the risk of losing their seats if the government is toppled and an election is called. Other barriers to vigorous backbench opposition to the government's foreign policy also exist. Members of Parliament are often unable to develop informed opinions about foreign policy issues because of the pervasive secrecy which surrounds Whitehall, which makes it difficult for them to provide a credible challenge to governmental policy. In addition, since foreign policy considerations have rarely won votes in post-1945 Britain, backbenchers have numerous incentives to focus their attention on domestic issues.[51]

Thus, the government customarily has fairly wide latitude in foreign policy formulation, but the possibility that backbench dissent could impact the coalition-building process in the Cabinet, perhaps by swaying reform-minded ministers, is nevertheless present. In fact, in interviews in the 1960s, senior civil servants claimed that backbench attitudes were the single most important influence on policy outside Whitehall's walls.[52] There are, of course, a number of political considerations which affect the potency of backbench opinion, particularly the size of the ruling party's majority, the extent that backbench opinions coalesce, and the nature of backbench leadership.

The main party in opposition must be taken into consideration as well. The structure of the British political system, with an ingrained tradition of adversarial politics and an electoral system which typically produces a clear one-party majority, ensures that the opposition is much less influential than the government's own backbenchers. Nonetheless, the opposition often helps to shape public debate on a policy.

By either supporting policy initiatives or taking them to task, the opposition may also have an impact on the types of policy options open to the government. Consequently, views articulated by opposition leaders will also be noted as an important factor affecting the context within which government policymakers operate.

The articulate public, that small group of journalists and scholars with a steady interest in foreign affairs, has a similar ability to indirectly influence policy formulation. This layer of elite opinion tends to center on a tightly woven group based in London which includes analysts associated with policy institutes such as the Royal Institute of International Affairs, newspaper editors, and foreign correspondents for the quality press.[53] The influence of the articulate public varies, but it is clearly not as consistently important as the government's backbenchers. It plays a largely ancillary role comparable to that of the opposition party.[54] It can politicize an issue, and, by doing so, potentially boost reformers in the Cabinet. Critics in the press and academia can also offer plausible policy alternatives, and if they succeed in generating controversy over the issue, the size of the winning coalition ultimately required for policy change may shrink.[55] Thus, this layer of elite opinion can have a palpable, but nonetheless indirect, influence on the coalition-building process. As seen in Figure 2.1, preferences within the articulate public are the only societal level pressure analyzed.

Attitudes on the overseas military role at one further layer of opinion in the British polity, that of the mass public, might have been examined. In a democracy where governments must win elections, public opinion inevitably carries substantial weight. That said, the consensus among scholars is that mass public attitudes had little impact on the formulation of foreign and defence policy in the first decades following the Second World War. Passive, even deferential, acceptance of the foreign policy course charted by the government was common. And when popular attitudes did diverge from those of the government, they more often than not reflected opinions expressed by segments of the articulate public.[56] This should not imply that foreign policy initiatives were invariably given blanket support by the mass public at this time. Dissent, sometimes very vocal, was registered, with the activities of the Campaign for Nuclear Disarmament in the late 1950s and 1960s being a prominent example. But such opposition was more often the exception than the rule, and it rarely persuaded government decision-makers or changed policies.[57] Hence, while popular opinions are occasionally referred to in this study, they are not systematically traced.

Finally, the last domestic factor analyzed is the oft-neglected role that institutional change plays in the coalition-building process. The state, after all, is not simply a collection of policymakers and mandarins; it is also, as G. John Ikenberry observes, 'a piece of strategically important terrain, which shapes the entire course of political battles.'[58] Perhaps most importantly, the state's institutional framework provides access to the policymaking arena and it also limits such access.[59] It can thus be assumed that alterations in Britain's foreign policy machinery might have affected the construction of a winning coalition in two principal ways: either by limiting the access that opponents of reform have to the decision-making arena, or by enhancing the political capacities of reformers within government. Such changes may, of course, be mutually reinforcing.

Analyzing the institutional determinants of policy as well as the impact that changing strategic views, elite attitudes, and political maneuvering had on the east of Suez decision provides a more realistic appreciation of the interaction between agents and structures. As Walter Carlsnaes observes, there is an 'increasingly widespread recognition' in the international relations literature that '...human agents and social structures are in a fundamental sense intertwined entities, and hence that we cannot account fully for one without invoking the other.'[60] Tracing the interaction of agents and the structure they operate within may provide a less than parsimonious explanation of Britain's east of Suez decision and the factors that cause states to abandon overseas roles more generally. But as recent scholarship demonstrates, the formulation of foreign policy is a complex process which is best understood through the use of flexible and integrative analytical frameworks. Focusing on only one set of explanatory variables or level of analysis will inevitably fail to provide a comprehensive grasp of the realities involved in foreign policy change.[61] Thus, while the multi-layered approach taken here may have costs in terms of economy, these are effectively counter-balanced by the gain in explanatory power.

In sum, relevant potential influences from three levels of analysis – system, state, and society – are incorporated into the research framework of this study. The ways in which these pressures affected the coalition-building process are not, however, analyzed throughout the post-1945 era. As the next section reveals, policy change is a discontinuous process, with change most likely to occur when the political system is under great stress. For that reason, periods of crisis in Britain's post-1945 east of Suez policy are the explicit focus of this study, as it was during these periods that the impulses for change reached their zenith.

LONGITUDINAL COMPARISON

In other words, this study is limited not only to certain explanatory variables, but also to key decision-making episodes. It centers on three transitional periods in postwar British foreign policy: the immediate postwar transition, from 1945 to 1947, which included Indian independence; the Suez crisis of 1956 and the re-evaluation which followed; and Britain's severe financial crises of the late 1960s. Among others, D.C. Watt identifies these intervals as the three 'learning periods' of post-1945 British foreign policy.[62] These learning periods, or as they will be referred to in this study, transitional periods, were times of adjustment in British foreign policy. In each of these junctures, long-standing assumptions about Britain's role in the world were punctuated by the reality of relative economic and political decline. Crisis was a key characteristic of each interval, and in each, leaders became aware that familiar signposts which had long guided British foreign policy were disappearing, signposts which had been erected in a different era, when a prominent British presence on the international scene was unquestioned.[63] A chief concern at each of these junctures was Britain's future role in the world. Doubts were raised not only about Britain's ability to maintain an overseas military network, but also about the benefits that accrued from such a role.

In analyzing these transitional periods, the intricacies of specific episodes of crisis are not of concern. Nor are the effects that such episodes had on the body politic as a whole. It is the reappraisal of the nation's fundamental overseas interests following periods of crisis, particularly with regard to the east of Suez role, that is of interest. For that reason, the transitional periods examined will not be of uniform duration. The re-evaluation sparked by crisis may have a relatively immediate impact or it may drag on for some time.

No matter how the impact of crisis was felt, there can be little doubt that these three junctures represented the most serious episodes of questioning the east of Suez role after 1945.[64] The first transition period, the passage into the postwar era from 1945 to roughly 1947, was characterized by unforeseen difficulties and uncertainties. Statesmen had to adjust to Britain's reduced status in the world, at least in comparison to the two new superpowers, the United States and the

Soviet Union. Complicating this difficult transition was the loss of what Victorian statesmen cherished as the 'grand base of British power in the east,' India.[65] Historians have often criticized the postwar Labour government for not abandoning the overseas military role when India, long the hub of the empire, was granted freedom.[66] Of course, the illusion of continued power which went along with victory in the Second World War helped to conceal the realities of Britain's material weaknesses in the early postwar period, as did the hope for a rapid postwar economic recovery and some form of continued world leadership.

A second, and much more important, cornerstone of the British Empire in the twentieth century was the Suez Canal. Britain's first postwar Foreign Secretary, Ernest Bevin, considered the canal to be the 'jugular vein' of the empire.[67] Perhaps not surprisingly, then, a major crisis would erupt when Egypt unilaterally nationalized the canal in 1956, despite the fact that the Churchill government had agreed to withdraw British forces from the canal region some two years earlier. In making this decision, the Churchill government was acting in part on the belief that in the nuclear era Britain's overseas forces should not be overly concentrated on the sprawling Suez base. This argument notwithstanding, the episode would soon devolve into Britain's most severe diplomatic humiliation of the twentieth century. The Suez crisis was a traumatic shock for Britons, policymakers and public alike, which upset common views on the country's position in world affairs.[68] The deep sense of failure associated with this affair and the introspection which followed in even the highest levels of government marks the second major transition period in postwar British foreign policy.

Even though consciously planned, the withdrawals from India and the Suez Canal, two former latchkeys of the east of Suez role, were clearly blows to British strategic planners. But more than that, the periods of crisis which surrounded these departures sparked serious reappraisals of the country's overseas military role. In each instance, important questions were raised within the corridors of power about whether Britain should, or indeed could, continue to maintain a permanent military presence in the Indian Ocean area. The third transition period examined, the country's financial crises of the late 1960s, forced British decision-makers to do more than simply rethink the world role. Two of the most prized symbols of the country's greatness, sterling's parity and the east of Suez network, were surrendered during the sterling crises of the late 1960s. These three transition periods are compared to determine how a winning coalition supporting retrenchment was formed during the last crisis, in the 1960s, and not during the crises of the previous two decades.

These transitional periods are concentrated upon because of the magnitude of the policy change examined. Basic principles which had long guided Britain's foreign policymakers were uprooted with the withdrawal from east of Suez commitments, changing forever the character of Britain's role in the world. Transformations of this sort tend to be episodic in nature, occurring only in conjunction with crises. For, 'the reappraisal of general principles occurs only', as Michael Brenner observes, 'in the face of great pressure.'[69]

During non-crises periods, numerous impediments to change such as sunk costs, hidebound bureaucracies, and deeply-rooted belief systems prevent dramatic redirections of policy.[70] Incremental change tends to be the norm during such periods. Crisis disrupts the normal flow of policymaking, causing leaders to question the efficacy of long-standing policies and policymaking practices. It is at these moments that the inadequacies of existing goals and doctrines are suddenly illuminated. In crisis, therefore, the obstacles to change are removed at the same time that the impulses for change surge.[71] To explain a major transformation of policy such as retrenchment, it is thus logical to concentrate on periods of crisis.

Focusing on three transition periods in post-1945 British foreign policy does neglect notable events in the evolution of Britain's overseas military role. But, for reasons given above, none of these events would be expected to result in a major transformation of east of Suez policy, such as retrenchment. And, in fact, none did. A solid example is found in the 1952 Defence Policy and Global Strategy Paper, which was perhaps the most significant instance when dramatic change was contemplated outside of the three transition periods. This report, long considered a turning point in post-1945 British strategic thinking, was written by the Chiefs of Staff at the behest of the Churchill government. It called for a fairly substantial shift in British defense priorities. The Chiefs argued that Britain's prestige and its military credibility should be staked on the nuclear deterrent, thus allowing considerable reductions in conventional forces. Significant savings were anticipated in the defense budget if the program were adopted. Yet, although it marked a watershed in British strategic thinking and it provided a much needed overarching framework for British defense, it never become a blueprint for policy in the early 1950s, perhaps because this was a relatively tranquil period in British postwar history and drastic change was felt to be unnecessary. More importantly, the Global Strategy Paper never challenged the underlying assumption that Britain must of necessity maintain a military presence in the Indian Ocean area. Even if it had been implemented, a major chain of bases would have remained east of Suez.[72] Thus, the example of the 1952 Global Strategy Paper illustrates that what holds true elsewhere also holds true for Britain's post-1945 foreign policy. Periods of calm are rarely conducive to truly dramatic policy change. Or, as Kenneth Boulding captures this phenomenon more colorfully, 'man is a strange creature who is incapable of seeing the handwriting on the wall until his back is up against it.'[73]

Thus, this research approach entails analyzing five explanatory variables in each of three transition periods in Britain's post-1945 east of Suez role. Such a longitudinal approach to understanding foreign policy decisions is what Alexander George has termed a 'structured, focused comparison.'[74] This study is structured because it concentrates on three roughly similar events – transition periods in Britain's east of Suez role – which have different outcomes. It is focused because analysis is limited to five explanatory variables (in addition to the 'constant' variables of relative decline and crisis) when explaining why the outcomes differ.

A structured, focused approach has both theoretical and methodological advantages. Methodologically, analyzing a limited number of variables across three cases allows greater confidence in the relationship between the explanatory variables and the outcome, in this case British retrenchment. Moreover, a study of successive crisis periods within the same country, in this case with each crisis separated by roughly only a decade, controls for much of the variance that may be present in cross-national studies or analyses of very different temporal domains. In other words, there is less chance that confounding variables will undermine the findings of a longitudinal study of the same country because social, political, and economic background variables can be expected to be more similar than they would be in cross-national analyses.[75]

The distinctive theoretical contribution of such a longitudinal study is a result of its approach to explanation, which is more inclusive than foreign policy studies focusing on a single decision-making episode. Analyzing successive crises demonstrates the effect of what one perceptive scholar calls the 'shadow of the past' on foreign policy.[76] Longitudinal studies appreciate that a policy's past molds its present shape as well as the alternatives open to decision-makers attempting to reformulate it. When a particular policy course is chosen at a particular point in time, T1, both institutions and rules are created to guide the further evolution of the policy, thus limiting policy options at a subsequent point in time, T2. That is, past policy choices lead to the creation of individual positions and institutions responsible for maintaining the policy program, and after these programs become established, they exhibit the typical characteristics of bureaucratic inertia that make policy change discontinuous. Policy canalization also makes it impossible to backtrack and implement an unselected policy option from an earlier interval (T1) both because the policy arena has been altered by previous policy choices and the policy environment invariably transforms over time.[77] Consequently, the historical sequence of a policy becomes crucial to explanation.

This channeling process is often neglected in the study of foreign policy, particularly in studies of foreign policy change.[78] Foreign policy studies tend to concentrate intensively on a single decision, which may last a few weeks or a few months, or less frequently they employ statistical analyses which include a large number of cases.[79] Each of these types of study has shortcomings. In case studies of a single foreign policy decision, history is often visualized as the short-term pressures which decision-makers must immediately respond to. Of necessity, statistical studies of many cases tend to concentrate on a handful of variables while trying to find statistical relationships. Such statistical analysis may be done without a thorough analysis of the political dynamics within the decision-making arena. The crucial defect of both of these approaches, however, is that the decision-making arena is treated as a static variable.

A longitudinal study recognizes the pliability of the decision-making arena and that policies are path-dependent. Using two examples relevant to this study, foreign policy institutions can be reformed and strategic doctrines can gain and lose favor over time, and either could potentially open or close policy avenues for decision-makers. The longitudinal study employed here captures the interplay between earlier crises and their responses, institutional transformations, and the evolution of strategic ideas. This approach broadens the scope of analysis, enabling the analyst to capture the underlying, historical causes of foreign policy change which can be as, and often times more, important than the immediate day-to-day pressures policymakers come under when making critical foreign policy decisions.

Moreover, since the weight of the past is not uniform, a longitudinal view helps to distinguish between what Arthur Stinchcombe labels

Decline and the Politics of Retrenchment

'constant causes' and 'historic causes,' the latter of which are termed 'bounded causes' in this work. As has already been discussed, constant causes are long-term pressures on decision-makers which have far-reaching consequences for the polity as a whole, whereas bounded causes are short-term pressures the impact of which tends to be limited to a specific policy area. Students of foreign policy must comprehend both the bounded and the constant causes of major policy changes such as Britain's withdrawal from east of Suez, because neither provides a sufficient explanation alone.[80] Since constant and bounded causes are inexorably intertwined as a policy unfolds historically, this argument should not be surprising. Perhaps more importantly, distinguishing these two types of causes and weighing their relative importance will help to build a more precise understanding of the mechanisms involved in British retrenchment.[81]

ORGANIZATION OF THE ARGUMENT

The following chapters analyze the three transition periods in postwar British foreign policy highlighted above. Chapter 3 discusses the transformed international political and strategic landscape which Britain's first postwar government faced in 1945. The 1945–51 Labour government's attempt to adjust to this dramatically altered international terrain is traced in Chapter 4, where particular attention is paid to the internal debate over whether Britain should, or indeed could, continue to maintain an overseas military role.

Chapter 5 analyzes the second transition period in British foreign policy, the Suez crisis in 1956 and its aftermath. The Suez crisis was a tremendous blow, which raised new doubts about Britain's world role both within Whitehall and among the public. In this chapter, the more immediate controversies over the nation's overseas role within the government are examined. Chapter 6, on the other hand, is devoted to the long-term implications of Suez which had relevance for the overseas military network. The most notable changes in the wake of the Suez débâcle are the dramatic rise of anti-British sentiment in the Indian Ocean area, the reorganization of Britain's foreign policy machinery, and the revision of fundamental assumptions about the military's role abroad.

Chapter 7 provides an analysis of the third transition period in post-1945 British foreign policy, the sterling crises of 1966–8. The focus of this chapter is the interaction between crises and the coalition-building process which eventually culminated in the east of Suez decision. Chapter 8 concludes the study. In this chapter, the theoretical threads woven into this work are tied together, offering an analytical framework which provides a comprehensive explanation of Britain's withdrawal from the east of Suez role and offers considerable insight into similar transitions from world power.

3 The Return to Normalcy: Postwar British Strategy

Britain emerged from the Second World War among the ruling trinity in the world, one of the 'Big Three' wartime victors. But the country's position at the conference tables of world diplomacy obscured the reality of diminished power. Britain had, in effect, given its all to win the war, exhausting domestic industries and selling off many of its overseas assets. The country was devastated economically. Yet, the perception of world power remained, both in the minds of officials and in the perception of the general public. That Britain, which had just emerged victorious from the most destructive war in its history, would continue to maintain the trappings of international power was almost universally accepted at this time. In many sections of British opinion, the extensive network of bases east of Suez was considered the most vital testament to Britain's greatness.

Yet, British statesmen could have chosen other means to buttress the country's international status. As Peter Taylor and others claim, 1945 was a decisive turning point in British history, where a fluid international environment provided a number of alternatives for Britain's foreign policymakers.[1] To decision-makers at the time, the tides of history surely must have seemed to flow in divergent directions, and the Cold War pattern which eventually emerged appeared far from inevitable in 1945, 1946, or even 1947. It is at this point, during the uncertain postwar years when Britain's weaknesses were readily apparent, that Britain's overseas military role was most likely to be reshaped in a dramatic new way.[2] Yet, even the impending independence of India and the loss of the mighty Indian Army, with all that this meant both strategically and sentimentally to Britain's planners, did nothing to change Britain's policy course. No major reappraisal of Britain's overseas military role was undertaken in the late 1940s, and policy continued to be based on old notions which valued the security of the lines of communication to the empire above all else.

Decision-makers of this era are often criticized in the literature on British foreign policy for not grasping the inherent weakness of the country's postwar economic and military position and subsequently scaling down overseas commitments. In hindsight, the reasons why British leaders did not carve out a new and more limited overseas military role at this point seem transparent. The postwar international environment was widely considered too unstable for long-term planning, particularly with the advent of nuclear weapons. The country's foreign policy machinery was excessively fragmented during this period, which prevented not only the development of a coherent global strategy, but also a critical re-evaluation of the world role. In addition, the pivotal strategic and economic role of the Middle East was brought into sharp relief from 1939 to 1945 and resource-rich Africa appeared to offer limitless possibilities for economic expansion at this time. The chain of bases, outposts, and fueling stations stretching from the Mediterranean to the Far East was crucial to guard the economic riches of these two regions. Perhaps most important, habits of imperial thinking persisted which assumed that British predominance east of Suez was both inevitable and just. As long as such ideas remained, a substantial withdrawal from the overseas military role would be difficult, if not impossible.

Yet, despite the existence of seemingly overwhelming grounds for staying east of Suez, the decision to do so aroused controversy. While it was generally accepted in Whitehall that Britain's positions east of the Suez Canal would be restored to more or less what they had always been, this was not the case in the broader political arena. A Labour government with a sizable parliamentary majority took power in July 1945, and many of its supporters felt that the country's military and colonial holdings overseas were incongruent with the socialist principles being pursued at home. An intense debate ensued at the highest levels of the government, with the Prime Minister, Clement Attlee, emerging as perhaps the harshest critic of the Britain's extensive overseas military role. As we shall see, Attlee's sustained criticism did not prompt a thorough appraisal of Britain's fundamental interests and its capabilities overseas, and the eventual outcome was far from revolutionary.

To fully understand the variables which eventually compelled British leaders to abandon the east of Suez network, it is necessary to grasp why the Prime Minister's campaign to reshape Britain's overseas role along radical lines eventually faltered. With such an understanding, the immense obstacles standing in the way of even a partial disengagement from Britain's world role in the postwar period become clearer. In the following pages, the uncertain and relatively unthreatening international environment of the early postwar years, from 1945 to early 1947, is outlined. Overseas policy was, as we shall see, for the most part guided by imperial instincts and the need to respond to immediate events at this time. Chapter 4 discusses the opposition to the overseas military role posed by the Prime Minister and the Labour Party, and the reasons why such early challenges to the world role ultimately failed.

THE POSTWAR WORLD

The term 'superpower' was gaining currency in 1945, and at the time it was applied to Britain as well as the United States and the Soviet Union. But Britain's dire economic condition after the war was widely recognized both within the country and without. At Potsdam in July 1945, Churchill claimed that Britain was the 'world's greatest debtor.' Nevertheless, Britain's postwar leaders never questioned whether Britain was a world power; Britain's greatness was accepted as an article of faith. It was widely assumed that Britain's economic enfeeblement was only a temporary consequence of the war. A Foreign Office (FO) survey of Britain's postwar prospects in March 1945 concluded that despite the country's inevitable economic troubles, Britain still had high prestige, a high level of armaments, and a critical political and geographic position in the world. All of these assets, it was thought, could be used to recover Britain's former economic prowess. The statement concluded that 'the essential task of diplomacy [is] to make clear that the United Kingdom can and will overcome its difficulties, otherwise other countries will say the lion is in his dotage and try to divide up his skin.'[3] Neither the Labour Cabinet nor the foreign policy establishment ever questioned this analysis. Consequently, although it was recognized to be a long uphill struggle, the pre-eminent goal of the country's foreign policy in this period was to rebuild Britain's economic strength and its standing in the world.[4] What specific policies should be pursued in order to reach this goal were, as we will see, disputed by ministers from 1945–6. Given the rapid flow of international events after the war, it was not easy for policymakers to determine which was the right path for Britain in the postwar world. The greatest element of uncertainty arose from the fluidity of relations among the Big Three before 1947.

At this time, the stance of the Soviet Union was the chief concern of British decision-makers. Since the USSR's strong position in the heart of Europe in 1945 was the most striking difference from the European situation in the interwar era this is understandable. Throughout 1945–6 Soviet expansionist aims and a perhaps inflated postwar perception of the British Empire created a growing number of disputes between the two countries. In eastern Europe the USSR did not honor the British interpretation of the Yalta agreements, which consisted of democratically elected governments in the region that would be naturally friendly to the Soviet Union. Soviet insistence on massive reparations from Germany hampered the progress toward a peace settlement in Europe and, from the British point of view, needlessly prolonged the four-power occupation in that country. The new appeal of communism in states such as France and Italy caused much apprehension in British foreign policy circles at a time when most western communist parties were closely tied to Moscow. Outside Europe, British policymakers were troubled by the Soviets' attempt to gain a foothold in the Mediterranean, which was seen as a crucial link in the lines of communication to the empire. The Soviets were attempting to gain territorial concessions from Turkey which, among other things, included control of the Dardanelles.[5] They were also pushing at postwar international conferences to gain trusteeship over Italy's colonies in northern Africa. Perhaps most ominously, Moscow had failed to withdraw its troops, as agreed, in early 1946 from the neighboring state of Iran, which was a long-standing area of Anglo-Russian rivalry.

Whether these actions by the Soviet Union were interpreted in light of the country's habitual obsession with its own security or as part of an invidious expansionist plan, they certainly created a mood of apprehension within Britain's foreign policy establishment over Soviet aims. The Chiefs of Staff had identified the USSR as Britain's main threat since at least 1944, while the Foreign Office (FO) remained cautiously optimistic that some form of Anglo-Soviet-American condominium could be reached. By at least the opening months of 1946 the FO had slowly came round to the Chiefs of Staff's pessimistic view of Soviet intent. A special 'Russia Committee' was established in the FO to monitor Soviet actions, and this Committee soon developed a very hard-line attitude toward the USSR.[6] In an influential memo, this group concluded in April 1946 that 'the Soviet Government, both in their recent pronouncements and in their actions have made it clear that they have decided upon an aggressive policy, based upon militant Communism and Russian chauvinism.'[7] After a series of bruising meetings with Soviet representatives, the Foreign Secretary, Ernest Bevin, came to agree wholeheartedly with this view. Neither the FO nor the military believed that the Soviets wanted war, given their considerable human and material losses between 1941 and 1945. But it seemed that Moscow was willing to take advantage of the disarray in postwar Europe to expand its influence by all means short of war.[8]

At the same time that distrust of the Soviet Union grew, Anglo-American wartime collaboration unravelled. British plans for the postwar period had assumed the continuation of strong ties with the United States, but they were always tempered by an underlying fear of an American retreat into isolationism as had happened in 1919. The abrupt ending of Lend-Lease with victory over Japan in August 1945 demonstrated that these fears had substance. Over the next two years, relations with the United States became increasingly strained. Although there were many reasons for the growing tension, Robert Holland succinctly captures the essence of the Anglo-American parting of the ways in 1945 and 1946. According to Holland, 'the Americans and the British were each trying to get a headlock on the other' as they worked together to mold the postwar international order.[9]

American policymakers were determined that, given the scale of the US wartime contribution, Britain should follow the US lead in postwar negotiations. After all, it was widely accepted in Washington that Britain's halcyon days were over. As Admiral Leahy, Truman's military advisor at Potsdam, told the President, Britain was 'prostrate economically' and 'relatively impotent militarily.'[10] Yet, this did not mean that the Americans wanted to undermine Britain's overseas military role. After 1941, the US acquired a strategic frontier in the Western Pacific, running from Alaska through the Aleutian Islands and Japan to the Philippines. Between 1945 and 1948, US grand strategy centered on domination of the Western Hemisphere and the Atlantic and Pacific Oceans, with, for the first time in the nation's history, far-flung bases to project American power globally. Seen through this Atlantic–Pacific lens, the Indian Ocean did not figure prominently in American strategy. The American Chiefs of Staff had, moreover, concluded by March 1946 that Britain's position in the east of Suez area should be bolstered because it was a major bulwark against communist aggression in the area.[11] Yet, it was still far from clear that this view was widely shared in the American administration.

For their part, the British took a somewhat patronizing view of American diplomatic efforts after the war, believing that the United States' initially conciliatory stance toward the Soviet Union was due in part to a fundamental lack of historical understanding and an inability to grasp the complexities of international affairs.[12] But the most worrying aspect of the United States' naive view of world affairs for British policymakers was their reluctance to support their closest ally, which had suffered tremendously during the war. Of special concern was America's apparent unwillingness to lend Britain support in three areas – the defense of Europe, the atomic bomb, and finance.[13]

In the summer of 1945, the United States seemed to British observers to be overly preoccupied with domestic demands to 'bring the boys home' and to return to normalcy. US troops in Europe were quickly run down from 3.5 million in June 1945 to 200 000 two years later. Worse still, Washington seemed to be more concerned with restoring order in Asia than in Europe, leaving a weary Britain to confront the Soviet Union on numerous fronts spanning Europe and the Middle East.[14] Added to this apparent lack of interest in the future shape of Europe was the unilateral American decision to halt collaboration in atomic matters. Agreements with the US secured by Churchill and Attlee guaranteed future cooperation, but Truman reneged in 1946 in the face of a nationalist Congress. That August the US President signed the McMahon Act which effectively ended meaningful atomic cooperation between the two countries. Not unnaturally, the British Cabinet was enraged.

More significant was the dispute over a postwar American loan. Because of the country's tremendous exertions during the war, Britain was for the most part insolvent in 1945. It was estimated at the time that Britain had lost at least one-quarter of its national wealth between 1939 and 1945, or £7300 million. A crucial component of this calculation was the sale of foreign assets valued at approximately £4200 million to help pay for the war. For more than a century Britain's balance of payments had depended heavily on the 'invisibles' earned from such overseas assets, making their loss a particularly hard blow from which the British economy would not soon recover.[15] Given these conditions, the Treasury estimated that exports would have to increase by 75 per cent just to regain the living standard of 1938. But far more was asked of the postwar Labour government than a return to the status quo of 1938. At home, Labour leaders had promised a 'People's Peace' which included the creation of a comprehensive welfare state. Abroad, Britain had to maintain a high level of mobilization while tension mounted with Russia over postwar settlements in Europe and the Middle East. And this manpower abroad was desperately needed to fuel industrial recovery.[16]

Thus, American financial help was thought to be essential to overcome the problems of postwar adjustment. John Maynard Keynes, the Treasury's negotiator, was dispatched to Washington to secure a loan, which he felt would be substantial (around $8 billion) and interest-free given Britain's wartime sacrifices. Such hopes proved unrealistic. After much hard-bargaining, a loan of $3.75 billion at 2 per cent interest was eventually procured. Britain's Lend-Lease debts, worth some $21 billion, were also written off. In return, the United States demanded that Britain ratify the 1944 Bretton Woods agreement on the international monetary system and make sterling convertible into dollars within one year.[17] Not surprisingly, the agreement did not receive a warm reception in Britain. Robert Boothby, a Conservative MP, denounced the package as 'an economic Munich' when it was forced through Parliament in December 1945, and the attitude of the general populace was little different.[18] Given such inauspicious beginnings, Anglo-American tensions grew only worse in the early postwar years.

British policymakers thus found themselves in an unenviable position in the immediate postwar period, with growing anxiety over Russian aims and uncertainty over what type of role the United States would play in the postwar world. Relations among the Big Three in 1945–6 seemed to suggest that the ultimate outcome of the Second World War would be a fragmented international order. In November 1945 Bevin claimed that 'instead of world cooperation we are rapidly drifting into spheres of influence or what can be better described as three great Monroes,' a reference to the Monroe Doctrine of 1824 which staked out American hegemony in Latin America.[19] Uncertainty over America's global role would remain until at least the middle of 1947, when the Marshall Plan started to assuage British fears over a splintering world order.

Added to the apprehension which existed over relations among the Big Three, Britain was saddled with a number of costly and time-consuming postwar responsibilities. The biggest financial burden was the occupation of Germany. The failure to reach international agreement on a peace settlement required the occupation troops to stay, and, so long as they did, each occupying power had to provide for the needs of the populace in their zones. Britain controlled the area most heavily damaged from the war: northwestern Germany, including the Ruhr. Given the destruction in this area, the burden of providing the zone's food needs was immense. In July 1946, the Cabinet was compelled to ration bread in Britain, a measure avoided in even the blackest days of the war, in order to maintain the flow of US wheat to Germany – wheat which had to be purchased using scarce dollars from the American loan.[20] Fortunately, the US and Britain agreed to combine their two zones in that same month and to promote German industrial recovery. Still, the 'bizone' that was formally established in January 1947 did not remove all of the financial burdens and it increased tensions with the Soviet Union.

British arms were also charged with establishing political and economic order throughout South and Southeast Asia. With several countries in the area on the verge of civil war and the entire region devastated economically and short of food, this was an immense task. Perhaps most important, rice production had to be quickly restored to pre-war levels in order to avoid famine in a number of areas, including India and Malaya. In many ways, in this part of the world rice was as vital for reconstruction as coal and wheat were to Europe.[21] In addition, British troops undertook the responsibility of maintaining order in India as the subcontinent progressed toward independence, a process which the Labour government initiated almost immediately after taking power.[22] In the eastern Mediterranean, British forces were involved in an increasingly taxing civil war in Greece and an almost insoluble predicament in Palestine, where Jewish and Arab inhabitants had very different interpretations of Britain's 1917 promise to establish a Jewish homeland in the area.

The details of the Palestinian quandary need not detain us here, since they have been treated exhaustively elsewhere.[23] But, by re-igniting the flames of Arab nationalism, the Palestinian issue would have important ramifications for Britain's east of Suez position in the future. Since the British were the pre-eminent external power in the region, they bore the brunt of Arab nationalist outrage for years to come. Even among moderate Arab leaders, the value of ties with Britain depreciated rapidly after the events of the late 1940s. For over 30 years, British statesman had sought the friendship of a number of Arab states for strategic and economic reasons, impressing upon them the benefits to be had from security ties with the UK. But, when British patronage was put to the test over the Palestinian issue, especially during the 1948–9 Arab-Israeli war, it was found to be of little worth.[24] Emotions also ran high in the United States over the Palestinian issue, where President Truman, perhaps courting the Jewish vote, asserted that an independent Jewish state must be established. Yet, the United States did not offer to assist in the maintenance of law and order in the mandate and did not open its own borders to Jewish immigration. Consequently, Palestine proved to be yet another sore spot in Anglo-American relations, one which prompted Attlee to complain that the Americans were 'forever laying heavy burdens on us without lifting a little finger to help.'[25]

Thus, the international arena was remarkably fluid during the early postwar years. British policymakers were attempting to navigate the country's foreign policy course in unusually uncertain and largely unchartered waters. At the same time, they had vast postwar responsibilities to carry out. Until the outline of the postwar international order gradually became clear, it was difficult to assess what Britain's proper role in the world should be. Many in the foreign policy establishment felt that any attempt to reshape global strategy would be futile in such an uncertain environment. In these circumstances, it was widely agreed in Whitehall that it would be wise to hold on to Britain's overseas possessions. Soviet belligerence in particular added to the perceived need to maintain Britain's overseas military role until the shape of the new world order could be more readily discerned. Policy thus evolved along traditional lines in the early postwar years, with the east of Suez network playing much the same role in British political and strategic thought as it had for over a century and a half. Yet, the uncertainty of the postwar international political environment was far from the only reason a thorough reappraisal of Britain's global role was not initiated.

THE BARRIERS TO REAPPRAISAL

The void in Britain's overseas strategy in the early postwar years can also be explained by the lack of any immediate military threat. Although tension with the Soviet Union was palpable in 1945–6, British military planners felt confident that the Soviets would be incapable of waging a major war for some years to come.[26] One British admiral declared in the *Sunday Times* on 1 December 1946: 'Never since Trafalgar has there been a time that sea security, and all that it means to our nation and empire, seemed less endangered; never has it given strategists less anxiety.'[27] Following interwar practice, the government adopted the ten-year rule in the winter of 1946. The rule instructed the Chiefs of Staff to plan on the assumption that Britain would not be involved in a major war for at least a decade. Thus, in the swiftly moving, but nevertheless unthreatening, postwar international environment, a critical re-evaluation of British strategy did not appear immediately necessary.

The unforeseeable impact of nuclear weapons on warfare also spoke against trying to devise long-term strategy in the early postwar years. Until the potential of this momentous new weapon could be ascertained and the international political environment stabilized, the government took a cautious approach to military strategy overseas, as the Defence White Papers of the period demonstrate. Attlee admitted that the 1946 Defence White Paper was 'something of a stopgap'; the 1947 statement stated that it was 'yet another transitional year'; while the 1948 White Paper claimed that new weapons were an 'emphatic reminder of the need to preserve a flexible policy and a warning that there must be no rigidity in decisions about the future role of the three services.'[28]

Yet, even if political and strategic conditions had been more predictable, there were other obstacles preventing the careful reanalysis of Britain's global role at this time. Perhaps most important, Britain's foreign policy machinery was ill-prepared to develop either clearly defined foreign policy goals or a global military strategy. In the chief body for the formulation of foreign policy, the Foreign Office, a deeply ingrained tradition of empiricism prevented the development of long-term goals. Attempts to use analytical frameworks to assess the country's long-term international interests were consistently resisted in the department, because it was assumed that the international arena was far too volatile to plan for indeterminate future events.

Although a Permanent Under-Secretaries Committee was established in the Foreign Office (FO) in 1949 to determine long-term priorities, it proved to be largely ineffective. Not only did this committee challenge time-worn practices in the department, it was hindered by a lack of permanent staff and the constant pressure of immediate problems.[29] Perhaps the most concise summary of the FO worldview, a worldview which persists even today, is that given by Harold Macmillan during his brief stint as Foreign Secretary in 1955. At a meeting over the conflict in Cyprus the future Prime Minister frankly explained to the Greek and Turkish delegates: 'We are a very empirical people. We try to deal with the facts as we see them. Nothing is permanent in the world.'[30]

FO empiricism was far from the only impediment to the development of a coherent global strategy in late 1940s Britain. A number of other departments had overlapping jurisdictions with the FO, making it very difficult to see Britain's overseas policy in the round. Until 1947, three departments were responsible for colonial affairs: the Indian Office, dealing with matters affecting the subcontinent; the Dominions Office, handling relations with Canada, Australia, New

Zealand, South Africa, and Ireland; and the Colonial Office, which managed all other colonial policies. After Indian independence in 1947, the India Office was merged with the Dominions Office to form the Commonwealth Relations Office (CRO), but the piecemeal approach to colonial affairs remained.

The lack of a unified focus is even more evident in defense. In the late 1940s, the three armed services remained for the most part separate empires, preventing the formulation of a coherent, long-term military strategy. Churchill took the title Minister of Defence during the Second World War, but it was not until the new Labour Prime Minister, Clement Attlee, came to power that the Ministry of Defence (MoD) was formally recognized. Yet, the MoD was a weak body at this time with an extremely small staff. The three service departments – the Royal Navy, the Royal Air Force, and the Army – remained intact and kept their full constitutional powers. Individual service ministers were still responsible to Parliament for the expenditures of their services, which in effect meant that the Defence Minister was armed with only his own persuasive powers when trying to coordinate policy among the branches of the military. At the end of the day, the Ministry was capable of little more than assisting inter-service committees in the late 1940s.[31]

At the political level, the Defence Committee was designed to be the central body where foreign and military policies were analyzed to determine future needs. Established in 1946, the Defence Committee essentially was the interwar Committee of Imperial Defence bestowed with a new title.[32] The Prime Minister chaired the committee, with the ministers of overseas departments, the Chiefs of Staff, and the armed service ministers present. In 1945 and 1946 the committee was, as we shall see, the site of an intense debate over Britain's global strategy, and as such it was briefly a very important forum. Unfortunately, it encompassed too many vested political interests to earnestly tackle fundamental policy questions, much less to chart the country's future global strategy. Beyond the anomaly of the first two postwar years, the committee was rarely able to accomplish anything beyond choosing between competing weapons systems and resolving disputes over the allocation of resources among the three service departments. As in the past, the broader outlines of policy were typically provided by the Prime Minister, the Foreign Secretary, and perhaps one or two other senior ministers.[33]

Thus, because of excessive fragmentation and an aversion to long-term planning, Britain's foreign policy machinery was rendered incapable of formulating a single, coherent global strategy. Worse still, Whitehall at this time was overwhelmed by the sheer volume and complexity of Britain's postwar responsibilities. Officials were literally swamped with paperwork. Professor James Meade of the Cabinet's Economic Section noted in his diary in 1945: 'the coincidence of the end of the war with the beginning of the new Labour government has put a strain of work on the central Whitehall machine such as I cannot remember since I came to Whitehall in 1940.'[34] The situation did not soon improve. In 1949 the Cabinet was warned that 'the increased volume of international work was already in danger of imposing intolerable strains on the machinery of national government.'[35] Whitehall as a corporate body seemed in the late 1940s to be in a state of semi-permanent exhaustion. Sir William Strang, who would become Permanent Under-Secretary at the Foreign Office in 1949, provides a first-hand account of the effects of excessive fatigue on his performance:

> The mind revolted against the reading of discourses and articles that had no immediate bearing on day to day problems. The next resistance erected would be against aimless discussion at large about foreign affairs...the mind was attempting to shed all but the inescapable tasks of dealing with essential interviews or with the flow of papers.[36]

It is reasonable to assume that Strang's predicament was common in the foreign policy bureaucracy. In these conditions, fresh thinking on the broader elements of Britain's overseas role was not likely to come from officials. If any reassessment of Britain's global strategy was going to take place in the early postwar years, it would have to be initiated by the nation's political leaders.

INDIA'S INDEPENDENCE AND THE RETURN TO 'NORMALCY'

It is hardly surprising, in this context, that policy was allowed to simply evolve in the early postwar years with little or no contemplation of the nation's fundamental interests or capabilities. The crux of British overseas planning at the time was, in a sense, a return to normalcy. Though it was recognized that it might take the country years to recover fully from the war, it was rarely, if ever, doubted in the foreign policy establishment that Britain's old positions in the

Middle East and the Far East would be restored, for the most part, to their pre-war splendor.[37] This also meant a return to traditional notions of Britain's overseas military role. The need to defend the main lines of communications to the empire and the Commonwealth was again assumed to be the essential prerequisite of British defense.[38] Even the impending loss of India, with its military installations, barracks, communications facilities, ports, and airstrips did not cause British strategists to pause and reconsider the broader elements of global strategy in the postwar world. Perhaps most important, Britain would no longer have the Indian Army, a strategic reserve of a quarter of a million men which, with the Royal Navy's capabilities to move them to troublespots, British world power had largely depended on for over a century.

There are a number of reasons why the withdrawal from Britain's largest and traditionally most pivotal possession left, as Phillip Darby puts it, scarcely 'a ripple on the placid surface of British political and strategic thinking.'[39] The pressure of immediate events in the east of Suez area offers a partial explanation. Not long after the signing of the Indian Independence Act in 1947, Britain found herself drawn into a counter-insurgency operation against communist guerrillas in Malaya which was to last 12 years. There was little use in discussing the utility of Britain's overseas military role when a war had to be won. As had so often been the case in Britain's imperial past, the problem at hand, Malaya, diverted attention away from more searching questions on the country's global strategy. The outbreak of the Korean War in June 1950 had a similar effect.[40]

Also, by this time defense tasks in the Indian Ocean area included much more than the traditional duty of safeguarding India. A great number of British colonies remained in the region after the subcontinent had gained its freedom. Moreover, former colonies, such as Burma and Ceylon, agreed to sign 'run down' agreements with Britain which guaranteed the newly formed state's external security during a transitional period. Such agreements were said to allow former colonies sufficient time to develop stable political and economic systems without the worry of external aggression. They also soothed anxieties in Whitehall by giving the impression of an amicable parting. Although India did not agree to such an arrangement, it seems that British military planners assumed that they would be bound to help defend India in the event of an external attack and prepared accordingly.[41]

More important than continuing obligations in the Indian Ocean region was the gradual shift in the geographic focus of London's strategic view. After generations of service there, many British still had a deep sentimental attachment to the Indian subcontinent in the 1940s. But by this time the centerpoint of Britain's east of Suez strategy had shifted decisively to the West. Since roughly the end of the First World War, the Middle East, marked particularly by the sprawling military complex on the Suez Canal, was the true hub of the British Empire.[42] The importance of Britain's position in the Middle East was only further underscored during the Second World War, when the region served as the central staging post for air communications throughout the world as well as a base from which to attack southern Europe.[43] Added to this, of course, was the gradual realization of the magnitude of the oil reserves in the region.[44] In a note written for the Cabinet in 1949, the Foreign Secretary, Bevin, summarized the multiple reasons why 'in peace and war the Middle East is an area of cardinal importance to the United Kingdom, second only to the United Kingdom itself.' 'Strategically,' the paper explained, 'the Middle East is a focal point of communications, a source of oil, a shield to Africa and the Indian Ocean, and an irreplaceable offensive base. Economically, it is, owing to oil and cotton, essential to United Kingdom recovery.'[45]

The Middle East's function as a shield to Africa was especially important in the mid-1940s. Immediately after the war British policy-makers produced a plan to develop this resource-rich region in an attempt to provide a much needed boost to the metropolitan economy. Bevin would even proclaim that by developing Africa, Britain could 'have the United States dependent on us and eating out of our hands in five years.'[46] There was also a call from many quarters at this time for the creation of a great colonial army in Africa to replace the Indian Army, but the War Office consistently argued that scarce military dollars were best spent training British conscripts.[47] It is somewhat paradoxical that at a time when the postwar Labour government was granting a number of South Asian states their independence, government ministers simultaneously began to expound on the extractive possibilities of colonial empire in crudely imperialistic tones. The vision of an African-led economic boom would fade by the late 1940s after many well-publicized failures, such as the attempt to produce groundnuts in the inhospitable terrain of Tanganyika in order to reduce Britain's shortages of oil and fat.[48] Nonetheless, the possibilities that the African colonies were thought to hold in the early postwar period worked to soften the blow of Indian independence.

Thus, the loss of India did not dampen the imperial ambitions of British statesmen. On the contrary, the empire was very much alive in decision-makers' minds in the late 1940s, despite the fact that a Labour government was in power. The Cabinet accepted wholeheartedly the idea of an extractive empire in Africa and the Middle East. With rare exceptions, officials in the foreign policy bureaucracy did as well.[49] The necessary backbone for such an imperialist policy was British naval power from the Mediterranean to the Indian Ocean, and the bases and fueling stations which buttressed the naval presence. Peter Hennessy pithily summarizes how postwar colonial and strategic commitments became intertwined in the minds of British policymakers:

> The Cabinet's grand strategy for the Middle East... was bound up with the guts of imperial policy post-India, part of that cherished notion of an oil and mineral rich Empire from Cape Town to Iraq which could sustain Britain in its great powerdom long after the Indian Army marched to a different drumbeat.[50]

Of course, imperial impulses were not the sole justification for the east of Suez role after the war. There was also an important strategic rationale for Britain's positions along the east of Suez network as well, as has been outlined in the case of the Middle East.

The renewed vigor in the pursuit of colonial enterprise after the war underscores perhaps the most important reason why the east of Suez role remained unaltered in the late 1940s. The global role simply remained too interwoven with British self-identity, both among leaders and the populace, to permit a radical change such as substantial military withdrawal.[51] Several generations had been brought up to regard the Mediterranean, the Red Sea, the Persian Gulf, and much of the Indian Ocean as being as much under British control as the English Channel. It was not so easy to close the chapter. Sir Oliver Franks, the British Ambassador in Washington from 1948 to 1952, explains what was a common view among British policymakers in the late 1940s:

> We assume that our future will be of one piece with our past and that we shall continue as a Great Power. What is noteworthy is the way that we take this for granted. It is not a belief arrived at after reflection by a conscious decision. It is part of the habit and furniture of our minds: a principle so much one with our outlook and character that it determines the way we act without emerging itself into clear consciousness.[52]

It is this deeply ingrained belief in Britain's greatness which offers the least palpable, but probably the most accurate, explanation for the continuation of Britain's overseas military role in the postwar period.

Additionally, this deep-seated and almost universally held belief had only been further set with victory in the war and, at least from the British point of view, the relatively smooth transition of power in India. Or, perhaps it is better put that this notion was not dislodged by the clinical reappraisal of a country's global role which often follows a crushing military defeat.[53] The 1946 Defence White Paper made this point abundantly clear when stating: 'We could not abandon our responsibilities in many parts of the world. To do so would have been to throw away the fruits of victory and to betray those who had fought and died in the common cause.'[54] Given this mindset, a critical re-evaluation of Britain's global role was unlikely in the foreign policy establishment of the late 1940s, and a reversal of policy may have been virtually impossible.

Subsequently, the Middle East remained, in the words of William Roger Louis, 'a region honeycombed with British military installations.'[55] The region was now considered the main prop of Britain's position in the world, but British policymakers were no more willing to relinquish other sections of the great chain of military installations and fueling stations which lay east of Suez.[56] Soon after 1945, the entire network of bases was quickly re-erected essentially in its pre-war form. Not surprisingly, the dawn of the Cold War did little to change Britain's traditional orientation toward its overseas military role. The east of Suez commitments were simply remolded to fit the new strategic context. The traditional argument that Britain's sea routes had to be protected was generalized into the importance of maintaining open lines of communication between the two chief concentrations of power in the non-communist world, Europe and North America on one hand and the Far East on the other. Additionally, the Middle East was now considered a useful base from which to attack the industrial and oil-producing regions in southern USSR. This strategy was, in essence, a small variation on Britain's traditional interest in latchkey bases around the world and in the ability to pose a threat to the soft underbelly of Europe.[57] Therefore, postwar British strategy east of Suez remained remarkably similar to the course pursued since at least the time of Waterloo, with concentration placed on a lengthy string of bases stretching from the Mediterranean to the Far East, a general defense system which would remain largely intact until the late 1950s.[58]

The early postwar years were thus cautious ones, when leaders appeared to cling consciously to traditional conceptions of Britain's overseas role. Continuity seemed the rule of the day. But the outward appearance of a relatively smooth period of transition, bereft of any serious contemplation of change, is deceptive. Given that this was the first majority Labour government in British history, it could perhaps be expected that some doubts about the overseas military role would be raised in Cabinet. One well-placed critic was especially important. This was the Prime Minister, who proved to be a tenacious and radical opponent of Britain's extensive overseas commitments. Throughout this uncertain period, Attlee called for the withdrawal of British troops from the Middle East and a more conciliatory approach toward the Soviet Union. The result was a fierce and relatively lengthy quarrel between the Prime Minister and the foreign policy establishment over Britain's global role. For a myriad of reasons, many of them discussed in this chapter, this row never produced a thorough reappraisal of Britain's basic economic and military interests east of Suez. As a result, policy continued to evolve along pragmatic lines.

Nonetheless, a summary of this debate is necessary to fully understand the variables which would compel British leaders to abandon the east of Suez role slightly over two decades later. The following chapter outlines the internal struggle over Britain's global strategy in the early postwar years, and the factors which would eventually cleanse the Labour government of its radical momentum.

4 Holding Course: The Labour Government of 1945–51 and the Struggle over Strategy

1945 marked a dramatic swing to the left in domestic politics in Britain, encouraged in part by the widespread admiration of the struggle of the Soviet Union against Nazism.[1] A Labour government came to power committed to the creation of a welfare state and an extensive program of nationalization. Many backbenchers also heralded the long-awaited arrival of a socialist foreign policy, which would not only bolster Britain's international standing, but also would revolutionize world affairs. The slogan 'left understands left' was used frequently by Labour campaigners in 1945 when international issues were raised. Perhaps not surprisingly, the foreign policy establishment greeted this phenomenon with undisguised apprehension, and a pervasive gloom spread over the Foreign Office after the 1945 election. Orme Sargent, soon to become Permanent Under-Secretary at the Foreign Office, pessimistically foresaw 'a Communist avalanche over Europe, a weak foreign policy, a private revolution at home and the reduction of England to a 2nd-class power.'[2] As we have seen, such anxieties were unfounded. Britain's foreign policy followed a well-trodden, traditional path after 1945, particularly with regard to the east of Suez role.

The Labour Cabinet and nearly all segments of opinion within the party accepted Britain's great power status. As one of the postwar victors, it seemed Britain had finally earned the right to have both 'greatness' abroad and a more just society at home, embodied in the 'welfare' state. Britain's economic woes in the early postwar years were, after all, widely accepted to be merely an unfortunate and temporary consequence of the war. Yet the types of policies which should be implemented to buttress the country's great power position were hotly debated on different levels in the Labour Party hierarchy. Within the government, the Prime Minister attempted to redefine Britain's overseas military role, and backbenchers soon began to feel that the government's foreign policy had somehow been commandeered by traditional interests in the state. To many Labour supporters, it seemed that a golden opportunity to overhaul Britain's role in the world, and international affairs more generally, was being missed. Even though such opposition to the country's overseas military role would ultimately have no impact on policy, it did confirm some of the less extreme fears of Sargent and others in the foreign policy bureaucracy.

To understand the variables which eventually caused British leaders to withdraw from the east of Suez role, it is essential to grasp the reasons why vigorous opposition to the world role failed to affect policy in the late 1940s. In the pages that follow, the debate over Britain's global role in the early postwar years is outlined along with the severe crises which would check the Labour government's radical momentum in 1947. In somewhat paradoxical fashion, these crises would ensure that the east of Suez role would retain its traditional scope and character. First, however, it is necessary to discuss the balance of political power in Prime Minister Clement Attlee's regime. To fully understand why British foreign policy followed a path of continuity in the late 1940s, one must comprehend the structure of authority in the postwar Labour government.

THE 1945–51 LABOUR GOVERNMENT

As Kenneth Morgan makes clear in his authoritative study on the 1945–51 Labour government, the Attlee regime operated within a unique background of consensus, both within the Labour movement and in society more generally.[3] Wide agreement on Britain's priorities provided an undergirding of bedrock for the Labour government to carry out its policies. In the Labour movement, the unions, the National Executive Council, and the Parliamentary Labour Party (PLP) all shared the same basic goals as the Cabinet: nationalization, regional development, and most importantly, the creation of a welfare state. A vision of a better future following two devastating global wars in the first half of the century was common to practically everyone in the country. And, although there might be disagreement over the particulars, the Labour government's initiatives seemed to be progressing toward the 'People's Peace' all wanted.[4]

In part, this unique period of unity and coherence of purpose in the Labour movement stemmed from the sustained dominance of the Cabinet over the government, the parliamentary party, and its supporters.

Throughout the life of the Labour government, the center of power rested with a handful of key ministers who were largely unfettered in steering the nation's policy. This ruling inner group included: Attlee, Ernest Bevin, Herbert Morrison (the Lord President), Hugh Dalton (the Chancellor until 1947), and Stafford Cripps, who succeeded Dalton at the Treasury. Almost no major government decision was taken without this inner Cabinet being involved, either collectively or apart.[5] Moreover, the Cabinet as a whole was uncommonly cohesive in the early postwar years, particularly for a Labour regime. Ministers genuinely believed that they stood at a critical junction in history, with a unique opportunity to reshape British society and perhaps even international relations. Tremendous burdens, of course, went hand in hand with such hope for change. The weight of history thus seemed to bear down upon the Labour Cabinet, and they responded by coalescing into a common front in the belief that they were leading Britain into a new, and it was hoped better, era.

History's shadow fell upon the Attlee regime in another important way. The unfortunate legacy of Ramsay MacDonald's minority government of 1931 hung like a pall over the regime. The MacDonald government fell when bitter internal divisions prevented it from reaching agreement on policy during a time of national crisis. There is little doubt that ministers in the 1945 government remembered this humiliating episode vividly, and the common memory worked to unite the Cabinet still further.[6] Not only was the 1931 episode perhaps the most dramatic event in Labour's history up to this point, but this was also a Cabinet of seasoned, and relatively elderly, Labour warriors. Until a Cabinet reshuffle in 1947, the entire government consisted of men and women at least in their late fifties and sixties.[7]

A further factor that added to cohesion of the Labour Cabinet in the early postwar years was the absence of factional rifts. This can be partially explained by the mood of unity which prevailed, but more important was the fact that the Labour Party's left-wing was virtually powerless in Cabinet. The left had only three ministers to safeguard its interests. The most powerful of these was Aneurin Bevan, the Minister of Health. Although he would eventually split with his colleagues and resign in 1951, ostensibly over the reinstatement of charges for dentures and spectacles, his attitude toward the government up to that point was one of solidarity. He accepted the government's relatively cautious, and, after 1947, economically austere, policies as a necessary step to rebuild the nation after the ravages of war. More strident steps toward socialism could only be made, he believed, when prosperity was restored. He had no sympathy for left-wing critics of the government, and he toed the party line, and often even enthusiastically supported, the government's major foreign policy decisions.[8] Thus, given the spirit of camaraderie which existed in the Cabinet and the rare moment of cohesion within the Labour movement as a whole, all policy levers rested in the hands of the inner Cabinet.

In the formulation of foreign policy, the key actor throughout this period was indisputably the Foreign Secretary. Much more than Attlee, Ernest Bevin embodied the spirit of the Labour government with his pugnaciousness and his bulldog patriotism.[9] He was the most influential trade union leader of his time and as such his commanding presence in the Cabinet guaranteed crucial union support for governmental policy. It was perhaps because of his unique political constituency that Attlee typically followed in Bevin's wake in the formulation of foreign policy. The Prime Minister would later tell Kenneth Harris, his biographer, that he felt that foreign policy was the Foreign Secretary's preserve. After all, Attlee explained, 'you don't keep a dog and bark yourself.'[10] Yet, Bevin did not confine himself to matters of diplomacy. He took a leading role in Cabinet discussions regardless of the subject and was pivotal in most Cabinet decisions.[11]

The common notion that Bevin was the dominant voice in the Cabinet on matters of overseas policy is reinforced by the contrasting personae of the Prime Minister and his Foreign Secretary. Bevin was physically imposing and had a dynamic, aggressive temperament. As Kenneth Morgan states, given his dominance over the trade unions, Bevin 'embodied in his own titanic personality the solidarity of Labour.'[12] By contrast, Attlee had an unassuming manner and a marked tendency toward understatement. While Bevin confidently thundered out opinions on practically any issue raised in Cabinet, history has recorded an image of Attlee quietly sitting at the top of the Cabinet table, summarizing discussions but rarely if ever initiating policies of his own.[13] Given the wide variance in their public demeanors, it is not surprising that Attlee is often thought to have had very little influence on foreign policy. Sir Alexander Cadogan, Permanent Under-Secretary at the Foreign Office until 1946, provides a valuable glimpse of the outward image of the two men at Potsdam, the first international conference they attended after taking office. Cadogan observed that even at this early date, 'Bevin...has a tendency to take the lead over Attlee, who recedes into the background by his very insignificance.'[14] One clear exception was Indian affairs, an issue in which Attlee had much experience and tended to dominate Cabinet decision-making.

Despite their differing personalities, Attlee and Bevin had a close working relationship which was politically essential to each. Bevin's loyalty was unquestioned, and this would prove critical when the government ran into rough waters and an attempt was made to remove the Prime Minister. The steadfast political support of the most powerful member of his Cabinet must have been a significant source of strength for Attlee. The benefits Bevin derived from the relationship were just as important. Only the Prime Minister had the authority to grant Bevin the wide powers which he enjoyed, which included the authority to formulate all aspects of external policy. And, after the conventional outlines of Bevin's foreign policy became apparent, Attlee vigorously defended his Foreign Secretary from critics within the Parliamentary Labour Party (PLP). Having never been a backbencher himself, Bevin was a rather unskilled parliamentarian. He had brooked no opposition when leading the nation's largest union, the Transport and General Workers' Union, and he viewed his backbench critics with undisguised contempt. More than once Attlee, an old party hand, had to diffuse tension between backbenchers and his uncompromising Foreign Secretary.[15]

Until Bevin was weakened by ill-health in 1950, practically all of the activities of the Labour Cabinet revolved around the Attlee–Bevin axis. Their close political relationship formed the heart of the Labour government, and they tended to play a decisive role in Cabinet decisions regardless of the policy issue.[16] The left-wing Labour MP Michael Foot claims that, 'In fact, often enough Bevin *was* Attlee. It would be folly to overlook the powerful authority of this composite figure.'[17] And Bevin's biographer, Alan Bullock, goes so far as to claim that the relationship between Bevin and Attlee was among the most successful political partnerships in British history.[18]

As we shall see, this image oversimplifies the first years of the Labour government, when Attlee and Bevin had sharp differences over defence policy. But when examining the government's full life, the conception of unity between these two men is largely accurate, particularly with regard to international affairs. Since Britain's foreign policy course was ultimately shaped by ideas jointly held by Bevin and the foreign policy establishment and not by the undemonstrative Attlee, it is not difficult to understand how time has merged the images of these two key figures in the postwar Labour government.

For our focus on Britain's east of Suez role, however, the most relevant aspect of the relationship between Attlee and Bevin is perhaps their greatest area of conflict. The two men had very different worldviews, which soon developed into a lengthy debate over the future of Britain's overseas military role. This debate, which reverberated throughout the foreign policy bureaucracy, marked the most significant challenge to Britain's traditional global role in the first two decades following the war. The concepts which would guide the country's global strategy in the new postwar era were hotly disputed, and an earnest attempt was made to redefine Britain's role in the world.

ATTLEE'S CHALLENGE TO THE GLOBAL ROLE

Although it is rarely emphasized in studies of the Labour government, upon entering office in 1945 Prime Minister Attlee had the most extensive foreign policy background in the Cabinet.[19] He simultaneously became Labour's chief spokesman on defense affairs when he became party leader in 1935. A Labour Party Defence Committee was quickly established soon after, with modern technology's impact on defense strategy as its primary focus. The future Prime Minister took a keen interest in air power, and the views he developed at this time would color his perspective on Britain's defense requirements in the first critical years of his premiership.

In addition, Attlee's perspective on world affairs carried much of the idealist baggage common to the labor movement of the 1930s. In an often quoted passage published in 1937, Attlee claimed that 'there is a deep difference between the Labour Party and the capitalist parties on foreign as well as on home policy, because the two cannot be separated. The foreign policy of a government is the reflection if its internal policy.'[20] The Labour Prime Minister was firmly committed to the creation of a new supranational organization, which he hoped would have the ability to use force to discourage and to halt potential aggressors. Attlee felt that it was crucial to place strategic areas which could potentially cause friction among the great powers under international control. Only in this way, he believed, would it be possible to ensure great power cooperation in a world body. Thus, Attlee's internationalism was not founded on starry-eyed idealism. He recognized the faults of the interwar League of Nations and offered an astute assessment of the steps which would be necessary to create a powerful supranational organization. The new Prime Minister felt it imperative that such an organization be created. He told the Commons on 22 August 1945 that with the advent of nuclear weapons, 'we are now faced with the naked choice between world cooperation and world destruction.'[21]

Experience in the wartime coalition did not dampen Attlee's enthusiasm for such internationalist goals. But with Britain narrowly scraping by during the war, Attlee had little opportunity to develop his views or to press them on the Cabinet. Yet, as the end of the war drew near, Attlee began to try to convince his colleagues of the necessity of a fresh approach to Britain's foreign policy. Twice in spring 1945 he used his chairmanship of Cabinet committees to challenge fundamental assumptions of British strategy. The Deputy Prime Minister suggested that Britain should begin curtailing its role in the Middle East while trying to persuade other powers, especially the United States, to assist in security arrangements in the region. At this point, Attlee was firmly rebuffed by Anthony Eden, the Foreign Secretary, who reiterated the familiar notion that Britain's lines of communication to the empire were vital to the country's material well-being and must be maintained at practically any cost.[22] But Attlee's ideas nevertheless caused great concern in the foreign policy establishment. British strategic planning for the postwar period was already operating under the assumption that the Soviet Union was Britain's most likely potential adversary, and Eden's reply echoed the fears of Soviet expansion into the Middle East, which were prevalent in the foreign policy bureaucracy.[23]

Attlee nevertheless returned to what would prove to be a consistent theme at the Potsdam Conference in July 1945, where he was present as Churchill's 'friend and counsellor.' Attlee thought that Churchill and Eden were taking far too pessimistic a view of both the Soviet Union's intentions and the United Nations during the proceedings. There was, according to Attlee,

> A danger of our getting into a position where we and the Russians confront each other as rival great powers at a number of points of strategic importance... We ought to confront the Russians with the requirements of a world organisation for peace, not with the needs of the defence of the British Empire.[24]

Attlee went on to emphasize that the Joint Planners' report on postwar strategy relied far too heavily on obsolete notions of imperial defence dating from what he saw as the bygone naval era.[25] He considered Britain's lengthy chain of naval bases scattered across the globe to be of little relevance in an age whose defining characteristic would be air power.

Eden again bluntly rebuked the Deputy Prime Minister's remarks. Such idealist aspirations seemed hardly appropriate to the Foreign Secretary and his officials at a time when the Soviets were pressing to get a foothold in the Middle East by gaining control of Italy's former northern African colonies. But Attlee would not be deterred. He then wrote to Churchill, carrying his argument much further. He maintained that in order to build a lasting world peace, British leaders would have to take the Soviet viewpoint into consideration in the ongoing negotiations. After all, Attlee explained, 'Our claim that we occupy these positions [in the east of Suez area] as trustees for the rest of the world that can trust our disinterestedness is not likely to be generally accepted.'[26]

Churchill did not have time to respond. Both he and Attlee returned to London on 25 July to be present for the result of the general election. It would be Attlee and Bevin who would return to Potsdam. Thus, the sole person in the wartime government actively seeking to revise the traditional principles of British foreign policy now became Prime Minister, which not unnaturally created much apprehension in the foreign policy establishment.

Attlee immediately put the issue to the Cabinet, challenging his colleagues either to seek to make the United Nations an efficacious body or to continue to 'act on outworn conceptions.'[27] The centerpiece of his plans was again the abandonment of British military positions in the Middle East. Yet, the Prime Minister's bold proposals ran against the prevailing attitude in Whitehall. Bevin in particular believed that Britain's positions in the eastern Mediterranean, the Middle East, and the Far East were sacrosanct, as did his officials in the Foreign Office. Lord Listowel, India Secretary from 1947 until the Office was abolished in 1948, accurately described Bevin as 'at heart an old-fashioned imperialist, keener to expand than contract the Empire.'[28] To Hugh Dalton, the Chancellor of the Exchequer, Bevin's fascination with the Middle East was apparent in practically every Cabinet discussion.[29] A.V. Alexander, the first Minister of Defence in the Labour government, held much the same outlook as Bevin on Britain's overseas role and how vital it was to the fabric of the nation as a whole.[30] For their part, the armed services seemed genuinely stunned by the Prime Minister's propositions and his refusal to amend them. Viscount Alanbrooke, the Chief of the Imperial General Staff in 1945, expressed the sentiment of the Chiefs of Staffs at this time:

'We were...shaken by Attlee's new Cabinet paper in which the security of the Middle East must rest in the power of the United Nations.'[31] By this time, the Chiefs of Staff had concluded that Britain's international interests could best be safeguarded by maintaining the string of bases running from the Middle East to the Far East.[32]

From this point on an intermittent, but nevertheless intense, debate raged between the Prime Minister and the foreign policy bureaucracy on Britain's global role. The debate would last over a year and a half. Throughout this period Attlee was influenced by private briefings from the innovative strategist Sir Basil Liddell Hart.[33] Buoyed by such advice, the Prime Minister, as Alan Bullock records, 'showed himself to be a radical and persistent critic of the services' plans.'[34] In the early months of 1946, Attlee decided to press the point much more vigorously in a series of Defence Committee meetings. In his diary, Dalton records the broad outline of the Prime Minister's strategic vision at this time:

> Attlee is pressing on the Chiefs of Staff and the Defence Committee a large view of his own, which aims at considerable disengagement from areas where there is a risk of clashing with the Russians. We should...pull out, from all the Middle East including Egypt and, of course, Greece. We should then constitute a line of defence across Africa from Lagos to Kenya, and concentrate a large part of our forces in the latter. We should face the prospect of going around the Cape in war-time and, the future attitude of India being somewhat uncertain, we should put a large part of Commonwealth Defence, including industries, into Australia. We should thus put a wide glacis of desert and Arabs between ourselves and the Russians. This is a very bold and interesting idea and I am inclined to favour it.[35]

This statement underscores the somewhat conciliatory approach Attlee took toward the Soviet Union in the early postwar years and his appraisal of the limitations economic difficulties were placing on British strategy. He was convinced that Britain's strong position in the Middle East was more likely to precipitate than to deter hostilities with the Soviet Union. In taking this stance, the Prime Minister was indisputably challenging the main currents of opinion on Soviet ambitions in the foreign policy bureaucracy.[36] Yet, he showed no signs of acceding to intense and persistent internal criticism.

It was not only the desire to create a stable, peaceful relationship with the Soviet Union which compelled the Prime Minister to argue so consistently and robustly for a reduction in Britain's overseas military role. He also believed that Britain's military planners placed too much emphasis on naval power, which he recognized to be a legacy of Britain's naval pre-eminence in past centuries. Attlee argued that Britain's bases in land-locked seas like the Mediterranean and the Persian Gulf were now assailable from the air, a vulnerability which greatly diminished their strategic value.[37] To provide adequate air defense would make the overseas bases increasingly costly, and Attlee did not believe the UK economy could support the heavy military presence abroad which the Chiefs of Staff were demanding as it was, either in the long or the short term.

In the ongoing debate in the Defence Committee in early 1946, the Chancellor, as we have seen, agreed that Britain could no longer afford an extensive overseas military presence.[38] Herbert Morrison, Lord President of the Council, also supported the Prime Minister's view, creating a powerful triumvirate in favor of change. But Bevin and the Chiefs of Staff refused to buckle under Attlee's pressure and the issue remained unresolved. By this time Bevin's view of the Soviet Union had hardened and was the complete reverse of that of his Prime Minister. The Foreign Minister told the Cabinet on 3 May 1946 that 'the danger of Russia has certainly become as great as, and possibly even greater than, a revived Germany.'[39] The Chiefs of Staff remained in a state of bewilderment over Attlee's actions, which the First Sea Lord, Andrew Cunningham, described as 'past belief.'[40]

It was becoming apparent, given such gridlock between the Prime Minister on the one hand and Bevin and the Chiefs of Staffs on the other, that some type of reformulation of Britain's defense priorities overseas was becoming increasingly necessary. As the internal debate wore on, Britain had been deprived of a coherent defense policy. Of course, the fluid international environment and the multiple strains on the foreign policy bureaucracy also hindered attempts to set clear priorities for overseas policy. Up to this point, the military had accepted the traditional view that control of latchkey naval bases in the Mediterranean and the Indian Ocean was vital to British interests, and was a sufficient military strategy in and of itself. During the interchanges of early 1946, the Chiefs of Staff were finally persuaded that a new interpretation of Britain's global strategy was necessary, if for no other reason than to quell Attlee. They now embraced the Prime Minister's vision of air power and turned it upside down, using the concept to undermine Attlee's arguments. In early April the Chiefs of Staff argued that there was 'little or no obstacle to a Russian advance to the western seaboard,' particularly after American demobilization. The only effective British deterrent against Soviet aggression was therefore the threat of long-range air strikes launched from the Middle East against vital industrial centers in southern Russia. From the Chiefs of Staff's point of view, then, maintaining the bases in the Middle East was vital to British security.[41]

This new military rationale eroded Attlee's strategic case, but it was based on an assumption that he plainly did not share: that the Soviet Union was Britain's chief potential enemy. Attlee remained skeptical, but he agreed that firm conclusions on the country's global strategy should await the outcome of the Paris Peace Conference scheduled to run from 29 July to 15 October 1946. Little in the way of positive results came from the Paris meetings, and as the situation in both Greece and Palestine steadily worsened toward the end of 1946, the Chiefs of Staff attempted to reassert their strategic doctrine. As was always the case in this early period, Attlee stood fast. It seemed at the beginning of 1947 that the long process of internal debate might drag on for some time. As long as it did, Britain would be deprived of a clear defence policy for the east of Suez area.[42]

The struggle eventually climaxed in early January 1947 when the Prime Minister sent Bevin a long memorandum restating his key strategic ideas, which Alan Bullock claims was 'the most radical criticism Bevin had to face from inside the Government during his five and a half years as Foreign Secretary.'[43] In the memorandum, Attlee concluded that the Chiefs' new approach to the Middle East was little more than a 'strategy of despair.'[44] He argued that Britain was materially too weak to deter the Soviet Union effectively with the threat of air strikes from the Middle East. Once again, he felt that such a strategy increased the probability of tension between the USSR and Britain.

Bevin's reply was sharp in tone. The Foreign Secretary accused Attlee of having strategic ideas which were tantamount to appeasement. Given all of the negative connotations which hung over such a policy in postwar Britain, this was an extremely forceful reposte. Although this surely caused Attlee to pause, it seems that his will was not broken until the increasingly intransigent position of the Chiefs of Staff became apparent.[45] According to Montgomery, who became Chief of the Imperial General Staff in June 1946, a few days after Bevin's terse memorandum the Chiefs of Staff privately informed Attlee that they planned to resign in unison if he continued to oppose them on the necessity of holding the Middle East. After that, 'We heard,' Montgomery records, 'no more about it.'[46]

Attlee's capitulation to the views of the Chiefs of Staffs and Bevin in January 1947 was the result of many factors. Perhaps most important, real world events gradually undermined many of Attlee's assumptions. By mid-1946 he had begun to recognize the limitations of the United Nations, particularly considering the blocking power of the Security Council veto. Also, the premier was able to witness the increasingly belligerent stance of the Soviet Union at first hand at the Paris Peace Conference in late 1946, which he attended at the last moment when Bevin fell ill.[47] Soviet diplomats at this meeting may have given Attlee reason to question his views on the Soviet leadership and their international ambitions.

Also, it may be that, after gauging the increasing rage of the Chiefs of Staff and his most powerful ally in the Cabinet, Bevin, the Prime Minister eventually concluded that this was a battle which he could not win. It was apparent that Whitehall was not prepared for such a radical reformulation of Britain's role in the world after emerging victorious from one of the most perilous struggles in the country's history. Officials throughout the foreign policy bureaucracy no doubt shuddered at the mention of Attlee's proposals, which, in many of their eyes, represented a drastic diminution of Britain's great power status. One further factor proved to be important in stripping Attlee of his radical inclinations. In the winter of 1946–7 the government was in the midst of a fuel crisis which would soon devolve into a much broader economic crisis. As we shall see, in the context of such crises, the Prime Minister's political clout depreciated rapidly. The energetic and original policy initiator of the early postwar years would soon vanish, never to return.

Not long after Attlee retreated into what Robert Holland calls 'the enigmatic shell which subsequently became the hallmark of his official temperament,'[48] Bevin was able to declare to the Commons:

> So far as foreign policy is concerned, we have not altered our commitments in the slightest... His Majesty's Government do not accept the view... that we have ceased to be a great Power, or the contention that we have ceased to play that role. We regard ourselves as one of the Powers most vital to the peace of the world, and we still have our historic part to play.[49]

This statement is widely quoted in studies of the period to demonstrate the strong elements of continuity which characterized the Labour government's foreign policy and the government's strong desire to retain Britain's overseas military role in the face of such sweeping changes as Indian independence. Emphasis should be given, however, to the fact that this well-known speech was not made until 16 May 1947, after the nearly 20-month internal struggle over global strategy had finally been won by Bevin and the foreign policy bureaucracy.

Among other things, the lengthy internal debate on Britain's world role illustrates that the Prime Minister had bold and innovative policy ideas which he pursued vigorously during his first 20 months in office. Kenneth Younger, a junior minister in the Home Office and then the Foreign Office in the late 1940s, describes Attlee as 'the extreme outside left member of the Cabinet.'[50] But Attlee pursued his initiatives in a relatively quiet way, primarily outside of the Cabinet and far from the public eye. The disagreements between Attlee on the one hand and Bevin and the Chiefs of Staff on the other were hashed out mainly in private memoranda and in the Defence Committee. Perhaps because of this, the political alliance which had developed between Attlee and Bevin was never in doubt during the debate. For example, it appears that Attlee prudently refused to undermine Bevin in Cabinet meetings when the Foreign Secretary was abroad, even on issues where the two strongly disagreed. Private quarrels with Bevin were a very different matter than disputes in front of the full Cabinet. In the latter setting, the Prime Minister perspicaciously recognized that his political mainstay must be supported.

One example is the Cabinet's discussion of a paper from Bevin on 7 May 1946, while the Foreign Secretary was in Paris meeting with his Soviet counterpart, Vyacheslav Molotov. This was during the height of the controversy in the Defence Committee over Britain's role in the Middle East. Bevin's report essentially followed the same lines as Churchill's Fulton speech of two months prior, calling for the creation of a combined western strategy to stall the Soviet Union's inevitable expansionist tendencies in Western Europe. The Foreign Secretary's plan drew criticism from a number of ministers, particularly Emanuel Shinwell, the Minister of Fuel and Power, and Bevan on the left, who felt that the Foreign Secretary was exaggerating the Soviet threat. Dalton, the Chancellor, also disapproved because of the additional expenditures Bevin proposed in Germany. Interestingly, only Attlee came to the defense of his Foreign Secretary at the meeting, although his own conception of the Soviet Union at this time was clearly more akin to that of Shinwell and Bevan.[51] As this example illustrates, the argument over Britain's world role rarely, if ever, reached the full Cabinet. Cabinet cohesion remained throughout this period, largely because the attention of ministers remained anchored to the problems of domestic reconstruction and the creation of the new welfare state in these early postwar years.

Thus, despite fierce opposition from the Prime Minister, British foreign policy proceeded seemingly unmoved down the path of continuity. The Labour Cabinet quiescently accepted that it was vital for the country to retain control of the lines of communication to the empire. And, given this assumption, an extensive network of bases strung from the Mediterranean to the Far East was thought to be integral to British security throughout the late 1940s.

Attlee's critique of Britain's global role was certainly the most influential of the time. Yet, uneasiness and even outrage over the country's traditional foreign policy was widespread throughout the labor movement. Along with the support the Conservative opposition provided the Labour government's foreign policy, this swelling dissent provides an important backdrop to the internal debate over global strategy. Although the Cabinet retained firm control over policy in this period, the impotence of Labour backbenchers and the broader Labour movement at this time helps to explain further the traditional character of British foreign policy in the late 1940s.

SWELLING OPPOSITION WITHIN THE LABOUR PARTY

Not unexpectedly, the opposition benches received the Labour government's foreign policy warmly. No better example of this can be found than in the efforts to update Conservative policies in the late 1940s. To many in the Opposition, the crushing defeat at the polls in 1945 underscored the need to redefine Conservatism for the postwar period. The public had to be made aware of the differences between the two parties and the benefits that could be gained through Conservative government. Churchill, the Leader of the Opposition, did not share this opinion, for he felt it better to wait until the new Labour government's gloss began to fade before offering detailed policy alternatives. He eventually acquiesced to the groundswell within his party, led by such men as R.A. Butler and Anthony Eden, which called for clearly articulated Opposition policies. The result was a series of policy statements on specific issues, which culminated in the publication of the official Opposition program in 1949, *The Right Road for Britain*. What is interesting about these declarations is that they emphasized domestic policies, particularly how the Conservatives planned to improve upon the new social and economic structures created by the Labour government. Calls for any real change in foreign and defence policy were noticeably absent.[52] So long as Bevin's more traditional interpretation of Britain's overseas interests prevailed in the Labour Cabinet, the opposition would offer few critiques of the country's foreign policy. Perhaps not surprisingly considering the storm which raged behind closed doors on the government's overseas policy, the Conservatives' main point of censure was that a coherent global strategy had not been produced by the government.[53] This was a legitimate criticism from which the Labour government could not be absolved. But, as has been mentioned, given the rapid pace of change in the global strategic environment, it may have been difficult to produce a lasting framework for defense policy in any case.

While commended by the Opposition, the Labour government's defence of the status quo in foreign policy was certain to generate opposition in many quarters of their own party. Pressure for a 'socialist foreign policy,' which would reflect the same radical change as Labour's social reforms at home, was insistent after 1945. While the precise content of a socialist foreign policy was always somewhat ambiguous, it had long played a prominent role in Labour Party rhetoric. The 1945 general election campaign was no exception in this regard.

One consistent theme of advocates of a socialist foreign policy was the eschewing of traditional, elite-based power politics in favor of an open diplomacy between peoples. The 'real' interest of peoples, it was said, was the same in every country. The roots of these sentiments lay in the peace crusades of Richard Cobden and others on the radical left in the mid-nineteenth century.[54] Moreover, the abrogation of power politics was often thought to be intertwined with and ultimately necessary to build a just, socialist society in Britain. As a young Hugh Dalton asked while a junior minister in the Foreign Office in the late 1920s: 'What use to create an Earthly paradise that enemy aircraft will bomb to smoking ruins, or to begin the building of a Socialist Commonwealth on a foundation of planks stretched across a precipice?'[55] Thus, socialist principles of social justice, fraternity, and cooperation had to be infused into the international order for any truly socialist experiment in Britain to succeed. Although he tended to be more moderate than many in the party, Attlee's desire to avoid direct confrontation with the Soviet Union was a reflection of Labour's traditional distrust of power politics.[56]

Another common and related theme was the need to eradicate international capitalism, which was thought to be inexorably linked with war. Imperialism was considered a distasteful manifestation of capitalism in many quarters of the Labour movement, but it was not universally condemned in the party. The corollary of such anti-capitalism was a fear and distrust of the United States among many on the left-wing, because the US was felt to be the citadel of international finance capitalism.[57]

The degree to which Labour supporters accepted such socialist aspirations after the travails of the Second World War varied greatly. Obviously, the trade union leadership had for quite some time been guided by much more orthodox sentiments. Under Bevin's direction, for example, the unions moved toward rearmament in the 1930s long before the political wing of the party.[58] In the Parliamentary Labour Party, the desire for a socialist foreign policy found voice in two distinctive groups. First was a small fringe of fellow-travelling Marxists who adamantly called for much closer ties to the Soviet Union. Although vocal, this group drew little support and its leaders were eventually expelled from the party in 1948 and 1949.

A much larger grouping consisted of over 50 MPs headed by figures such as Richard Crossman, Michael Foot, and Ian Mikardo. This group argued that Britain should steer clear of Cold War pressures; it also sought greater governmental support for socialist and democratic movements in Greece, the Middle East, and elsewhere.[59] Michael Foot summarized the core belief of this circle at the opening of the 1945 Parliament. He claimed that Britain stood at the zenith of its power and glory because it had 'something unique to offer' international politics – a 'third force' between communism and capitalism. If the country would only combine the 'economic democracy' of the Soviet Union with the 'political democracy' of the West, Foot asserted, Britain could have the moral leadership of the world.[60] Among other things, this illustrates that even the left-wing of the Labour Party accepted Britain's great power status as an article of faith at this time. These views also differed considerably from Attlee's internationalism. Whereas the Prime Minister sought a more effective supranational organization to preserve the peace, an inherent nationalism underlay the proposals for a 'third force' in the world which Britain would naturally lead.

These two leftist groups combined in November 1946 to put forward an amendment calling for a 'socialist alternative' to the two superpowers, which was the first serious challenge to the government from the parliamentary party. Fifty-six MPs (out of a total of 393), mainly on the left, signed the amendment. A further 70 abstained from the motion that the government put through. In a separate amendment, 45 Labour MPs voted against the continuation of peacetime conscription, which the government felt necessary given the country's extensive postwar responsibilities. Although there was little sign of sustained, organized opposition at this point, the revolt caused alarm in Cabinet. It prompted a scathing attack on the PLP from Bevin at the 1947 annual conference, by which time the rebellion had petered out.[61] A more organized revolt soon formed, however, in the 'Keep Left' group, a coterie of some 15 MPs who met regularly in the Commons to urge the government to adopt an independent course in foreign policy. Crossman and Foot were prominent members of this gathering. But even as it was forming the group was swimming behind history's tide. As the Cold War enveloped Europe, marked especially by the coup in Czechoslovakia and the Berlin blockade in 1948, the 'Keep Left' group splintered. Many of the group, including Crossman and Foot, were driven into support of the American alliance by the stark choices imposed by East–West hostility.[62]

In general, the party leadership remained firmly in control, and such revolts caused them little embarrassment. The government retreated in the face of backbench pressure only once, and this was over the historically sensitive issue of conscription. Even in that case, the government would later reverse its policy to support its original plan of an 18- rather than a 12-month period of national service.[63] Not surprisingly, Bevin was particularly unwilling to listen to, much less accede to, the views of left-wing backbenchers. His sentiment was surely reflected in the words of one of his supporters who told left-wing critics that 'they would learn more if they spent more time in working-class pubs than in attending gatherings of Bloomsbury Bolsheviks.'[64]

Part of the explanation for the occasional parliamentary revolts lay in the changing character of the party. The make-up of the PLP became significantly more middle-class after the war. Whereas before 1939 elementary schooling was the norm, after 1945 over 100 members of the PLP held university degrees and more than a third were professionals – lawyers, doctors, university lecturers, teachers, and journalists. Moreover, 253 of the 393 Labour MPs in 1945 had entered the Commons for the first time. Since government posts were filled with party stalwarts, it was perhaps inescapable that some frustration would be expressed by green, energetic backbenchers who had little hope for promotion into the government. The natural outlet for such frustration was foreign affairs, since the government's domestic policies were widely supported in the party. Nonetheless, the infrequent backbench revolts of this period were never more than a minor irritant for the Cabinet. By contrast, the next Labour government to take power, that of Harold Wilson in the 1960s, would have much difficulty keeping control over the increasingly articulate and ambitious ranks of middle-class professionals in the PLP.[65]

Yet, in many ways the PLP's limited impact on the leadership is deceptive. Throughout the government's life, a lingering unease existed among Labour supporters over the country's foreign policy course. There was a genuine and widespread feeling that a Labour government should implement a foreign policy very different from that which would be put in place by a Conservative regime. A Labour government should, it was widely believed, be more actively committed to internationalism and initiatives that would promote peaceful cooperation between nation-states than was the case. The maintenance of both colonial and overseas military outposts did not fit well within this framework. Although it was scarcely noticeable in the relatively serene context of postwar policymaking, grassroots disaffection was growing dramatically at this time.[66] Criticism of Labour's foreign policy flooded into Transport House, the central office of the Labour Party, from union members and the constituency parties. But it was smothered effectively by the party's General Secretary, Morgan Phillips, who used his influence to reinforce the government's position.[67] After the Attlee government lost power, such widespread, but suppressed, dissent would broaden eventually into an intense debate over foreign and defence policy. The deep rift which emerged in the early 1950s on these issues would do perhaps irreparable damage to the Labour Party. But, during the Attlee government's tenure, such dissent was scarcely perceptible.

The support that Churchill and Eden consistently gave to Bevin's policies only added to the trepidation of many in the labor movement. The enthusiastic backing that traditionally right-wing newspapers gave to the government's foreign policy also was disturbing. Yet, after the ordeal of the war and experience in the wartime coalition, bipartisanship on foreign policy seemed to be interwoven into the fabric of British politics in the late 1940s.[68] The crucial test of bipartisan attitudes at this time was the Middle East. The Conservatives surely would have castigated the Labour government if Attlee had won his battle to disengage from the Middle East. As we know, this never happened. The Labour government staunchly supported Britain's world role at every turn, and Churchill and Eden were more than willing to support such a policy.[69]

Moreover, the Labour government enjoyed remarkably broad support in the press regardless of the issue. Of the serious newspapers, the *Manchester Guardian* backed the government throughout its lifetime. *The Times* was astonishingly pro-Labour between 1945 and 1947. And although it gradually began to turn away from the government following the economic troubles in 1947, it could not be counted as being firmly in the Conservative camp until about 1950. The *Observer* was also broadly in sympathy with the government, particularly before 1948, as was *The Economist*.[70] Perhaps not surprisingly, the only sustained criticism of the government's external policy came from the two main outlets of the Labour Left, the *New Statesman* and *Tribune*, the latter edited by Michael Foot of the 'Keep Left' group.[71]

Yet, as we have seen, neither left-wing criticism nor the internal struggle of the Prime Minister ultimately had any effect on the country's policy course. Britain remained firmly committed to the east of Suez role after the Second World War. Ironically, it was the first sign that the twin goals of 'welfare' and 'greatness' were severely straining the British economy, the convertibility crisis of 1947, which ensured the survival of Britain's world role. As we shall see, this crisis purged the Labour government of its radical momentum.

THE 'ANNUS HORRENDUS' AND THE END OF RADICAL MOMENTUM

Within two months of Bevin's confident assertion in May 1947 that Britain still has 'its historic part to play', the Labour government was engulfed in a severe economic crisis which proved to be a decisive turning point for the administration. The fundamental problem was Britain's currency. The cause of the economic travails of summer 1947 would mark a consistent theme in Britain's postwar history: the lack of international confidence in the British economy, as refracted through sterling.

Until early 1947, the Labour government had been riding on a crest of success and popularity. The economy showed every sign of a boom in 1946. Exports recovered strongly from the war, up 111 per cent from the 1938 level. Particularly impressive were British exports in metal goods and chemicals, two symbols of industrial strength. Of course, with the devastation in Europe and Asia after the war British industries had very little competition outside of the United States. Even so, by all indications it appeared that the postwar revitalization of Britain's industrial base would proceed at a rapid pace.[72]

In early 1947, the bottom fell out of this boom. The year proved to be an unmitigated economic disaster. Britain's already inadequate infrastructure for coal production and distribution was thrown into crisis by the country's most severe winter of the century. Bitter cold and snow blanketed the British Isles for over two months. It proved impossible to transport coal by road, rail, or sea. Soon power stations had to be closed with disastrous consequences for industry. For a government which prided itself on economic planning, the episode was deeply humiliating. But it was only the beginning of what would be a series of humbling crises for the Attlee regime.[73]

Unfortunately, the fuel crisis added to the shortages in important raw materials that British industry had been coping with since the war, and by the spring of 1947 exports began to drop off sharply. As exports fell, dollars began to flow out of Britain at an alarming pace. Britain was simply exporting much less to dollar markets than it was receiving. A global shortage of food and raw materials had left the United States virtually the sole supplier and, worse still, American prices rose sharply in early 1947. The result was catastrophic. In the first six months of 1947 roughly $1890 million was swept away, over half of the American loan of $3750 million. It seemed that the 1945 loan, intended to stabilize the British economy through to 1951, would run out sometime in 1948 or even sooner.[74]

Worse still, a number of foreign policy crises deepened in that bleak winter. By late February 1947 the Cabinet, 'in a mood of panic akin to 1939,' was compelled to make a series of fateful decisions.[75] It was decided that on 31 March the British embassy in Washington would inform the State Department that Britain would no longer be able to continue its military and financial aid to Greece and Turkey. Dalton's financial arguments and Attlee's strategic doubts prevailed over the continued objections of Bevin and the Chiefs of Staff on this issue.[76] If the United States wanted to prevent the spread of communism in this area, it would have to carry the burden itself. In that same month, the United Kingdom referred the ongoing problem of Palestine to the United Nations. With mounting costs and British public outrage at the terror tactics practiced by some Jewish guerrilla groups, which included the bombing of the King David Hotel in Jerusalem and the public hanging of two young British sergeants, the government decided to surrender the Palestine mandate completely in September. Not long afterwards, British forces ignominiously retreated 'bag and baggage' from this portion of the Levant.[77]

It was also in late February that Attlee announced that, come what may, Britain would withdraw from India no later than June 1948. The date was soon brought forward, with the official transfer of power taking place on 15 August 1947. Despite the carnage which accompanied the partition of the subcontinent into two new states, India and Pakistan, the government's handling of the transfer of power generally has been perceived in Britain as a notable achievement. This feeling was reinforced when the new nations promptly joined the Commonwealth. But the loss of what had been the jewel of the British empire for well over a century was still a devastating psychological blow to many Britons, and a tangible sign of the country's waning power.[78]

After these momentous decisions in early 1947, the Labour government's position seemed to be crumbling on all sides, and disaster loomed on the horizon. As the economic situation deteriorated, the pre-arranged date for sterling's convertibility, 15 July, was fast approaching. Convertibility, again, was a condition Britain agreed to in order to secure the American loan in 1945. Sterling would have come under tremendous strain with convertibility even if the British economy had been healthy. In the circumstances of July 1947, with gold and dollar reserves running out and the balance of payments position eroding, convertibility proved to be unbearable.

Yet, the ensuing débâcle was not anticipated in London, either in the government or in the City. It was widely believed that convertibility's blow would be softened by a number of transitional arrangements the Treasury had made with sterling holders overseas.[79] This did not prove to be the case. Within days of convertibility's announcement there was a massive outflow of capital from London, far surpassing the first half of the year when the situation was already serious. In the month following the announcement the drain of dollars averaged $135.5 million a week, compared to roughly $77 million a week in the second quarter of the year.[80] By mid-August, British officials and ministers had to rush to Washington to get permission to reimpose the controls that they had previously agreed to remove. The episode indicated how fragile international confidence in the British economy already had become.[81] Moreover, it had a profound impact upon the government. A regime which seemed to carry all before it in early 1947 was now shaken to its core.

There were very few successes for the government in what the Chancellor labelled the 'annus horrendus'.[82] The government initiated thorough and effective agricultural reforms, transport and electricity were nationalized, and the Marshall Plan was announced in June 1947, the latter being a particularly bright point in a bad year. But, overall, the government was reeling from a nearly constant state of crisis throughout much of 1947. Labour slumped in the opinion polls and, as has been seen, the press started to lose faith in the government. The cohesion which had up to this point typified the Cabinet dissolved as bickering between senior ministers became almost constant. As the year wore on the government seemed to become steadily more exhausted, with the pinnacle of despair perhaps being the convertibility crisis. During this long year, as Kenneth Morgan observes, 'the strength and vitality of the Labour government fled, never really to return.'[83]

Not surprisingly, severe financial and foreign policy crises soon created a political crisis. The Prime Minister came under increasing criticism from nearly every corner of the Labour movement for his inability to offer firm leadership during the disastrous year. At a meeting of the PLP on 11 August the Prime Minister encountered an unprecedented degree of opposition, most notably over his lack of drive to boost exports and the government's heavy defense spending. He reportedly offered to resign at this point, but was dissuaded from doing so by his Cabinet colleagues. Yet, Attlee was exhausted and felt deeply the humiliation of the government's predicament. Worse still, there was wide speculation in the press that his ouster was imminent. As the Prime Minister was apparently well aware, these reports were based on the backroom maneuvering of some the heaviest hitters in his Cabinet. During a period spanning from at least July through September, Sir Stafford Cripps, Herbert Morrison, and Hugh Dalton were actively trying to remove Attlee. The only question that seemed to remain, for these men at least, was who would be the successor. The most obvious candidate, Bevin, refused to take any part in such betrayal. Such a firm stance by the government's most influential minister was perhaps the chief reason a palace coup was avoided in the dreadful autumn of 1947.[84]

Nonetheless, from this moment forward Attlee appeared less obviously in command. It appears that he receded into the silent, pipe-smoking, almost anonymous figure sitting at the top of the Cabinet table which studies of the Labour government typically recall. In fact, it might be questioned whether Attlee had any real impact on policy after this point, save for the important decision over the war in Korea in 1950.[85] The ramifications for the overseas military role were obvious. The most radical critic of Britain's east of Suez role in the Cabinet had been drained after a prolonged struggle with the foreign policy establishment and then completely undermined politically and, according to some observers, psychologically by a series of grave crises. Britain's overseas military role would not be questioned in the central governmental machine for the rest of the Labour government's life. In fact, it was not until the late 1950s, following the Suez débâcle, that the overseas military role was again seriously challenged from within the government.

Yet, the Prime Minister's political retreat was not the only reason Britain's overseas military role was never again challenged in the Labour government. Other factors compounded the impact of the Prime Minister's silence. Foremost among these is the Cabinet reshuffle that followed the convertibility crisis, which altered both the complexion of the Attlee regime and its priorities. A Cabinet shake-up seemed necessary given the widespread criticism of the government, and the subsequent reshuffle in September pushed the Cabinet even farther to the right. Shinwell, the minister politically responsible for the fuel crisis, was demoted out of Cabinet. With 'Red' Ellen Wilkinson's accidental death earlier in the year, Bevan was now the sole representative of the left in the Cabinet. The young MPs promoted to junior ministerial positions, such as George Brown and Patrick Gordon Walker, also tended to be from the right, sealing the shift in that direction. The chief victim of the crises was Dalton, the formerly confident, breezy Chancellor. Stafford Cripps, stern and evangelistic, replaced Dalton in November, signalling a substantial change in the mood of the government.[86]

It was immediately evident that the austere Cripps gained the most from this shift in the balance of Cabinet authority. Attlee's and Dalton's stars had clearly fallen in the calamitous year, and Morrison's political clout was considerably weakened as well. It was Morrison's Lord President's Committee which had been charged with Economic planning, and hence the unmitigated economic failure of 1947 reflected poorly on the Lord President. Bevin remained a unique and powerful force in Cabinet, but as we shall see, his foreign policy had reached a new pinnacle with the restoration of the Anglo-American alliance in mid-1947 and his energies were increasingly absorbed over the coming years by the monumental task of laying the groundwork for the North Atlantic Treaty Organization (NATO).

In this political vacuum, the Chancellor had the decisive say on domestic matters in the Cabinet, and his image was soon superimposed on that of the government as a whole.[87]

With Cripps' ascendancy, the age of austerity had been ushered in. Succinctly capturing the aura which surrounded the post-1947 Labour government, Kenneth Morgan describes it 'a curious, evangelical regime of Cromwellian severity.'[88] The government seemed to exhort the nation to practice the same self-sacrifice and discipline which undoubtedly governed the grim, puritanical Chancellor. Added to this moralistic stance, Cripps' economic program stressed cutbacks and retrenchment, which seemed necessary to bring the balance of payments into equilibrium and to bridge the dollar gap.[89] Many thought Cripps' economic policies bore a striking resemblance to a siege economy. Rather than a multilateral trade regime, the economy now rested securely in a closed trading bloc based on the sterling area and the European Payments Union. The government also was clearly on the defensive politically during Cripps' era. It appeared to struggle to hold on to the political ground which already had been won. Under such a weary, cautious regime, bold policy initiatives could not be expected. Britain's foreign policy would remain on its traditional course.

Paradoxically, as the government stumbled from crisis to crisis in 1947, Ernest Bevin was just reaching his stride in the Foreign Office. Yet the Foreign Secretary's endeavors would prove to be yet another factor preventing any further attention being given to Britain's overseas military commitments. The turning point for Bevin came with the announcement that Britain could no longer afford to support Greek government forces in their ongoing civil war. This bombshell was well-timed because American thinking had been slowly stiffening with regard to the Soviet Union, particularly as pessimistic cables poured in from the chief American representatives in Moscow, Averell Harriman and George Kennan.[90] The result was perhaps the most significant transformation of American foreign policy in the country's history, embodied in the Truman Doctrine. Uncertainty over the role America would play in world affairs was promptly swept away when the Truman administration agreed to take up the burden in the eastern Mediterranean. Not long after, in June 1947, the Marshall Plan was announced, which was a bright ray of hope in a generally dismal year for the Attlee government.

The Marshall Plan was a critical watershed in Bevin's foreign policy. Up to this point, his policies appeared fumbling and unsure, perhaps in part because of the ongoing debate over Britain's global strategy within the government. After mid-1947 and the announcement of Marshall Aid, nearly all of Bevin's considerable energies were directed toward the same goal, a goal which the Foreign Minister had been striving to achieve since 1945: the creation of a comprehensive regional security system for Western Europe which included the United States.[91] Since the end of the war, the Foreign Secretary's paramount fear was an American withdrawal from the European continent similar to that which had occurred in 1919, with disastrous results. American involvement was crucial, Bevin believed, because the terrain of European defence was strikingly barren: Germany and Italy had no armies and that of France remained untried. In Europe, Britain alone was capable of defending the gains of the Second World War from potential communist aggression.

As the United States' desire to assume the responsibilities of global leadership became more apparent, Bevin's foreign policy not unnaturally gained a new clarity and confidence. The groundwork that Bevin helped to lay for the distribution of the Marshall Plan aid eventually would culminate with the creation of NATO, which is often considered the crowning achievement of Bevin's diplomatic career.[92] Disputes of the early postwar years, such as that over Palestine, receded into the background as a broader framework for economic and military cooperation was erected with the United States. Except for minor disagreements during the Korean War, which would generate some lingering mistrust, the Anglo-American alliance would remain on relatively firm ground until the Suez crisis of 1956.

Not only the Foreign Secretary's attention was becoming increasingly fixed on Europe during this period; after the announcement of the Marshall Plan and with the progress toward NATO, popular and press attention were as well. Events in 1948, particularly the Czechoslovakian coup and the Berlin blockade, riveted the public's gaze on Europe. Years of what seemed to be extraordinary peril, when war could break out at any moment, followed these events and would last until at least the end of the Korean War.[93] Britain's east of Suez role was not a significant consideration for the public in such a tense climate of Cold War confrontation.

In addition, since Europe was widely considered the most likely site of East–West confrontation, British military planning also was increasingly focused on the Continent.[94] Because of the legacy of the Second World War, a common assumption in Whitehall was that modern war would of necessity be total war. As was the case in

1939–45, countries would be compelled to devote their entire national capacities to winning a global struggle. In such a scenario, the east of Suez commitments could not figure prominently. When they were given consideration, it was as part of a broader strategic picture which had central Europe as its main focus. Given this neglect, old notions on the need for open sea lanes continued to dominate British strategic thinking on the east of Suez role[95] – with, of course, the Cold War strike-capability of Middle Eastern bases welded somewhat incongruously on top of this predominantly naval framework.

Europe figured increasingly prominently in another way as the late 1940s wore on. The idea of a more closely integrated Western Europe was debated fairly widely throughout the lifetime of the Labour government, and the integration movement gained particular momentum throughout Europe after 1947. This debate also diverted attention from the overseas military role, although only slightly. It may even be argued that the importance of Britain's overseas role was only magnified as a result of the controversy over the possible creation of a united Europe. There were many reasons that the idea gained legitimacy after 1945, including: the need to heal the wounds of the Second World War; the desire to assert European independence in a world increasingly dominated by the superpowers; the perceived need to bind Germany into a cooperative framework within Europe; and the growing political influence of men such as Jean Monnet, the French economic planner, who had been an advocate of the idea since before the war. Although Bevin labored tirelessly to create a united defense structure in Europe, both he and the government took a skeptical and ultimately dismissive view of European political and economic integration. Above all, the Labour government did not want Britain to be lumped in with the pedestrian countries on the Continent. Britain had emerged victorious from the war and remained a world power. The ideal of a united Western Europe, it seemed to many, was better suited for countries whose national pride had been broken during the war. Labour leaders made it perfectly clear that they wanted nothing to do with a federal Europe as talks on this prospect proceeded. If one digs a little deeper behind the almost xenophobic stance of the British government, appropriate fears of European economic competition, particularly from a revived Germany, are unmistakable at this time. Although it could scarcely have been anticipated in the late 1940s, the European enterprise eventually would develop into a legitimate alternative to the east of Suez role for British policymakers. Yet, it would take a further two decades of

British relative economic decline before this fact was appreciated by Britain's leaders.[96]

HOLDING COURSE

Thus, with public and official attention focused on Europe, fundamental questions about Britain's interests and its capabilities east of Suez were neglected. By the end of the 1940s, supporters of the overseas military role had weathered persistent and radical criticism from the most powerful figure in the government. Whitehall, it seemed, was not ready to accept a dramatic reduction of its overseas military role, particularly when the country had just emerged victorious from the most destructive war in its history and was still widely considered to be among the most influential nations in the world. The Chiefs of Staff and the Foreign Office were particularly astonished by the Prime Minister's tenacious criticism of Britain's role in the Middle East. Their opposition, combined with the swift flow of postwar events, ensured that Britain's role in the east of Suez area would not change. Growing grassroots disgruntlement in the Labour Party over the course of British foreign policy did little to change this equation, largely because power within the party was concentrated in the hands of a few men.

It should be emphasized that Attlee did not advocate the complete abandonment of the east of Suez network. He still believed ardently in Britain's international greatness, as is evinced by the decision to build atomic weapons. He also appears to have raised few objections to the deepening of Britain's colonial interests in subSaharan Africa. Nevertheless, his proposal to reduce Britain's overseas military network to bases on the eastern coast of Africa and the western coast of Australia, supplied in wartime by a naval route around the Cape, was a dramatic reformulation of Britain's traditional role in the area. If he had succeeded in persuading the government to abandon the most crucial component in the east of Suez network at that time, the Middle East, common perceptions of Britain's world role would have been altered. After such a dramatic transformation, officials might have begun to look at Britain's overseas military role through lenses less clouded by sentiment and the longing for international prestige. The myth that Britain's overseas bases were intrinsically valuable may have been questioned more often both among government officials and in the populace. If this were the case, future reappraisals of Britain's interests east of Suez would have been much easier. As it was, though, Attlee was considered an ill-informed and unwelcome intruder on foreign policy matters in Whitehall. The east of Suez network remained intact, and the extensive chain of bases continued to be widely conceived as one of the cornerstones of Britain's greatness.

Perhaps more than anything else, it was the continued belief in Britain's great power status which prevented a dramatic reformulation of British foreign policy after the Second World War. It was clear to the government that the country was in dire economic straits, but for a considerable time this was regarded to be only a temporary consequence of the war. By the late 1940s officials began to grasp the long-term damage the war had done to the British economy, and that full recovery and growth would be much harder than they had imagined. Even at this early date the margins for fiscal error were extremely small because of the ambitious pursuit of both 'welfare' at home and 'greatness' abroad. Rationing of a number of basic food items persisted until the early 1950s, and even the cost of small initiatives, such as the dispatch of a battalion to Eritrea, was of concern to the Cabinet. But the time for really big decisions had not yet arrived. It was not yet apparent that Britain's expansive domestic and international goals would prove to be too heavy a burden on the country's frail economy. The argument over 'guns versus butter' would not begin in earnest in Britain until the late 1950s. Before that time, it seemed that Britain, as one the most powerful countries on earth, could afford both.

5 Reappraisal: The Suez Crisis and its Aftermath, 1957–60

The Suez crisis is often claimed to be a watershed in postwar British history. The operation to retake the Suez Canal was among the most significant British military ventures in the twentieth century, and it was perhaps the most humiliating. The belief, both at home and abroad, that Britain was a world power of the first rank is commonly thought to have been stripped away by failure in this episode. Yet, while the events of late 1956 were a stunning blow to Britain's international prestige, the significance of the crisis for the east of Suez role is less than one might suspect. In fact, with regard to the country's overseas military role, the years immediately following the Suez débâcle did not mark a sharp break with the past. The main lines of Britain's policy east of Suez remained remarkably steady in the late 1950s.

The Suez episode nevertheless helped to precipitate important changes which, over time, would contribute to the decision to withdraw from east of Suez. For example, the increasing precariousness of British bases overseas from the late 1950s on is closely connected to the surge of anti-British nationalism which the Suez adventure sparked throughout much of the Indian Ocean area. Substantial transformations in Britain's foreign policy machinery and in the country's strategic doctrine in the mid-1960s also have roots in the débâcle on the banks of the Suez Canal. If Suez can be seen as a watershed, then, it is largely because developments which had their genesis in the events of October and November 1956 would later gain a momentum of their own.

There was little change in British politics in the immediate aftermath of the Suez episode, in the late 1950s and early 1960s. Britain's economic and diplomatic rejuvenation following the crisis was remarkably swift. The government recovered its equanimity with surprising speed as well. A resurgent mood among both the populace and political leaders by the late 1950s seemed to indicate that the Suez affair was an idiosyncratic, almost anomalous, event. An attempt was made to re-evaluate Britain's fundamental interests in the world following the shock of the Suez episode, but those officials who argued that the country should rein in its overseas military role, and perhaps even abandon it, encountered a wall of political indifference at this time. As in the past, British policy was allowed to evolve pragmatically in response to external events, and this led, perhaps not unnaturally, to an emphasis on security operations east of Suez. In sum, the postwar tranquillity of British politics, centered on a consensus on 'welfare' at home and 'greatness' abroad, was not disturbed radically by the trauma of the Suez crisis.

In the following pages, the blow which the Suez crisis represented for both British policymakers and, perhaps even more so, the public is outlined. The structure of power in the Macmillan regime is also described. For, as we shall see, it is chiefly to the successes of the Macmillan government, and to the beliefs held by the Prime Minister himself, that one must look to comprehend Britain's foreign policy path in the late 1950s. Particular emphasis is given to the Sandys Doctrine, the government's mainly unsuccessful attempt to restructure Britain's defense apparatus and to curb military spending in 1957, and to the exhaustive, but extremely secretive, reviews of Britain's world role which were initiated in that same year.

Perhaps more than any other phenomena of the late 1950s, these secret reviews demonstrate why the Suez episode had virtually no effect on the country's overseas commitments. Not only do these reappraisals of Britain's world role illustrate how perceptions of foreign bases were beginning to change in Whitehall, they also underscore the reasons why opponents of the east of Suez role ultimately failed to influence policy in this period.[1] In many ways, the heated discussions in the clandestine committee rooms of these reviews were a microcosm of opinion throughout Britain following the shock of Suez. Fervent calls for a reduction in Britain's seemingly overextended world role marked the initial stages of this review process, but they were soon subsumed by more traditional interpretations of Britain's global interests as the nation's political, economic, and strategic position recovered in the late 1950s.

THE SUEZ EPISODE

On 5 November 1956, British and French paratroopers landed at Port Said on the Sinai Peninsula in Egypt. Within 24 hours they had captured the port and began moving inland. It was a fateful episode for postwar Britain. Working in collusion with France and Israel, the British invasion was the Eden government's response to Nasser's nationalization of the British- and French-controlled Suez Canal Company in July of that same year. Although Britain had already agreed in 1954 to evacuate British forces from the Suez base by mid-1956, every shade of British opinion demanded some sort of immediate action in response to the Egyptian act of bravado. Churchill, as he had done so often in the past, summed up the national mood when he told his doctor: 'We can't have this malicious swine sitting across our communications.'[2] The Prime Minister, Anthony Eden, who by 1956 was an ill and perhaps even an unstable man, appeared to be swept up in the atmosphere of rabid nationalism which washed across the country. Even the Labour Party leader Hugh Gaitskell initially acknowledged that Britain might have to use force, if such action was sanctioned by the UN.[3]

For many in Parliament, particularly the government's backbenchers, Nasser's action seemed to harken back to the dark days of lawless aggression in the 1930s.[4] Eden, who had resigned as Foreign Secretary in 1938 in protest at the policies of the Chamberlain government, publicly compared Nasser to Mussolini, and declared that Britain could not again fall into the trap of appeasing dictators. He was convinced that British influence in Africa and Asia would be undermined permanently if Egypt was allowed to commandeer the Suez Canal. Despite repeated warnings from the Eisenhower administration that they would not look favorably on the use of arms, Eden eventually concluded that Nasser's action could not be allowed to go unchecked.[5] Like his colleague Harold Macmillan, then Chancellor of the Exchequer, he decided that it would be better to see Britain 'go down against Egypt with all flags flying rather than submit to the Suez despoliation.'[6]

Unfortunately for Eden and the country, a little over two days after British troops had landed on the coast of Egypt, Britain did 'go down' in the operation, suffering a bitter diplomatic defeat at the hands of their erstwhile American allies. Under heavy economic pressure from the United States, the Eden Cabinet was compelled to call a ceasefire in Egypt on 8 November. Britain's gold and dollar reserves were expected to fall by over $300 million in the month of November under the crippling American pressure, and this would undoubtedly have a huge effect on international confidence in sterling.[7] To many in the Cabinet it seemed that the nation's economy was teetering on the brink of insolvency. The humiliating retreat from Egypt which followed would have far-reaching consequences for Britain.

Among other things, popular perceptions of the country's role in the world were jarred by Britain's political and diplomatic failure at Suez. Although British policymakers had known of the country's underlying economic and military weaknesses for some time, the public image was of a country that was still among the world's pre-eminent powers. The defiant stand against Hitler in 1940, victory in 1945, and postwar recovery only reinforced this popular perception of greatness. As David Reynolds pithily put it, 'for an Egyptian ex-colonel to twist the lion's tail, and get away with it, was a palpable and lasting blow to national self-esteem and international prestige.'[8] Beyond this, the Suez fiasco, as it has come to be seen in retrospect, also disrupted the standard lines of postwar British diplomacy. It brought about the most severe fissure in Anglo-American relations since the Second World War and placed the future of the 'special relationship' in doubt. It opened up a chasm in the Commonwealth between those backing and those denouncing Britain's actions. It made Britain a pariah at the United Nations, an especially acrid turn of events in an organization that Britain had helped to found. It exposed the vulnerability of sterling to American economic pressure and raised fears that an independent foreign policy might now be a thing of the past. It revealed the limitations of British military power and the dubious value of overseas bases in times of crisis. For, although the British forces worked with admirable efficiency once on the ground, the approach to Egypt was slow and cumbersome.[9] The Suez crisis also generated sharp political differences at home. As at the time of Munich, friendships were split and anger seemed to return to postwar Britain. Although the temperature would fall rapidly after the ceasefire, it would be some time before a sense of national unity would be restored. And finally, along with Eden's declining health, the Suez episode led to a change of premiers and threatened to topple the government altogether.[10]

Inheriting this tumultuous situation was Harold Macmillan, whose elevation to Number 10 was the most immediate consequence of the crisis. Macmillan's unwillingness to apologize for the invasion and his determination to portray it in the best possible light, and even as a victory of sorts, was perhaps the key reason he emerged from the murky selection processes of the Conservative Party. He was the leading protégé of the country's great war hero, Churchill, and he appeared to offer a degree of calm reassurance to a party and a nation which were reeling from the most devastating political blow in living memory.[11]

Not surprisingly, the Suez episode would cast a long shadow over the early years of the Macmillan government. The overriding objective of policy was to repair the political and economic damage done to the country in the last months of 1956. Questions were raised about the utility of maintaining an extensive overseas military network in the wake of Suez, in the press, in academic forums, and most importantly, in the government. To understand why Britain's overseas military role scarcely changed after this dramatic failure, it is first necessary to outline the broader political background of the immediate post-Suez years.

THE POST-SUEZ POLITICAL SCENE: MENDING FENCES ABROAD AND CONSOLIDATING POWER AT HOME

In the unstable political climate which followed Suez, it was widely believed that Macmillan's premiership was a stopgap which would last just weeks or months. Bitterness pervaded Parliament in the early months of 1957. Always outspoken on the opposition benches, Aneurin Bevan called it 'the squalid Parliament' because of the 'lingering stench of Suez about the place.'[12] The Tory ranks were in disarray over the entire affair, and party morale reached its postwar nadir. Gallup polls consistently were against the party, a fact repeated in by-election results for 18 months.[13] The new Prime Minister thus had inherited exceptionally adverse, if not outright explosive, political circumstances.

Yet, Macmillan entered office with great enthusiasm, determined to revive the flagging fortunes of his party and to repair the damage done to Britain's international prestige. To many observers his outwardly calm demeanor, which had often looked dull in normal times and at lower government posts, seemed to mesh perfectly with the needs of the time.[14] Macmillan soothed the nation by re-affirming Britain's greatness in a Churchillian manner. In his first public broadcast after becoming Prime Minister, on 17 January, he called for an end to defeatist talk of Britain being a second-rank power: 'What nonsense. This is a great country and do not let us be ashamed to say so...there is no reason to quiver before temporary difficulties.'[15] The new Prime Minister simply carried on as if the Suez crisis had never happened. And his confidence and showmanship would soon help to reinvigorate both the Conservative Party and the nation.

His most pressing task was to choose his Cabinet. This he did carefully, for while he did not want to disown Suez, he also recognized that fresh blood had to be brought into the government. To the surprise of many, Macmillan kept Selwyn Lloyd, the most obvious scapegoat for the Suez débâcle, on at the Foreign Office. Retaining Lloyd was a symbol of Macmillan's refusal to apologize for Suez, and since Lloyd was not known to be a man of bold ideas, it was also a signal that Macmillan intended to manage foreign affairs himself and to take an active lead in his government. He also planned to keep defence matters closely under his control, which meant replacing Eden's Minister of Defence, Antony Head. The new Prime Minister's desire to dominate overseas affairs led him to place the only minister with political clout approaching his own, R.A. Butler, in the Home Office. To fill the post of Chancellor of the Exchequer, which Macmillan had held, he promoted Peter Thorneycroft, an outspoken figure whom he had respected as President of the Board of Trade under Eden. It was a fairly substantial reformulation of the Cabinet. After March 1957, only four ministers remained from the 1951–5 Conservative Cabinet, and most of Macmillan's team consisted of relatively young men who had entered Parliament in the 1950s. The government thus bore the unmistakable personal stamp of the new Prime Minister.[16]

As a result, it was not long before Macmillan established authority over his Cabinet colleagues, many of whom were still somewhat unnerved by the Suez episode. To several observers it seemed that Macmillan had an innate need to lead, and he ran the Cabinet in an informal but business-like way. Unlike his predecessor Eden, he did not interfere in departmental management. By allowing ministers to carry out policies unhindered after a decision had been reached and then backing them to the hilt, Macmillan created a powerful cult of loyalty in the Cabinet. The new, relaxed, trusting atmosphere reinvigorated the Cabinet, boosting the ministers' morale in the trying period which immediately followed the Suez episode. 'It is impossible,' wrote Lord Kilmuir, the Lord Chancellor, 'to overemphasise the personal contribution of the Prime Minister to the renaissance of the government.'[17] The Chancellor of Duchy of Lancaster, Charles Hill, would later say that he thought Macmillan's 'chairmanship of the Cabinet to be superb by any standards. If he dominated it (he usually did) it was done by sheer superiority of mind and judgement.'[18] Macmillan's transcendence in Cabinet is important for understanding Britain's foreign policy path following the Suez crisis. For once he had consolidated his power within the Conservative Party, there was no alternative leadership or policy.[19] In contrast to the Labour government of the late 1940s, one need look no further than the Prime Minister to grasp the general outline of British foreign policy in the late 1950s. If a substantial change in the country's international posture was to occur, it would have to be supported, and most likely initiated, by Macmillan.

But it was only after the parliamentary debate over the terms with Egypt in May that the Prime Minister felt sure he had gained firm control over his party. Often called the Suez debate, this episode marked the final stand of the right-wing diehards on the Tory backbenches. The original 'Suez rebels,' who began their protest over three years earlier when the Suez base began to be evacuated, were depleted by this time. Their leader, Captain Charles Waterhouse, had left the country to defend the empire's glory in Rhodesia. Perhaps their most outspoken member, Julian Amery, had joined his father-in-law's government. Subsequently, in the vote on the Suez measures, only eight Conservative MPs voted against the government and a further 14 abstained – a remarkably timid protest. With this vote the Macmillan government convincingly demonstrated that it had won the loyalty of its backbenchers, and questions over the government's survival soon faded.[20] As Leon Epstein observes, 'the crucial political fact about the Suez crisis was the support of the Government by Conservative MPs, including some who never wanted to go into Egypt and some who never wanted to come out.'[21] The Suez debate foreshadowed the unyielding backbench support which would remain during the somewhat turbulent political period which followed the débâcle in Egypt.

Macmillan learned a key political lesson during the Suez debate, one which he would not soon forget. He triumphed over his critics at this time by reaffirming Britain's greatness in the world and, more importantly, by focusing attention on a fresh symbol of the country's international prestige – the nuclear deterrent. Fortuitously for the Prime Minister, on the first day of the debate over the terms with Egypt, the London papers were filled with news of the explosion of the British H-bomb on Christmas Island in the Pacific.[22] Possession of the hydrogen bomb became the badge of Britain's great power status, for it demonstrated that Britain's influence was at least equal to what it had been before Suez, if it had not actually grown. The Macmillan government would give repeated emphasis to the nuclear deterrent in its rhetoric from this point forward. Hence, it is no exaggeration to claim, as Anthony Sampson has, that 'the long trail back from Suez continued under the smokescreen of a mushroom cloud.'[23]

Yet, there was another element in the restoration of Britain's prestige after Suez which was as, if not more, vital than the nuclear deterrent – the healing of the breach with the United States. Macmillan recognized that the transatlantic relationship had to be restored if Britain were to recover its global influence. His first task as Prime Minister, as he saw it, was to mend fences with President Eisenhower and his Secretary of State John Foster Dulles. Although he made sure that he was not seen as a supplicant to the Americans, he lost no time in establishing friendly contact with Washington. As he soon discovered, the damage that Suez had done to the transatlantic relationship was not as great as had at first been feared. The Americans recognized that Britain remained an indispensable ally in the fight against world communism and were eager to retain close ties. After meeting with American leaders in Bermuda in March 1957, Macmillan was convinced that, as he told Australian Prime Minister Robert Menzies, 'things [were] back on the old footing' in the transatlantic relationship.[24]

In a follow-up meeting in Washington in October, Macmillan secured his most sought-after prize: the restoration of full Anglo-American atomic cooperation. By this time the American public's sense of invulnerability to nuclear attack had been shattered by Sputnik, the first space satellite, which the Soviet Union had launched earlier that month. After Sputnik, the need for warm and steady relations with another power suddenly became much more pronounced in Washington. Beyond atomic cooperation, joint working groups designed to coordinate Anglo-American policy across the globe were created during the Washington meeting, further institutionalizing the special relationship.[25] Over the next few years, the nonconformist tendencies in French diplomacy and the decreasing responsiveness of other West European democracies to US guidance led to an ever greater American appreciation of British fealty. Although there were the occasional bumps typical of any close association, the transatlantic relationship would remain on relatively solid footing throughout the remainder of the 1950s and well into the 1960s.[26]

With Anglo-American relations reaching a new postwar plateau and the Macmillan government's political position secured, the Suez episode was, at least in practical political terms, over by mid-1957. Incredibly, little had in fact changed. A Conservative government remained in power, continuing to affirm Britain's place at the top table of world politics. Moreover, the economic ramifications of the Suez crisis were limited at best. The British economy recovered rapidly from the crisis precipitated by American financial pressure in late 1956 and early 1957. By April 1957, Chancellor Peter Thorneycroft was able to deliver a very optimistic budget which emphasized expansionism. Exports had been revived, reaching a record level of £296.9 million in March, with car exports being particularly strong. A financial crisis did develop unexpectedly in late summer, but it did not reach alarming proportions. There was a run on the pound in August, causing a fall of more than $200 million in the gold and dollar reserves. But strong measures were taken in September, which quickly renewed confidence in sterling. The bank rate was raised from 5 to 7 per cent, and the clearing banks were told to restrict advances.[27]

Although the incident was marked by only moderate financial troubles, the brief crisis in summer 1957 would have ramifications for the country's military posture abroad. A fierce debate had erupted in the Cabinet over the September measures, with the Chancellor, Thorneycroft, forcefully arguing that severe expenditure cuts were necessary to stabilize the economy over the long term. But Macmillan refused to heed the Chancellor's call to reduce spending on social services, and his staunch defence of the postwar consensus at this juncture would set the tone for the government's approach to economic affairs.[28] There are probably many reasons why Macmillan felt that expenditure on social services was something of a sacred cow. Perhaps memories of conditions in his interwar constituency of Stockton, which he often spoke about, or his determination to follow the 'middle way' in terms of policy led to his firm stance on this issue.[29] Whatever the cause, it meant that the Prime Minister would insist that overseas spending bore the brunt of any proposed budget cuts in the future.

Thorneycroft would, however, continue his quest for substantial expenditure reductions even after the economic difficulties of the summer had subsided. He eventually resigned in January 1958 because his Cabinet colleagues refused to curtail what, in his mind at least, was run-away government expenditure. It was the first crisis in the Cabinet, and the only one of importance for the Macmillan government of the late 1950s.[30] Yet, the Cabinet rallied around the Prime Minister, in part because of the brusque manner of Thorneycroft's resignation, but also because ministers recognized that size cuts in welfare provisions would be politically disastrous. In the en the Prime Minister's political position was only further strengthened by the incident. It would be 1962, after a series of political setbacks and the Prime Minister's own health began to decline, before Macmillan's political ascendancy was again challenged.[31]

One reason Macmillan stood firm against swingeing expenditure cuts was his confidence that the economy would improve, and in the short term he proved to be correct. 1958 was a boom year. Industrial production reached new record levels, with steel doing particularly well. Over the next few years, the media seemed obsessed with the society's growing affluence, particularly how dramatically everyday life was improving in Britain with advances in technology. Bidding farewell to the 1950s, *The Economist* exclaimed on 2 January 1960 that Britain's slow postwar 'recovery was turning into a boom.'[32]

Yet such positive indications glossed over the continued existence of structural weaknesses in Britain's economy, which would reappear in the vicious form of the financial crises of the late 1960s and 1970s. The calamitous sequence of stop-go economic policies, which would take a considerable toll on Britain's economic growth over the long term, had begun in the mid-1950s.[33] Moreover, Britain's financial system, which continued to underwrite much of the world's trade in primary products, began to be racked repeatedly by losses in international confidence during that decade. An ominous cycle persisted throughout the 1950s, with vast sums of 'hot' money flowing out of London when international confidence in sterling waned, only to ebb back in when it became clear that no other financial center could offer, or wanted to offer, the skills, capacities, and the risks available in London.[34]

Macmillan recognized that although vibrant on the surface, the British economy still had underlying frailties. In one of his favorite historical analogies, he often compared mid-twentieth-century Britain to Elizabethan England. As he told Anthony Sampson in 1961, people often 'talk about the glories of the old Elizabethan age, but they forget that this was a time when Britain was politically very insecure, between much greater empires. We only kept going then by taking tremendous risks and adventures. It's more like that today – it's exciting living on the edge of bankruptcy.'[35]

All in all, though, while Britain's economic situation remained somewhat precarious in the late 1950s and early 1960s, economic pressures would not reach the crisis proportions that they had in the late 1940s and would again in the late 1960s. The economy expanded at a leisurely pace. Just fast enough, it can be seen in retrospect, to avoid searching questions over the country's ability to support its vast international and domestic commitments. By mid-1958, the economic upswing and the popular perception of affluence turned the polls to the government's favor. Buoyed by the country's economic growth, the Conservatives sailed through the election of 1959, increasing their overall majority in Parliament to 100 seats. They were helped by the lingering image of a Labour Party irrevocably split on issues such as the deterrent and nationalization, a legacy of the deep rifts which opened up after the Attlee regime lost power.[36] All things considered, the election was a remarkable triumph for Harold Macmillan, who had come to power in January 1957 with the expectation of only a brief tenure of office.[37] Instead, he had revitalized his party and led it to its largest postwar electoral victory.

Britain thus entered the 1960s in a confident mood. The sense of decline which was so prevalent at the time of Suez seemed to drift away.[38] Although this feeling of economic well-being and security would be relatively short-lived, it nevertheless helps to explain why Britain's overseas military role remained largely intact after the Suez débâcle. Britons, most especially the leading officials in the land, were once again convinced of their country's greatness. There was, after all, much tangible evidence which seemed to support this assumption. In 1960 Britain was one of only three nuclear powers in the world, it continued to maintain a substantial military presence overseas, and the economy, although clearly declining in relative terms, still appeared vibrant enough to support both 'greatness' abroad as well as 'welfare' at home. As we shall see, doubts raised during the Suez crisis over the country's world role would soon fade in the sanguine political and economic climate of the late 1950s and early 1960s.

DEFENSE REFORM AND SANDYS

If that 'old Social Tory,' as Macmillan was referred to as Minister of Housing from 1951 to 1954, refused to break out of the mold of postwar consensus by cutting spending on social services, he recognized nevertheless that savings had to be found somewhere.[39] Welfare spending would inevitably ratchet up with the passage of time, and the British economy was, as he well realized, already stretched to its limits by expansive policies at home and abroad. Since the former could not be cut, economies would have to be found in Britain's foreign and defense policies. Macmillan had, in fact, favored such a course for some time. As Chancellor, he bluntly informed Eden in March 1956 that 'it is defence expenditure which has broken our backs'.[40] During his brief stints at the Foreign Office and the Ministry of Defence in the Eden government, Macmillan had concluded that overlap and waste were rife in Britain's defense structure. Worse still, a coherent global strategy, which clearly defined Britain's interests in the world and the specific roles of the armed services, had still not been espoused.[41] The result was that, as Macmillan told Eden in a joint memorandum with the Defence Minister, Walter Monckton, in March 1956, 'we are spending a great deal on defences which are not really effective, and in some respects are little more than a facade.'[42] Upon assuming office, Macmillan immediately began to try to reshape Britain's military apparatus in a way that would make it more effective and less costly.

On 24 November 1956, shortly after the last shots had been fired at Suez, the future Prime Minister made his feelings on defense reform clear in a long 'Top Secret' memorandum to the Minister of Defence, Antony Head, who had replaced Monckton in October. The memo captured the essence of Macmillan's philosophy on defense affairs. Writing as Chancellor, Macmillan argued that in light of the Suez crisis the need for economies in government expenditure was urgent. Given the unprecedented humiliation associated with Suez, he asked Head, 'Should we not now re-examine the bases on which our present defence policy rests?'[43]

In the memo, Macmillan set out his ideas by reviewing the 'order of priorities' for Britain's defense, which had been outlined in the 1955 Defence White Paper. He felt that in the wake of the Suez crisis it was now impossible to support all of the goals set at that time. The first priority was 'to prevent a global war,' which meant in effect keeping a nuclear deterrent. Given the vast size of the superpowers' arsenals, Macmillan felt that Britain could never have a truly effective deterrent of its own. It had in many respects to rely on the American atomic shield, and thus he thought that Britain's nuclear weapons program need only be large enough to convince the Americans of the United Kingdom's sincerity as an ally.

On the second and third defense priorities outlined in 1955, 'to maintain and improve our position in the Cold War' and 'to win any limited war,' Macmillan felt that great savings could be found. He argued that Britain should undertake no sizable operations without assistance from its allies, most specifically the United States. Given the recent humiliation of Suez, this proposal was far from surprising.

He hoped that by renouncing any intention of using force unilaterally in large operations, substantial savings could be had in manpower and equipment. Such reductions obviously would have ramifications for the east of Suez role, as Macmillan suggested:

> We have to run some risks regarding our lines of communications; but if, as appears, we cannot be at all certain of using our present bases in time of war, is there any real object in paying out large sums for garrisons or as 'key money' to the local landlords? There may in any case be other, cheaper, ways of attaining our ends (especially if the Americans would help).[44]

The Suez operation clearly had raised a number of questions in Macmillan's mind on the utility of overseas bases, as it had throughout the foreign policy bureaucracy. But, as we shall see, the Prime Minister never took this line of thought so far as to consider a substantial disengagement from the area. Finally, he turned to the last priority – 'to survive a global war.' Here he felt that a considerable financial commitment was still necessary, which in effect meant that Fighter Command and the Navy should be strengthened considerably to provide defenses against bomber attacks and as a counterstrike capability.

Head, who was genuinely committed to the armed services, was appalled by the memorandum. Knowing that he could not implement such reforms, he quickly resigned after Macmillan became premier. Macmillan replaced him with a well-known hatchet-man of previous Conservative governments, Duncan Sandys. In making this choice, the Prime Minister left little doubt about his intention to reform Britain's defence apparatus.[45]

Macmillan's memorandum to Head symbolized the opening shot in what would soon be a vigorous debate both in the government and in the press over the relative merits of spending on 'guns versus butter.' In a note to the Prime Minister in August 1957, Macmillan's Principal Private Secretary, Frederick Bishop, summarized the dilemma that British policymakers began to grapple with at this time:

> If we disregard the economic effects, we could take every possible defence assurance. Then we might be safe from the military threat, but we would succumb economically. At the other extreme, we could take the risk of dispensing with virtually all of our defences, which would be economically safe, but militarily suicidal. No-one can say at what point either of these [extremes] would become a certain danger.[46]

The balance between economic solvency and disposable military might is a fundamental question in any state's grand strategy, particularly under conditions of economic constraint.[47] Although economies had been sought consistently by the Conservative governments of the early 1950s, worry over the balance between spending on guns or butter never became acute until the Macmillan era. Before 1957 it seemed that the country could afford its extensive commitments both at home and abroad, even though the economy was not expanding as rapidly as some of its continental neighbors. The Suez crisis in many ways shattered this myth, and brought new urgency to the need for undertaking economies. It was, after all, ultimately Britain's economic weakness which brought the nation to its knees in the affair, forcing the Eden government to put a halt to the military advance. And for all the country had invested in overseas positions, the country's performance on the battlefield was far from spectacular.[48] To many in the press and in Parliament it seemed that Britain was incapable of independently carrying out a major military operation in a world dominated by the superpowers. And this raised questions about why Britain had spent so much on an overseas military presence in the first place.

Another variant of the debate was the relationship between Britain's heavy military spending and the country's relative economic decline, which had become fully apparent by the mid-1950s. In the first low-level contact between US and British officials following the Suez crisis, on 15 January 1957, Sir Ivone Kirkpatrick, the Permanent Under-Secretary at the Foreign Office, made clear that worry over Britain's military burdens was increasing in Whitehall. He told his American audience:

> In the fight against communism Britain was the only country which was really making a substantial contribution whether in Germany or in the Middle East or in Hong Kong... In the race with Germany for the world's markets, the German runner was running in shorts and running shoes, while [Britain was] carrying a rifle and a pack and running in army boots. We were prepared to continue carrying the rifle but the time had come to discard the boots.[49]

Kirkpatrick's fears of economic competition from the European continent were based on the unfortunate, at least for Britain, economic realities of the day. At a time when continental products were beginning to challenge British exports, Britain was spending over 8 per cent of its GNP on defense, while France and Germany where spending roughly 6 per cent and 4 per cent respectively.[50] It seemed to many, both in and out of government, that the country's military load must be lightened. In February 1957, even the Joint Planning Staff called for a major reduction of Britain's overseas responsibilities, although the military would staunchly resist the spending cuts which lay ahead.[51]

Perhaps the harshest criticism of the overseas military role came from the Opposition benches. Throughout the late 1950s the Labour Party emphatically urged withdrawal from the country's overseas bases, or what Richard Crossman, a Labour MP and former member of the 'Keep Left' group, called the 'fag end' of imperial commitments. There are a number of reasons Labour opposed the commitments east of Suez at this time. For one, the numerous voices that had been calling for a socialist foreign policy but were muted during the Attlee regime grew louder and carried increasing clout once the party was in opposition. Thus, condemnation of the overseas military role reflected beliefs long held by a sizable contingent in the party. Few on the Opposition benches doubted that Britain should remain a world power, but many felt that the country's influence should be based on its economic, diplomatic, and cultural strengths rather than receding military power and overseas outposts. Censure of the east of Suez role was also expedient for the Labour leadership. Not only was it evident that the government was vulnerable in this area in the wake of the Suez crisis, emphasizing the overseas military network also focused attention on something other than unilateral nuclear disarmament. The latter was the subject of an intense, heated, and very public rhetorical battle which appeared to engulf the party in the latter 1950s.

Not all of the PLP or the rank and file agreed that the overseas military role needed to be pruned significantly, or even abrogated. A substantial number of Labour supporters felt that Britain's foreign policy should evolve along more traditional lines, as it had under the Attlee government, and that a true socialist foreign policy was unattainable given prevailing global conditions. But the PLP in large part toed the party line in this area, and during this period Labour MPs speaking in support of the overseas military role were extremely rare. Yet, despite this, and the fact that the Opposition focused considerable attention on the issue, the Labour challenge had very little impact. This is largely because their criticisms never cut very deep. Rather than an analysis of where a limited military presence abroad might still serve British interests and where such a presence was a liability, Labour simply charged that the imperial era had vanished and hence Britain should abandon the illusion of global military power and withdraw. The government replied by instinctively accusing Labour of 'scuttle' and a lack of nerve. The debate in Parliament was thus remarkably shallow. It did, however, put a charge in the political atmosphere surrounding the east of Suez issue in the late 1950s.[52]

The immediate result of the 'guns versus butter' debate and Macmillan's quest for defense economies was the 1957 Defence White Paper, the most drastic of all postwar White Papers. Although received as a shocking document at the time, it actually drew together a number of threads which had been emerging in British strategic thought since the early 1950s.[53] The central thrust of the 1957 White Paper, often called the Sandys Doctrine after the minister responsible, was to stake the credibility of British defense on the independent nuclear deterrent. In doing so, the Macmillan government could claim to be a great power internationally while simultaneously slashing the defence budget, as the United States had effectively done under Eisenhower's 'New Look' program in 1953. The most startling announcement was that conscription would be abolished, being phased out by 1960. The armed forces would be reduced from 690 000 personnel to 375 000 over a period of five years. This manpower reduction included decreasing the British Army on the Rhine by 13 000, and Home Defence would be dramatically cut on the assumption that the civilian population could not be protected effectively from the H-bomb. The east of Suez garrisons would remain much as they were, although obviously they would be much more thinly staffed. A considerable expansion of RAF Transport Command and the creation of a new Central Army Reserve in the United Kingdom would allow British troops to be transported quickly to trouble spots around the world. It seems that despite his earlier concern over the costs of the country's overseas military network, Macmillan intervened at this point to insure that British strength in the Far East and the Middle East would not be diminished significantly.[54] The financial savings for the year would not be dramatic, only £78 million. But over the long term the economic benefits were expected to be substantial.

The Sandys Doctrine helped to soothe fears of relative decline in the press and in Parliament, particularly on the Conservative benches. Reliance on nuclear weapons seemed to have a number of distinct advantages in the late 1950s. For one, an augmented nuclear arsenal seemed to guarantee that smaller states, like Egypt, would never again challenge Britain's authority. The limited applicability of nuclear weapons in what would soon be termed the Third World was not fully appreciated in 1957. Thus, political leaders in London thought that nuclear strength could restore what they saw as the 'natural order' in the Middle East and the Far East, which had been upset by the Suez episode. It was also thought that playing up the deterrent would allow Britain's voice to be heard more clearly in Washington and Moscow, which clearly had not been the case during the Suez crisis.[55] Beyond this, emphasizing Britain's atomic arsenal also had a large impact on the Conservative right-wing, whose steadfast belief in Britain's greatness had been so debased by recent events. For them and many others in the country, the government's new policy seemed to restore Britain's world status on the cheap. Randolph Churchill, Winston's son, summed up what many felt about the country's defence policy in 1958: 'Britain can knock down 12 cities in the region of Stalingrad and Moscow from bases in Britain and another dozen in the Crimea from bases in Cyprus. We did not have that power at the time of Suez. We are a major power again.'[56]

In many ways, reliance on the deterrent and on a better equipped, highly mobile military force seemed to gel with the post-Suez world. Events underscored this point, at least in the Middle East. In 1957, Britain successfully intervened in Oman to suppress a rebellion against the pro-British Sultan using air power and transported ground units. Macmillan's biographer, Alistair Horne, claims that Oman was an 'operation which [Macmillan] regarded with considerable personal pride to the end of his days.'[57] This should not be surprising, since a minor deployment of force proved that Britain could still make its influence felt in the Middle East. A risky operation in Jordan in 1958, where 2000 British paratroopers were dropped without the support of heavy equipment, also worked to demonstrate that Britain's newly streamlined forces could be effective in the country's old Middle Eastern domain. But the paramount example of a post-Suez campaign was Kuwait in 1961, where a massive British force was quickly assembled to prevent an attack from revolutionary Iraq, whose pro-British government had fallen in a revolt three years prior.[58]

At least initially, one factor that seemed to allow Britain to reduce conventional forces overseas was the growing US presence in the Middle East. In spring 1957 the 'Eisenhower Doctrine' was introduced, largely out of the fear in Washington that the Soviet Union might try to take advantage of Britain's weakened position in the Middle East after Suez. The doctrine guaranteed American military aid to Middle Eastern states who were under threat from external aggression related to international communism. Yet, despite the fact that the American presence helped to lighten Britain's heavy burdens, the increased US activity raised almost knee-jerk fears in Whitehall that America might be trying to supplant Britain in the region.[59] In December 1957, the Official Committee on the Middle East gave perhaps the clearest expression of Britain's approach to American activity in the Middle East: 'We should encourage the US government not only to back us in [our] effort' to restore British influence in the region, 'but to make it clear to the world that they are not replacing us in the area.'[60] Worries about the latter were unfounded. Washington had a continuing desire to maintain strong ties with Britain and to cooperate overseas. One example is an influential State Department paper on Britain's future prospects prepared before the Bermuda Conference, which concluded that 'we believe that the maintenance of the British position in the Middle East... is in the interests of the Free World.'[61] The Cabinet accepted that the increasing American presence in the region was intended to strengthen, not to weaken, Britain's interests east of Suez. In fact, the main complaint from the Prime Minister seemed to be that he wished the Americans would play their diplomatic cards in the Middle East more skillfully, reflecting a common, arrogant assumption in Whitehall of American naiveté and British sagacity in matters of diplomacy.[62]

Yet, US activity in the Middle East would soon recede. An American intervention into Lebanon in 1957 was considered in Washington to be a strong signal that the US would act if need be to prevent Soviet expansionism in the region. After this successful show of force, the Eisenhower administration turned its attention to other, more pressing, matters. It would be over a decade before the US would again take an active role in Middle Eastern affairs, leaving Britain once again the most visible power in the region.[63] But after 1957, Britain's role was much diminished in what had for over a half-century been its preserve. British planners now focused almost exclusively on the protection of the Persian Gulf and its oil, as British influence in 'Northern Tier' states in the Middle East such as Jordan and Iraq crumbled following the invasion of Egypt, with the ill-fated Baghdad Pact being officially brought to an end after the Iraqi coup of 1958.[64]

Although most post-Suez concern over Britain's overseas role centered on the Middle East, Britain also remained the dominant western actor in South Asia. The more mobile force structure devised by Sandys was assumed to be equally relevant in this part of the world. Consequently, although US influence had by this time become paramount in Pakistan, the Royal Navy was left relatively unchallenged on the Indian Ocean and Britain even signed a new defence agreement with India in 1961, replacing the old agreement which dated to 1898.[65] Furthermore, British arms were still present in Southeast Asia, where the garrison in Hong Kong and the naval station in Singapore remained, along with a chain of air bases stretching into the region from the Indian Ocean. Yet British policymakers were fully aware of the fact that at least since the end of the Second World War, it was American influence which really mattered in the Far East. Britain's inability to affect the course of events during the dispute over Quemoy and Matsu in 1958, despite the proximity of Hong Kong, served to underscore this point.[66] Thus, even after the blow delivered to British prestige by Suez and the Sandys Doctrine's reduction in conventional forces, Britain's east of Suez role clearly remained, although the country's dominance in parts of the Near and Far East was less certain than in the past.

Despite the fact that the Sandys Doctrine preserved the overseas military role, the reforms of 1957 met with significant opposition from the armed services and from some Cabinet ministers. Thorneycroft, for example, thought the cuts did not go deep enough. The controversy over the 1957 White Paper was so great that it ran to 13 'final' drafts before being passed through Parliament. The battle spilled over into 1958 and beyond. The armed services' stiff resistance to the reforms stemmed from the continuing belief among military leaders that the government's job was merely to provide the funds they required. The military leadership of the late 1950s clearly did not believe that the government's role included providing them with strategic rationales. Service leaders were also bitter that Sandys did not consult them when formulating the 1957 White Paper, relying instead on the advice of his own officials in the Ministry of Defence. As a result, Sandys' proposed cuts stirred up powerful emotions in the military, and the Defence Minister's bellicose attitude toward his uniformed subordinates only added to the acrimonious atmosphere.[67]

The eventual outcome of the dispute undermined the original purpose of the 1957 White Paper. Using their most potent weapon, the threat of resignation, the Chiefs of Staff would gradually succeed in the late 1950s in convincing the government that while *more* could be spent on the nuclear shield, it would be unwise to spend *less* on conventional manpower and equipment.[68] This result was foreshadowed when the decision to abandon the aircraft carrier role was reversed in 1957, despite Sandys' conclusion that carriers were 'expensive, vulnerable, and irrelevant to national needs.'[69] As the 1950s drew to an end, the Prime Minister became increasingly worried about the service backlash that his headstrong Defence Minister was creating, and the potential ramifications for military morale. After the 1959 election, Sandys was transferred to the Ministry of Aviation and later to the Commonwealth Relations Office. He was replaced by Harold Watkinson, a businessman who was known to manage his Cabinet portfolios in a more congenial manner. Thus, the armed services had by this time won the battle over the defense budget. Macmillan would later summarize the episode by saying: 'We failed, yes. The services were too strong.'[70] The phasing out of conscription would continue, but Britain's global commitments remained intact and spending on them began to rise dramatically.[71]

Thus, minor but extremely successful military operations east of Suez in the late 1950s and increasing technical problems in Britain's nuclear weapons program worked to underscore the argument that Britain should stick to tasks in which it was immeasurably experienced (in other words, policing the east of Suez area).[72] As Darby points out, by 1960 the east of Suez role had become much more prominent in British strategy:

> If anything, 1960 saw an increasing emphasis on Britain's role east of Suez. It is difficult to document the slight sharpening of focus, as it rested more on decisions taken regarding hardware and force structures than on any changed appreciation of the risks of conflict in the Indian Ocean vis-à-vis Europe. However, the gist of military thinking, the strengthening of Britain's strategically mobile capacity, the movement of some additional forces into the region, all indicate the government's tendency to upgrade the east of Suez role.[73]

By this time the limited applicability of nuclear weapons in small-scale wars was fully appreciated, most notably enshrined in the new US strategic policy of 'flexible response.' Flexible response postulated that limited conventional uses of force should be countered in a tit-for-tat strategy, graduating only very slowly up to the use of nuclear weapons.[74] This change in strategy by the West's leading power had undeniable repercussions on other states in the western camp, including Britain. It showed how quickly the Sandys Doctrine's reliance on 'big bangs and small bucks' was outdated, and that limited conventional uses of force would be invaluable in the West's struggle against communism. Although probably secondary to the lines of thought developing within Britain based on their own experiences east of Suez, US pressure on Britain to maintain its conventional strength in the Indian Ocean area began to push British policy even further in that direction, particularly after 1962.[75] Not long after, Labour in opposition even reversed its position on this issue, with the new party leader, Harold Wilson, extolling the virtues of Britain's conventional forces overseas and their contribution to both Britain's prestige and world security in the Commons.[76]

Thus, the most dramatic failure in postwar British foreign policy had virtually no impact on the scope of Britain's overseas commitments. Just three short years after the Suez crisis highlighted the limitations of Britain's overseas military network, government policy again stressed the east of Suez role. It is important to note, however, that this did not occur without some degree of consternation among senior officials in the foreign policy bureaucracy. While to many outside observers it appeared that British foreign policy recovered its equilibrium smoothly in the late 1950s, a vigorous debate was in fact raging in Whitehall, well-hidden from public view. Less than a year after British troops had evacuated the Suez Canal area, a series of sweeping and very secretive reviews of Britain's role in the world were launched.[77]

Since these reviews were the first exhaustive evaluations of Britain's world role since the end of the Second World War,[78] it is essential that they be outlined in a study on Britain's east of Suez network. They illustrate how British officials perceived the country's position in a dramatically transformed international arena, and how difficult it was for policymakers to determine which policy course Britain should follow in the midst of such marked change. A summary of these reviews also demonstrates how important political indifference was at this juncture in the maintenance of the overseas military role. The end result was, as has been seen, a foreign policy which in the late 1950s gradually re-emphasized the Indian Ocean role.

THE SECRET REVIEWS

In autumn 1957, Macmillan commissioned the first of a series of reviews on Britain's role in the world. Eden before him had tried to undertake a thorough reappraisal of Britain's overseas policy, but the re-evaluation ordered by Macmillan's predecessor never amounted to anything more than an attempt to economize. The country's basic defense priorities, the nuclear deterrent and the overseas military role, were taken as the starting point for Eden's attempt to reappraise, and hence they were never questioned seriously.[79] Perhaps because of the tremendous blow the Suez crisis had dealt to the nation's pride, the reviews initiated by Macmillan were more searching and more exhaustive.

In the reviews following Suez, senior civil servants representing each of the overseas departments – the Foreign Office, the Commonwealth Relations Office, the Colonial Office, and the Ministry of Defence, along with the Treasury – were instructed to meet and carefully weigh the relative costs and benefits of all aspects of Britain's overseas policy, even what up to that time had been considered inviolate planks of policy such as the east of Suez role. The participants were also directed to transcend narrow departmental views in order to provide an unbiased account of Britain's position in the world and its foreign policy prospects. A protective veil of secrecy would allow them to do so. Macmillan even went so far as to order the chairman of the Joint Intelligence Committee (JIC), Patrick Dean, to make sure that neither Britain's allies nor the full Cabinet knew what was going on.[80] Since these reappraisals of Britain's world role were carried out in such a clandestine manner, they will referred to as the 'secret reviews' throughout the remainder of this work.

There are a number of reasons why Macmillan initiated such a thoroughgoing reappraisal of Britain's world role. The most obvious was his continuing unhappiness over the fragmentation and biases inherent in Britain's foreign policy machinery.[81] Shortly before Macmillan took office, the Cabinet Secretary, Norman Brook, complained to Eden that past attempts to reach 'agreement on long-term [foreign and defense] policy... merely resulted in short-term compromises... [and] wasteful expenditure.'[82] As Brook's criticism illustrates, little had changed in the foreign policy bureaucracy in this regard since the late 1940s. Macmillan wanted to rectify this problem by creating a forum which would provide an even-handed assessment of Britain's foreign policy options. It may also be that the Prime Minister continued to have doubts about the country's east of Suez role, such as he had entertained as Chancellor.

Moreover, a fairly potent mood of neutralism swept the country in early 1957, with major newspapers and periodicals such as *The Economist*, the *Financial Times*, *The Times*, and the *Observer* beginning to question the benefits Britain derived from an extensive overseas military role.[83] A prominent Royal Institute of International Affairs study of the time on *British Interests in the Mediterranean and Middle East* argued that Britain should rely less on force and more on commercial, technical, and cultural influences to promote her interests east of Suez.[84] To many in the articulate public, the Suez episode seemed to underscore the fact that, in the world of the 1950s, international influence could not be gained through the use of force. Worse still, even if it could, Britain was shown to be incapable of brandishing its military sword independently of the superpowers during the Suez crisis. Given these apparently stark facts, many in the press and Parliament began to call for a fundamental re-examination of Britain's foreign policy. The Labour Party's attitude toward the overseas military network, described earlier, exemplifies this position. Despite his refusal to apologize for Suez and his repeated, almost habitual, declarations of Britain's greatness, Harold Macmillan agreed with these critics and it seems that his key foreign policy ministers did as well.[85] After the Suez débâcle, the basis of Britain's overseas policy did require re-examination. But the existence of committees set up to exhaustively reappraise Britain's world role could not be made public, no matter how much they seemed to correspond with the domestic mood. Whitehall had long stressed the importance of prestige in world affairs, and the damage that could be done to Britain's prestige if the country were found to be questioning itself and its capacities seemed real enough in the late 1950s.[86]

Thus, the first secret review of Britain's role in the world was commissioned in November 1957, producing a report entitled 'The Position of the United Kingdom in World Affairs' in June 1958.[87] The committee, chaired by Cabinet Secretary Norman Brook, consisted of the Permanent Under-Secretaries from the overseas departments and the Treasury. Interestingly, although nearly every aspect of Britain's foreign policy was scrutinized, the greatest controversy arose over the east of Suez role. A number of officials questioned whether Britain actually derived any positive benefits from such a role. One participant asked, 'Would, for example, our influence in the world be better assured by building up our economic strength rather than maintaining a world-wide military presence?' Another reminded his colleagues that 'the present strong economic position of Germany and America in the course of the 19th century were not built upon world power.'[88] British officials thus seemed to recognize that the basis of international influence was beginning to change in the mid-twentieth century. Military might alone was not sufficient; a thriving economy was also necessary both to support a military presence abroad and to ensure that a country's influence would be felt in the decades ahead. It is clear from the discussions in early meetings that the consensus among these powerful mandarins was for some form of withdrawal. Britain, it was argued consistently, was simply no longer capable of supporting an extensive military network abroad. Ideas of disengagement were carried so far that the delicate question of timing was even considered, as withdrawal had to be done in a way that would minimize any potential damage to Britain's prestige.

Yet, for reasons which remain clouded, opinion on the committee gradually swung back to favor maintaining the overseas military role. The outcome was a final report which vigorously defended the country's presence east of Suez. But in its tone and its language, the report also confirmed the fact that a heated debate over Britain's overseas military role had taken place. It stated that given the country's long history of world power and its far-flung trading interests, it was now impossible for Britain to retreat into the 'neutrality and comparative isolation of purely commercial powers such as Sweden and Switzerland.'[89] Such an emphasis on economic as opposed to military might is exactly what many members of the committee had proposed. Yet, the report went even further to confute such isolationist tendencies, arguing that despite the country's balance of payments problems, it was in the nation's interest to increase spending on Britain's overseas military positions. Since the defense budget had assumably been slashed to the bone under Sandys, the report concluded that if any economies were to be found, they would have to be in domestic expenditure.

It is unclear whether or not Macmillan agreed with the report's conclusions, particularly given his past attempts to curtail defence spending. But the Treasury was aghast. The standard Treasury line throughout the 1950s was the need to hold overseas expenditure constant in order to achieve a positive balance of payments. Not doing so, in the Treasury's view, would weaken foreign confidence in sterling and increase pressure on the reserves, with the ultimate result being the erosion of Britain's status in the world.[90] In two Cabinet meetings on the report, in June and July 1958, the Chancellor of the Exchequer Heathcoat Amory, argued forcefully against the report's conclusions.[91] He insisted that there was no room for further domestic cuts, a view which, as we have seen, resonated with senior ministers, particularly the Prime Minister. Not surprisingly, the Cabinet sided with the Chancellor. But it seems the Prime Minister was impressed with the types of issues which had been analyzed by this clandestine committee, and the energetic attempt to determine where Britain's true interests lie. Soon a much more ambitious review of Britain's future policy options was ordered, with precautions again taken to ensure that neither Britain's allies nor the full Cabinet would be aware of its existence.

Commissioned in June 1959, the 'Study of Future Policy' was essentially a continuation of the review process began in 1957. There were two stages in this review process. The first consisted of a working group overseen by Patrick Dean, chairman of the JIC, which included the Deputy Under-Secretaries from the foreign policy departments, as well as the Treasury and the Ministry of Fuel and Power (which was included to help determine how vital Middle Eastern oil was for the British economy).[92] Several subcommittees were set up under this working group to study functional problems, like nuclear proliferation and regional issues. Once completed, the working group's findings would be forwarded to a steering committee chaired by Norman Brook, which would be composed of the Permanent Under-Secretaries from the departments involved and the Chiefs of Staff. This represented the second and last stage of the review process, as the steering committee was to produce the final report for the Cabinet. The purpose of this elaborate committee machinery was to ascertain potential global transformations over the coming decade and their probable impact on Britain's international position. Using their interpretation of such changes, the committee would then be able to make recommendations on the path that the country's foreign policy should take in the 1960s. Originally it was hoped that such policy recommendations would be ready for the party which won the 1959 general election, but the review process took much longer than anticipated, with discussions continuing well into 1960.[93]

To make policy suggestions for the coming decade, it was first necessary to ascertain what Britain's relative economic and military power would be over this time period. This aspect of the review is important because it demonstrates not only that British officials were worried about Britain's international status, but that they grasped accurately the extent of Britain's economic and military decline in the late 1950s. For example, the review concluded that economically 'even if the United Kingdom's economy expands at the rate required to double national income in 25 years (2.8% [annual GDP growth]), we shall be left far behind, and our *relative* position vis-à-vis both the U.S.A. and Western Europe will have declined.' In terms of military might, the review argued that 'only the U.S.A. and the U.S.S.R....

have the strength to provide and sustain a complete global power apparatus. The United Kingdom, with its ageing population and dwindling possessions overseas, cannot even approach this status.'[94] The measures used to produce these estimates were uncomplicated. Gross steel production and electrical output were used to provide a general measure of economic strength, while output per head, population growth, and the proportion of national income channeled into defence were analyzed for military strength.

Using these estimates of Britain's weakening international position, the working group split into two polar factions over the policy course Britain should take in the future. One faction supported the maintenance of an active world-wide military role based on the Anglo-American alliance. The other argued that Britain's overseas military positions had become superfluous in the postwar era, particularly when Britain was dwarfed by the superpowers in terms of economic and military capability. This latter group also suggested that Britain's ties with the US might actually be strengthened if Britain withdrew into a regional role within Europe, since America had long supported closer European political cooperation. According to Michael Carver, who sat in on the working group for the War Office, the two most powerful departments in Britain's foreign policy establishment, the Foreign Office and the Treasury, argued forcefully for disengagement from the east of Suez role. Representatives from the Colonial Office were split on this issue, while the other members present favored the status quo.[95]

It seems that opponents of Britain's overseas military network won the battle in the working group. A number of startling proposals for limiting Britain's role east of Suez were forwarded to the steering committee. But perhaps because the Chiefs of Staff were included in the steering committee, the final report produced for the Cabinet was considerably watered down.[96] As in the first secret review, its conclusions were nearly the reverse of what might have been suspected given the discussions in the earlier meetings. Consistent with military thinking of the time, the final 'Future Policy' report stated that war in Europe had become improbable and that subsequently Britain should focus on winning small-scale conflicts in the Middle East and the Far East. While it was admitted that burgeoning nationalism was beginning to turn some of Britain's overseas facilities into liabilities, the group asserted that this did not mean that Britain's overseas commitments should be reined in. Instead, the report suggested that Britain should produce an even more mobile force structure than that proposed by the Sandys Doctrine. To support overseas commitments and to bring this more mobile force structure into being, the report concluded that defence spending should remain at roughly the same level, at around 7–8 per cent of GNP.

Despite the painstaking work which had gone into the 'Future Policy' review, it never served as any form of blueprint for Britain's foreign policy. The Cabinet considered the conclusions of the review at a single weekend meeting at Chequers, with the fate of the report being sealed when the Prime Minister was unable to attend at the last moment. In his absence, it is unlikely that ministers read the report seriously and as a consequence the meeting was much less productive than had been anticipated.[97] No policy decisions were taken on the country's overseas role at this meeting, which, as is the case for all non-decisions, was in effect a vote of confidence for the extant policy course.

Thus, any hope of a substantial redirection of policy, already limited given the diluted nature of the 'Future Policy' review's final report, gradually slipped away in an atmosphere of political indifference. Britain's international prestige by this time largely seemed to have recovered from Suez, and as long as the economy was buoyant, there seemed to be little reason for political leaders to make dramatic changes in Britain's overseas commitments. Although serious questions about the utility of Britain's military positions overseas were raised in the secret reviews, they were soon engulfed in the tranquil politics of affluence and consensus which characterized the Macmillan regime at the peak of its power, in 1959–60. As two astute analysts of this period, Vernon Bogdanor and Robert Skidelsky, have observed: 'the politics of consensus reigned supreme... [in the late 1950s, which, in effect]... imposed a moratorium on the raising of new and vital issues. For consensus also signified acceptance of traditional assumptions concerning Britain's political and economic role in the world.'[98]

All things considered, it should not be surprising that the more radical propositions in the secret reviews, such as complete disengagement, never influenced policy. Well before the 1959 election Macmillan, who dominated the foreign policy process, seemed to become enthralled with the more glamorous aspects of diplomacy. The enormous amounts of energy he expended trying to convince Eisenhower and Khrushchev to agree to what essentially would be a three-power summit meeting bears witness to this fact. Jetting off to discuss matters with American and, during a February 1959 trip to Moscow, Russian leaders seems to have been immensely satisfying to the Prime

Minister.[99] Perhaps more importantly, his attempt to act as an intermediary between Washington and Moscow throughout this period only underscored the continuing image of British importance in the world, while even a limited withdrawal from commitments east of Suez would have had the reverse effect. Thus, in many ways, the Prime Minister's former crusade to reduce Britain's defence expenditure in order to strengthen the economy vanished under the spotlight of high diplomacy. Once Britain's political and economic situation had stabilized after Suez, Macmillan was simply not prepared to abandon the overseas military role. Neither, it seems, were key members of his Cabinet.

The government was far from alone in this position. Political thinking on all points of the spectrum, including that of Labour Party intellectuals such as Anthony Crosland and John Strachey, tended to accept the political and economic assumptions behind Britain's world role as the 1950s drew to an end.[100] Some in the Labour Party continued to question the efficacy of military bases abroad, but the attitudes of the party leadership would, as we have seen, soon change. In any case, such dissenting ideas ran counter to the dominant mood in Britain at this time, which William Wallace summarizes well. Wallace observes that 'in the wake of the Suez campaign and in the long-awaited flush of post-war prosperity... the vast majority [of British], politicians and public alike... demanded a reassertion of Britain's traditional position.'[101] Britain in the late 1950s was enjoying what might be termed an Indian summer of world power. With what seemed on the surface to be excellent economic prospects and the continued appearance of greatness, there seemed to be no reason to scrutinize the country's changing position in the world. The national crisis of confidence brought on by the Suez venture faded in the resurgent atmosphere of the late 1950s. Or, perhaps it is more accurate to say, the crisis was postponed.

Nor was Whitehall immune to this renascent mood. The opposition to the east of Suez role expressed in the secret reviews was not at all common in the foreign policy bureaucracy at this time. There is little evidence, for instance, to suggest that either the Foreign Office or the Treasury ever consistently opposed the overseas military role in normal interdepartmental intercourse. Representatives from these departments who argued for a withdrawal from the east of Suez role during the secret reviews were either advancing a single strain of opinion within their respective ministries or they took to heart Macmillan's directive to transcend departmental views.

For example, in outlining Britain's essential interests east of Suez for the Prime Minister's Commonwealth Tour in early 1958, the Foreign Office concluded that 'in the Persian Gulf our position has withstood with welcome resilience the shock of the Suez crisis' and consequently, 'there is no reason to believe that the essentials of our position [in this area] will become less tenable or valuable in the future.'[102] Although British policy was now almost exclusively centered on the Persian Gulf rather than the 'Northern Tier' states of the Baghdad Pact, the Foreign Office continued to claim that Britain's interests in the Middle East were essentially the same as they had been in the late 1940s: 'to maintain the free flow of oil and freedom of communications and to oppose the spread of communism in the area.'[103] A continued presence in South Asia and the Far East was advocated by the Foreign Office at this time as well, although it was recognized that America's role, and in many areas its predominance, would continue to grow in both of these areas.[104]

In the Treasury, lower-level officials were beginning to question the burdens that overseas military spending placed on the British economy in the late 1950s. But the senior department has never been in the habit of making specific policy recommendations, and lower-level dissent over defense costs was consistently smothered by the department's senior officials at this time.[105] In fact, at one point during the 'Future Policy' review, the Treasury even accepted that the economy might benefit from increased military spending overseas if foreign aid and other incidentals were simultaneously cut.[106]

And one is hard-pressed to find opposition to the east of Suez network from other overseas departments during this period. It was generally accepted that the military network abroad was in the interest of the foreign policy bureaucracy. Commonwealth and colonial ties were reinforced by a British military presence in the Indian Ocean area and the armed services were bestowed with the budgets and the array of weaponry necessary to support a global military role. In sum, it seems that outside of the unique forum of the secret reviews, opposition to the east of Suez network was extremely rare in Whitehall.

Thus, Britain's overseas military presence weathered the shock of the Suez crisis and the questions about Britain's role in the world which necessarily followed. Yet, even though the secret reviews of Britain's world role were never translated into policy, they were nonetheless significant. They demonstrated that serious doubts existed in Whitehall, which were not present, or at least were not registered, before the Suez crisis. Although rarely voiced, these doubts would linger into the next decade, slowly growing into a potent force for change.

At the end of the day, the Macmillan government clung to a broad conception of Britain's overseas role because it felt that the foundations of Britain's greatness were too sturdy to have been seriously upset by the Suez crisis. Leaders in both main political parties were convinced that Britain was still a world power of the first rank, as were senior mandarins.[107] The idea that the east of Suez network somehow buttressed Britain's great power position persisted, even though the formerly great chain of bases was by this time rapidly thinning out. In part because of a surge in anti-British sentiment after the Suez invasion, the British military was forced to leave the Trincomalee naval base in Ceylon in 1957, Jordan in 1957, and, following the revolution in 1958, two air bases in Iraq. In 1960 Britain also decided to abandon a new base in Kenya, built at a cost of nearly £7.5 million.[108] Whether it was related to the Suez episode or not, a sweeping transfer of power in Africa was initiated in the late 1950s and early 1960s, of which the withdrawal from Kenya was merely a small part. By 1960 it had become evident that the last major bastion of British colonialism would soon disappear.[109] An important argument for the continuation of the east of Suez role evaporated along with it. If it could logically be said that overseas military positions served a colonial function in the late 1940s (perhaps a dubious proposition given Indian independence), this certainly was no longer the case in the late 1950s and early 1960s.

But the effective end of Britain's colonial empire and the gradual winnowing of the country's military network overseas did not cause leaders to conclude that the network itself was becoming untenable. Instead, these changes were merely seen as a challenge to British resourcefulness. James Callaghan, who sat in the shadow Cabinet in the late 1950s, summed up the post-Suez situation well: 'in the 1950s we were living in a fool's paradise, [for] we believed we were still an imperial power... the truth of our economic situation had not dawned on us.'[110] But, as we have seen, British policymakers had a prescient grasp of Britain's economic weaknesses at this time. More important than leaders' awareness of the country's economic situation is the fact that political support for disengagement from the world role had not yet become widespread. The foundations necessary for a winning coalition on this issue simply did not yet exist.

6 Setting the Stage: Longer-Term Implications of Suez

Even though British foreign policy shifted to emphasize the Indian Ocean role in the years following Suez, the questioning and uncertainty which became most apparent in 1956 would return. The Macmillan government suffered a string of political setbacks in the early 1960s: the failed bid to enter the European Economic Community in 1963, the costly failure of Blue Streak and dependence on American missile technology, by-election defeats, and a series of spy scandals which culminated in the Profumo affair. Added to this, Britain's economy ran into trouble again after 1961. Production and exports stagnated, and the country endured a series of balance of payments crises from 1961 to 1964. The economic satisfaction which characterized the late 1950s rapidly dissolved. Worse still, signs of the country's relative economic decline were becoming more difficult to ignore, with, for example, West Germany's postwar GNP first outstripping Britain's in 1960. The country's share of exports from the 11 major manufacturing countries fell from 20 per cent of the total to well under 14 per cent from 1954 to 1964.[1] Britain was feeling the pinch of increased economic competition in the early 1960s, perhaps in an acute form. As the 1960s wore on, legitimate questions about what Britain's rightful place in the world was, and what it should be, became increasingly widespread and germane. Eventually, such changes, along with the tremors which were working their way through the political system after the Suez débâcle, would create a mood of apprehension and expectant change in the mid-1960s.

In this context, British decision-makers modified a number of policies in an attempt to reverse what appeared to be accelerating relative decline. Change occurred in two of the variables focused upon in this study, and each of these transformations proved to be of considerable import in the decision to retrench from the east of Suez role. The country's foreign policy machinery was dramatically restructured in an attempt to generate economies and to produce policies of a higher calibre. One important outcome of this reorganization would actually reverse its framers' intentions and, as an unintended result, the institutional reshaping would have important ramifications for the world role. In addition, decision-makers' strategic conception of the overseas military role underwent change after the Suez episode. Although not immediately seized, the reformulation of overseas strategy would create new opportunities for the redirection of policy.

Of course, awareness of the country's dwindling international political and economic clout extended beyond the government. Support for the east of Suez role unravelled in the articulate public when it became apparent that the country's economic difficulties were not soon going to fade. The ranks of those opposing the overseas role grew steadily as the decade progressed, resulting in an extraordinarily polarized and fiery debate on the issue in the press, in Parliament, and in academic forums in the mid-1960s. Critics of the east of Suez role would eventually wear down the resolve of a Labour government far from convinced that Britain's days as a world power were numbered. But far more than economic exigency and internal pressure lie at the heart of the decision to withdraw from the country's overseas military network. Political maneuvering was also central in this process. In fact, it may be in the realm of politics that the key to understanding the east of Suez decision is most readily located.

The eventual outcome was that just three short years after regaining power, the party which orchestrated Indian independence in 1947 would now oversee the final dismantling of Britain's overseas military network. In no way, however, could this be described as an ideological victory for the Labour government or the gradual application of socialist principles to the nation's foreign policy. While serious doubts may have been raised over Britain's world role in the Attlee Cabinet, the same was not true of the government of Harold Wilson. The latter would retreat from the military role abroad unwillingly and under immense pressure.

In the pages that follow, the changes which occurred in the wake of the Suez crisis and which had a bearing on the decision to retrench are analyzed.[2] Examined first are the international changes sparked by Suez, which transformed the global political landscape in which British policymakers operated. The altering strategic terrain after 1956 provides an important backdrop for the policy adjustments that British policymakers began to initiate at this time. A description of the reshaping of Britain's institutions and the rapid evolution of ideas on the overseas military role following the events of 1956 follows. Then, the position taken on the east of Suez role by Labour decision-makers in the mid-1960s and the panoply of pressures that they consequently came under are outlined. The magnitude of the change in British foreign policy in the late 1960s can only be appreciated when one comprehends Labour decision-makers' conception of the world role and their ardent struggle to preserve it. Only in this way can the variables which eventually produced a dramatic shift in policy be fully grasped.

INTERNATIONAL TRANSFORMATIONS

The most momentous political change in the east of Suez area and perhaps globally during the postwar period was the rise of Third World nationalism. The myth of Western superiority had been shattered with Japan's defeat of the colonial powers during the initial stages of the Second World War, opening the way for this seismic shift in world politics. And as decolonization began in earnest in the late 1950s and early 1960s, an anti-imperial and anti-Western zeal spread throughout much of Asia, Africa, and the Middle East. This phenomenon, which eventually would mark the end of outright colonialism, increasingly constrained Britain's strategic options in the east of Suez area.

Anti-British sentiment in particular peaked in the wake of the Suez crisis. To Arab and Asian nationalists, the Suez invasion stripped the veneer of benevolent neutrality from British military activities in their lands, revealing London's long-suspected, base imperialistic aims. As a result, a nationalistic surge opposing Britain's presence swept the region in the late 1950s, with considerable effect on Britain's military strategy in the Indian Ocean area. A number of northern African and Middle Eastern countries, for example, promptly rescinded Britain's overflight rights.[3] This was a particularly troublesome turn of events since conscription was being wound down in the late 1950s and Britain increasingly had to rely on air-trooping – transporting a shrinking number of troops from one theatre to another by air. Worse still, British forces were evicted from a number of military outposts in the region after the Suez episode. British troops were asked to leave Jordan in 1957 and, after a revolution by nationalist army officers in October 1958, they were forced from two airbases in Iraq.[4] Also, British forces were expelled from the Trincomalee naval base in Ceylon in 1957, which was a vital link between the Middle East and the Far East for British forces. As such, it was a major loss. The British military was forced to scramble to find a substitute for this critical node along the east of Suez network, and they soon found one in an air staging post in the Maldive Islands.[5]

But perhaps more than any of these setbacks, Britain's attempt to build a new base for forward operations after the (already planned) loss of the Suez complex epitomizes the difficulties nationalism posed for post-Suez policy planners. After the Suez débâcle, the increasing problem of overflight rights meant that a large and stable base would be necessary in the east of Suez area to sustain troops and equipment. Although air-trooping would be increasingly necessary in the era of the all-volunteer force, overflight rights could not be relied on in times of crisis. Unfortunately for British policymakers, the search for a forward base would prove a long and arduous journey.

British military planners first began to improve garrison facilities in Kenya for this purpose. The Kenyan base had hardly been established (at a cost of £7.5 million), however, when it became clear that Kenya would gain independence much more rapidly than previously anticipated, and eventually it was decided to move troops and aircraft to a semi-permanent home in Aden, on the coast of southern Arabia.[6] Unfortunately, establishing a forward base in Aden only brought further problems. In the interwar period and during the early stages of the postwar era, RAF squadrons were sufficient for imperial policing in southern Arabia as they could strafe potentially rebellious tribesmen and frighten them away with their aircraft and bombs. Such extremely inexpensive methods of maintaining British dominance altered dramatically with the rise of Arab nationalism, and situating a major military base in Aden in the late 1950s only incited the nationalists further. Britain soon became involved in a full-scale civil war on the southwestern tip of Arabia in the 1960s, which culminated in the abandonment of Aden in 1967.[7]

By this time, Britain's postwar travails in the Indian Ocean area were drawing to an end. But perhaps better than any other sequence of events, the quest for a forward base in the late 1950s and 1960s illustrates the lengths to which British decision-makers went in trying to adapt to the changing tides of Third World nationalism. Post-Suez British decision-makers seemed to have felt that nationalism dogged their every action. When interviewing high-ranking civil servants and military officers in the late 1950s, DeWitt Armstrong discovered that nationalism weighed heavily on their minds.[8] In fact, they considered nationalism to be the chief reason that adjustments were made in Britain's role in the Indian Ocean. A.P. Thornton provides perhaps the most vivid portrait of the turbulence in Britain's world role after 1945, which only intensified after the Suez crisis and the subsequent rise of nationalist sentiment:

The Indian Army, underprop of British might in the Middle East, had gone. Some other must be found and fashioned. Genuine bases must be established. The soldiers were to wander, sometimes in imagination, sometimes in reality, from the Canal Zone to Kenya, from Cyprus back to Haifa, searching, somewhere along this inner circle, for security for the British Empire, for the protection of its communications and the safeguarding of its supplies of oil...[9]

Yet, any notion that rising nationalism forced Britain from their east of Suez commitments is too simplistic. Britain's military presence was acceptable in many quarters of the Indian Ocean area. As the decision to retrench drew near, some leaders actually lobbied strenuously for a continuation of Britain's military presence. Lee Kuan Yew, Prime Minister of Singapore, threatened economic reprisals if Britain withdrew, and his dismay was not atypical. It echoed in a number of capitals in the Middle East and in Southeast Asia (particularly Malaysia, Australia, and New Zealand, although the latter two at that time were not hotbeds of nationalist sentiment). Moreover, Saudi Arabia and the Gulf states offered on numerous occasions to finance a continued British presence in the area, an option never seriously considered in London.[10] In general, the context of Third World nationalism must be appreciated, for it often led governments in the Indian Ocean area to communicate with Whitehall using a very different voice than the one broadcast to the outside world.[11]

Other international transformations affected Britain's overseas commitments as well. In addition to the rise of anti- Western and anti-imperial sentiments, many states in the area, such as Egypt and Indonesia, were by the late 1950s and early 1960s arming themselves with sophisticated weaponry. The military forces with which Britain would have to contend were also better trained and organized, often with assistance from outside powers (primarily the Soviet Union and China). Given these changes, Richard Crossman, an outspoken left-wing Labour MP, quite correctly observed at the time that the defence of the scattered remains of empire was becoming more onerous than defending its earlier unity.[12]

Political and military transformations such as these strained British resources in the area and the situation was made worse because Britain's defence armory was shrinking as technological innovation drove weapons costs steadily higher. Also, with the end of conscription in 1957, there were fewer British troops overseas and fewer reserves in Britain to call upon if threats materialized east of Suez. Subsequently, the gap between the resources Britain allocated to the overseas military role and the nature of the commitments in the Indian Ocean area widened steadily throughout the 1960s.[13] And increasing the amount spent on the armed forces was out of the question in post-1945 Britain. Extensive social and political constraints prevented any substantial expansion of the defence budget.[14] Ultimately, the twin goals of 'welfare' and 'greatness' had to be balanced, one could not be allowed to undermine the other (and the 'welfare' system in particular could not be curbed). The political consensus which undergirded postwar British politics was, after all, predicated on the preservation of these two overriding goals of British policy as well as their harmony.

The ever-widening gap between Britain's capabilities and its overseas commitments in the late 1950s and 1960s created increasing tensions in the nation's east of Suez strategy. But such overstretch would not convince decision-makers that the overseas military role had to be abandoned. To the contrary, Whitehall seemed convinced that the numerous modifications made to streamline Britain's east of Suez network in the late 1950s and the 1960s would ensure its survival, despite an increasingly adverse environment. As Philip Darby observes, 'underlying much of the military thinking [of the time] there seems to have been an implicit assumption that the apparatus of global defence was being remodeled for the longer run, if not in perpetuity.'[15] Perhaps more importantly, during this period the leaders of both major political parties saw little reason why the new challenges in the Indian Ocean area should not be met.[16]

It must be remembered, after all, that up to this point the British had managed to muddle through despite a century or more of strategic overstretch. The pitting of 'short bayonets against long odds' had become something of a national sport.[17] Samuel Huntington, among others, maintains that strategic and geographic overextension may in fact be the natural state of affairs for great powers actively engaged in the world, such as Britain was after 1945.[18] It is, in a sense, standard operating procedure for nations at the top table of world politics. Not surprisingly, then, British decision-makers in the 1960s seemed to accept the growing gap between the nation's power and its policies as an inescapable but nevertheless innocuous given, even as the gap widened into a chasm.

INSTITUTIONAL CONSOLIDATION

One of the most visible domestic transformations in the wake of the Suez crisis was the reformation of British institutions. As Britain's relative decline grew more evident in the early 1960s, attention increasingly turned to the inefficiencies of the country's governmental machine. Calls for opening up the bureaucracy to outside expertise and reducing governmental secrecy became common.[19] The entire apparatus of Britain's bureaucracy was criticized by members of the Labour Party and academics, culminating in the Fulton Report of 1966–8. The aim of most of the organizational reform efforts in the 1960s was to reduce duplication and to add economies of scale through centralization. The consolidation of Britain's foreign policy establishment which eventually occurred would affect significantly the balance of political power in the government on the issue of the overseas military role.

Although it affected the entire foreign policy bureaucracy, this centripetal thrust was most marked in the organization of defence. The Suez débâcle and the tragedy of weapons procurement in the 1950s and early 1960s, where waste and inefficiency had been rampant, made a strong case for defense restructuring. Add to this the shedding of Britain's colonies and the skyrocketing costs of weapons, and a substantial reorganization of Britain's defense establishment appears inevitable. That it occurred in the early 1960s, and not at some later point, was principally due to the tireless effort of two men: Prime Minister Harold Macmillan and the Chief of the Defence Staff, Lord Mountbatten.

Having served as Defence Minister in 1954–5, Macmillan recognized the organizational flaws inherent in the defense structure. The Prime Minister was an ardent centralizer; he inspired a modest reorganization of defense institutions in 1957 and stood firmly by Duncan Sandys during the political struggle to implement it. Macmillan was deterred at this time from further consolidation of the defense apparatus by fears of the possible political storm which would follow and the potential harm to service morale. He knew that there would be stiff resistance to reorganization given the deeply ingrained traditions and loyalties of the armed services. Mountbatten had first advocated greater defense centralization in 1941, and thereafter his ideas evolved along these same lines. Since Mountbatten was a charismatic, outspoken, and very influential figure in the British foreign policy establishment, his position as Chief of the Defence Staff and his constant advocacy of centralization were crucial to defense reorganization. The impetus for reform also came from abroad. The United States, under Secretary of Defense Robert McNamara, was streamlining its defense establishment in the early 1960s, and Canada had already implemented a radical experiment which fully merged all of the components of its defense apparatus. In addition, if Britain was to ever participate in the European Economic Community and perhaps later in a united defense community, which seemed ever more to be a desirable goal for British statesmen, closer cooperation with continental partners would be necessary. Such cooperation would require tighter central control of defence.[20]

Even at the time of the limited restructuring under Sandys, Macmillan was convinced that reform must go much further. As early as 1959 he suggested that the tenure of his powerful Chief of Defence Staff should be renewed after his normal three-year term ended in 1962, so that Mountbatten could see through the reforms the Prime Minister was planning. By late 1962 these two reformers felt that the time was at last ripe. Given press and parliamentary calls for further savings in the military, the chance for a substantial reformulation of the defense establishment was upon them. A powerful ally was added when Peter Thorneycroft returned to replace Harold Watkinson as Minister of Defence. He was a forceful politician who shared the Prime Minister's penchant for organizational change.[21]

Faced with the inevitable opposition of the armed services, this powerful trio of reformers felt that a report from a respected senior committee was necessary to lay the groundwork for the restructuring of the defense establishment. Such a committee would provide an assumably objective seal of approval to the institutional consolidation favored by the Prime Minister and the Chief of the Defence Staff. For this purpose, the highly regarded architects of the 1947 defense reform, Lord Ismay and General Sir Ian Jacob, were brought in. These two men had worked together with distinction in the secretariat which served Winston Churchill in his capacity as Minister of Defence in the Second World War. They could be relied on to strive toward a more efficient organizational structure while simultaneously allaying the fears of the military.[22]

The Ismay–Jacobs committee completed its report in February 1963 and submitted it to the Prime Minister and the Minister of Defence. The government's defence reform package was announced in July of that year. It was immediately evident that the changes to be made were substantial. The first page of the government's program announced that from 1 April 1964 there would be a 'unified' Ministry of Defence under one Secretary of State for Defence (formerly the Minister of Defence), who held full 'authority and responsibility' throughout the MoD.[23] Thus, the service ministries were to be absorbed into the MoD, although distinct service identities would be preserved in separate departments. Service ministers, historically powerful in Cabinet, were downgraded to middle-level managers under the Defence Minister. They would be given functional duties along with their responsibilities to the branches of the armed services. In addition, the Admiralty Board and the Army and Air Councils were downgraded to sub-committees in the Defence Council. Chaired by the Minister of Defence, the Defence Council was intended to handle many of the political issues formerly dealt with by the Chiefs of Staff. The centralization of the defense apparatus was not absolute however. The Chiefs of Staff remained the key advisors on strategy and operations, and they retained their cherished right to have direct access to the Prime Minister either individually or as a group. Mountbatten had opposed bitterly the continuation of the influence of the Chiefs of Staff, advocating their full subordination to the occupant of his position, the Chief of Defence Staff. Finally, at the Cabinet level, the Defence Committee was renamed the Committee on Defence and Overseas Policy in an effort to get other overseas departments such as the Foreign Office to work more closely with the MoD in the formulation of defence policy.[24]

Ismay and Jacob felt their plan created an interim organization which subordinated the armed services to the MoD as a step toward the eventual goal of a completely integrated, functional Ministry of Defence. The greater control of research, development, and long-term financial planning by the MoD was heralded as one of the greatest benefits of the new structure. Such centralization was expected to reduce the overlap and waste which had plagued the military procurement practices of recent decades. Overall, even though a purely functional Ministry of Defence was not created, the 1964 reorganization was a remarkable reformulation of the country's defense apparatus given the intense desire of the armed services to preserve their independence. F.M.G. Willson calls the 1964 reorganization 'almost certainly the largest administrative merger ever to take place in British central government.'[25] Similarly, Franklyn Johnson, the historian of Britain's defense institutions, aptly describes the 1964 changes as 'the most fundamental peacetime restructuring of defence in British history.'[26]

The institutional consolidation of the defense establishment generally was received favorably by the press and the public. In Parliament, the objections of the opposition Labour Party were both mild and fleeting, which could be expected since the need for a stronger MoD had gradually become a Labour theme in the 1960s. The reorganization was, of course, not popular with the armed services, since it would considerably reduce their autonomy and decrease their access to the political tiers of government. Nevertheless, senior officers refrained from open criticism of the plan.[27]

After the modifications of 1964, continuous efforts were made to organize the services on a functional basis. Centralization was carried further in 1967 when the Ministers of State for the three services were replaced by two functional Ministers for Equipment and Administration.[28] After this change, the individual armed services – the Royal Navy, the Royal Air Force, and the Army – no longer had direct political representation in the government. This was the last major reorganization of defence in the 1960s, and it completed what had been a continual decline in the political influence of the armed services since 1939. Service ministers had been powerful actors in the Cabinets of the interwar period, but their influence had been reduced under the close wartime supervision of Churchill. Under Attlee service ministers were in the uncertain position of having Cabinet-level rank but not actually being a part of that body. In 1967, their political role was officially eradicated.

Although the reform of the machinery of defense was perhaps the largest institutional change of the period and the most trying for political leaders, it was only one area of institutional consolidation in the foreign policy apparatus of the 1960s.[29] Overseas policy was plagued by rival departments and conflicting jurisdictions in other areas as well. Before Indian Independence in 1947, three separate departments handled Britain's colonial affairs: the India Office, handling affairs on that subcontinent; the Dominions Office, handling affairs with Canada, Australia, New Zealand, South Africa, and Ireland; and the Colonial Office, which dealt with Britain's other overseas territories. In 1947, the Dominion and Indian Offices were merged to form the Commonwealth Relations Office. As part of the general trend toward institutional centralization in the 1960s, the Plowden Report of 1964 consolidated diplomatic representatives from the Colonial Office, the Commonwealth Relations Office, and the Foreign Office.[30] Henceforth, a single overseas emissary would represent these three departments in foreign countries. The report also confirmed that the merger of these departments was the eventual goal of policy. By 1966 the Commonwealth Relations Office had officially absorbed the Colonial Office, and two years later it was itself assimilated into the Foreign Office to create the Foreign and Commonwealth Relations Office. This process of consolidation reflected the steady contraction of Britain's territorial holdings overseas as countries within the empire gained independence. It also revealed the gradual awareness by decision-makers that for the first two-thirds of the twentieth century Britain's foreign policy machinery was inordinately fragmented and inefficient. In the institutional maze of Britain's overseas policy apparatus during this time, it was difficult to see the country's interests as a whole.[31]

There was a significant and not widely recognized consequence of the attempt to achieve economies and more effective policy through institutional consolidation in the 1960s.[32] As the foreign policy establishment contracted in that decade, so did the constituency within the government which had a vested interest in maintaining overseas military commitments. Two Cabinet-level departments which were intimately involved in overseas policies – the Colonial Office and the Commonwealth Relations Office – were abolished. The maintenance of the east of Suez military role was very much in the interest of actors in these departments. The constituency with the most invested in the east of Suez role, the military services, also lost access to the political arena.

It is important to note that the men who championed the institutional changes of the 1960s did not do so with any intention of dismantling the country's overseas military role. To the contrary, reformers such as Macmillan, Mountbatten, Ismay, and Jacob pushed through change in an attempt to strengthen the institutional machinery in foreign policy and defense. Consolidation was intended to reduce inefficiency. After these reforms and with the quantitative costing techniques increasingly borrowed from the US in defense matters, it was thought that Britain could again do more with less. By doing so, the country could maintain its overseas military network even as its economy continued to slip in comparison to its industrial rivals. Ironically, though, the changes which were meant to preserve the world role for the long haul contributed to its eventual demise. Although not an immediate cause of Britain's retrenchment, institutional consolidation in the country's foreign policy machinery decreased the number of officials and ministers with an inherent interest in maintaining overseas military commitments. The narrowing of this constituency eventually would make it easier for those calling for withdrawal to overcome the extremely potent mix of inertia and tradition underpinning the world role.

THE TRANSFORMATION OF STRATEGIC IDEAS AND GROWING OPPOSITION TO THE EAST OF SUEZ ROLE

At the same time that the institutional machinery of Britain's foreign policy establishment was being reshaped, conventional ideas about Britain's world role were undergoing transformation. Archaic ideas held in Britain's foreign policy establishment on the country's overseas bases were discarded and the benefits that the country derived from the overseas military role were increasingly challenged in the press and Parliament. Such questioning of the world role was undoubtedly a consequence of the growing awareness of Britain's relative decline and the failure associated with the Suez crisis, both of which helped to create a sense of uncertainty over Britain's international role.[33] After all, if Britain could not defeat a third-rank power like Egypt, then did the country truly sit at the top table of world politics? Also, if possession of an overseas military network did not provide the means for a successful operation against a regional power, then exactly what purpose did it fulfill?

Questions such as these became increasingly common in the articulate public and eventually in the government over the course of the 1960s. Ideas about Britain's overseas military role were in flux at this time. 'In the sphere of foreign policy,' Robert Holland observes of the 1960s, 'the old landmarks were evidently breaking up, even if it was not yet clear what the new ones were going to be.'[34] Since the landmarks fractured in distinct ways in the government and in the articulate public, the changing landscape of ideas in these two arenas will be analyzed separately.

In the government, the secret reviews of Britain's world role in the late 1950s seemed to exhaust any momentum for change that existed. Those opposing the world role had vented their opinions, and a firm policy course had been set for the early 1960s. Consequently, little criticism was voiced on the east of Suez role at this time.[35] Nonetheless, a more subtle change took place which not only altered policymakers' calculations on the overseas role, it created a new opportunity for policy change.

Following the Suez crisis, the view that Britain's strategic planners took of the country's network of overseas bases changed substantially.

A fundamental assumption which had guided British policy for decades was discarded: the assumption that fixed military outposts were inherently valuable and that they somehow buttressed the nation's greatness. The Suez episode was a powerful illustration that overseas garrisons no longer guaranteed success on the battlefield or the deference of local political leaders. Perhaps the best indication that British decision-makers perceived their overseas bases very differently was the emphasis on nuclear deterrence and increasingly mobile forces in the Sandys Doctrine.[36]

While the limitations of nuclear weapons were quickly revealed after the Sandys Doctrine was announced, increased mobility for the armed forces was stressed throughout the 1960s. It was consistently argued in foreign policy circles at this time that rapid response forces could replace many of Britain's expensive, vulnerable bases in the Indian Ocean area.[37] Yet, the emphasis on mobility in the 1960s meant only that Britain's network of bases east of Suez would gradually thin out, not that it would disappear. Key outposts such as Singapore and Aden would still be necessary for stockpiling supplies and for allowing troops to acclimatize to more torrid climates. Acclimatization was a large stumbling block for those who felt a strategic reserve in the United Kingdom would eventually replace the troops stationed overseas, as the British operation in Kuwait demonstrated in 1961. An army test conducted after the Kuwait episode concluded that while troops located in the area could carry out operations in the heat with little problem, almost a quarter of those flown in from the United Kingdom were out of action within five days and nearly all were ineffective after 12 days.[38] Also, a significant reduction of Britain's traditional land bases was not, it seemed at this time, feasible for political reasons. Bases were the army's principal stake in the overseas role. The delicate balance that had long existed between the armed services in terms of function, equipment, and manpower would be upset if overseas garrisons were curtailed. Politicians were acutely aware of the bitter rivalry among the armed services in postwar decades, and hence they naturally chose to tread lightly on the issue despite the additional political buffer that was soon to be provided with the centralization of the defense establishment.[39]

Overseas military installations thus in large part would endure. Yet, the conscious emphasis on strategic mobility in the east of Suez area, which was predicated on the notion that fixed bases were less useful and even somewhat anachronistic in the world of the 1960s, was nevertheless a significant shift in British strategic thought. It was an implicit recognition that Britain's greatness did not reprise solely in a network of overseas bases. The mystique which had been so carefully cultivated throughout the early part of the twentieth century around Britain's overseas bases had finally worn thin. British decision-makers subsequently took a more sober view of their outposts in the Indian Ocean area. In essence, the bases served an end – that of extending Britain's influence to the east of Suez area and protecting vital resources there. By the late 1950s it became widely accepted, for perhaps the first time since the turn of the century, that other means could be used to achieve this end.[40]

Although dispelling the myths surrounding Britain's overseas posts was not lent much weight at the time, in retrospect it appears vitally important. The range of policy options that decision-makers could pursue was suddenly and dramatically broadened with the new approach to Britain's bases abroad. Although the immediate outcome was the reduction of the number of military installations overseas, more radical policy change was becoming conceivable as well. In this way, this subtle change in strategic outlook can be characterized as the first step in a progression of thought which raised doubts about the east of Suez role. It must be remembered that the generation leading Britain in the late 1950s and early 1960s had been raised to believe, as Dewitt Armstrong records, that there was 'a close causal connection between naval bases, sea power, and Britain's greatness.'[41] Now these same leaders were uncertain whether Britain's network of bases abroad actually augmented the country's international influence and its prestige. Only one question could logically follow: 'What purpose does an overseas military role ultimately serve?'

Not surprisingly, this line of thought did not evolve rapidly in the foreign policy establishment. While the new strategic outlook marked a shift in perspective for policymakers which opened up unexpected policy options, it did not represent a radical reversal of their attitudes on Britain's world role. For governmental planners, improved mobility was a change designed to preserve the east of Suez role, not to raise doubts about it. As the literature on social psychology has convincingly demonstrated, consistent and unambiguous evidence is often necessary for individuals to discard firmly held beliefs, particularly if an appealing alternative is not readily at hand.[42] It can be surmised, although this study does not claim to offer systematic evidence on this point, that most British statesmen (and a large portion of the populace) continued to cling to ideas of British greatness.[43] This seems to be the case despite the increasing uncertainty over Britain's international position and, as we shall see, growing dissent over the east of Suez network in the articulate public. The most visible symbol of this greatness, along with sterling's position as a reserve currency, was the overseas military role; a role which had, after all, historically been very beneficial to the nation. While the international arena had changed dramatically in the decades after the Second World War, it was probably hard to believe that the benefits the country traditionally accrued from overseas commitments had evaporated as a consequence.

Thus, government policy and much political thinking remained anchored to the notion of a world role in the early 1960s. Moreover, a new, more coherent theory was developed to justify the overseas role at this time – that of international peacekeeping. Although Britain's economic and political interests were still the paramount reason for keeping the forces overseas, by the middle of the decade officials proclaimed that Britain was also serving the international interest by maintaining peace and stability in Indian Ocean area. Britain's stabilizing presence in this turbulent region was more likely to be accepted than that of other Western powers, and thus it could be argued that Britain was contributing to the construction of a nascent world security system.[44] Yet, this new, more amicable rationale for the east of Suez role remained vague, meaning different things to different policymakers. For many conservatives it was considered a link with the country's imperial past; for others it represented a new multilateral, multiracial role in the area. In a sense the concept was a smokescreen to cover the lack of clearly defined military strategy in the area. Without such a military strategy and with all three armed services seeing much to be gained by staying east of Suez in terms of hardware procurement and bureaucratic power, it is hardly surprising that British defense policy in the early 1960s actually placed renewed emphasis on overseas commitments. Stability in the Indian Ocean area was the basic policy goal agreed upon at this time, and more searching questions about Britain's capacities, its fundamental interests, and the changing international order were avoided not only by the government, but also by the Opposition frontbench.

While the military role abroad was quiescently accepted by the government, opinion on the country's overseas commitments began to splinter in the articulate public in the early 1960s. In comparison to the previous two decades, when critics of the east of Suez role were akin to lone voices in the wilderness, questions about the country's overseas role gradually grew more common. Liddell Hart's argument that Britain's bases abroad were merely 'crumbling sandcastles' is perhaps the most notable attack on the east of Suez role by a military strategist, but doubts also began to surface elsewhere.[45] In the press, *The Times*, in a highly critical article in August 1961, questioned how long Britain could afford to support a strategy which rested on a network of overseas bases. The article drew attention to the 'mystique of pins' on world maps in Britain's foreign policymaking apparatus, implying that the men managing Britain's overseas policy had lost touch with reality. In that same year the *Observer* likened Britain to a man whose umbrella had been torn to shreds by the wind but who still insisted on carrying the spokes. The spokes in this case were the remnants of empire, as embodied by the east of Suez role, and the wind represented the multitude of international changes to which Britain was attempting to adapt, especially rising nationalism and relative economic decline.[46]

Nevertheless, press criticism of the overseas role was far from consistent in the early 1960s. *The Times*, for example, had switched back to ardent support for the east of Suez role by 1962, after the limitations of nuclear weapons had become abundantly clear and an emphasis on conventional strength emerged within British and American foreign policy circles.[47] This illustrates that while deprecation of the world role was becoming more common in the articulate public, it was far from the predominant view at this time.[48] Consensus on the overseas military role was nonetheless slowly beginning to unravel in the early 1960s. Although it was scarcely perceptible at this stage, the tempest that would eventually emerge over the east of Suez network was showing its first, tentative signs of life.

By the middle of the 1960s the entire national mood appeared to swing.[49] C.J. Bartlett records that by the late 1960s Britain as a nation was 'becoming more introspective, more selective, more convinced that her resources were limited, and that her fields of action must be chosen with greater care and discrimination than in the past.'[50] Whether it was related to this shift in popular mood or not, the east of Suez debate began in earnest in this period. After 1965 a sustained attack on the east of Suez role was mounted in Parliament, in the press, and in academic forums, and controversy swirled over the issue of retrenchment.[51]

Criticisms of overseas commitments first articulated in the early part of the decade now burst to the forefront of the nation's political stage. Opponents of the east of Suez role argued that Britain's overseas military role not only disbenefited local peoples, it also was increasingly dangerous for Britain. According to such critics, Third World nationalism was a force which could not be reversed, and British forces overseas only acted as an irritant to local nationalism. Where Britain's military presence did not fan the flames of nationalism it only discouraged political and military self-sufficiency among newly independent nations. Hence, the east of Suez role was not creating stability in the region in the long run, it was inhibiting it. The military presence also was detrimental to the nation's interests because it would, over the long term, sour relations with many of the popular movements and governments in the region. Britain was thus, according to critics, too often siding with the feudal leaders of the region's past rather than the progressive nationalism of the future. Censure also came over the state of British forces in the area, which were said to be spread perilously thin. With the growing militarization of the Middle and the Far East, small conflicts could easily balloon into major ones which would be beyond the government's capacity to support.

Given such worries, the policy alternative typically offered by opponents of the east of Suez role was detached economic self-interest. A policy of open trade would be the best way, opponents of the overseas role maintained, to keep crucial raw materials flowing into Britain, to persuade nations in the region to buy British goods, and hence to preserve British influence in the area. Perhaps the two most consistent critics of the overseas role, Enoch Powell, the shadow Defence Minister, and Christopher Mayhew, a junior minister in the Admiralty who resigned over the east of Suez issue in 1965, made much of the commercial success of West Germany and Japan even though these countries had no military presence abroad. In short, critics argued that in the mid-1960s the drawbacks of the overseas military role had finally begun to outweigh its benefits.[52]

Yet, the traditional arguments for staying in the Indian Ocean area, which centered on strategic and humanitarian concerns, remained convincing. Advocates of the east of Suez role feared the emergence of a power vacuum in the Indian Ocean area after British withdrawal. British enemies, such as Arab revolutionary or communist-led governments might then rush to fill the void, toppling friendly regimes. In addition, Britain's economic interests in the area were said to be too vital to be left to the whims of the international marketplace. Britain still imported about 60 per cent of its oil from the Middle East in the mid-1960s. If Arab revolutionaries took power more widely in this area the sale of oil to the West might be curtailed even though it would be against the economic self-interest of these governments, and

British industry could ill afford such a calamity. Moreover, the presence of British troops was said to quell many long-simmering disputes in the region, which would likely spill over into bloodshed and perhaps even wider regional turmoil upon their departure.[53] Obviously, the two sides in this debate were more often than not speaking past one another. As a result, the period was characterized by pressures and opinions which were both intense and cross-cutting.

The emergence of a fierce and highly polarized debate over the east of Suez role after 1965 was a dramatic transformation in British political life which forms the context for the decision to retrench. Forceful arguments for disengagement eventually would erode the case for staying east of Suez. But, as can be expected in a foreign policy apparatus as insulated as Britain's, steady calls for withdrawal were far from sufficient to produce retrenchment. The effect that the east of Suez critics had on policy was further limited by extant assumptions on how overseas outposts served Britain's interests. More than any serious examination of the empirical evidence, such assumptions were based on wishful thinking and tradition in the mid- to late 1960s. Put simply, the government and its critics were viewing the overseas military role through very different lenses at this time.

Ironically, a government more committed to the overseas military role than any of its post-1945 predecessors took office during the east of Suez debate. The leaders of the Labour Party who won power in 1964 had no intention of eschewing traditional power politics in the hopes of making socialist foreign policy a reality. If anything, in its presentation of the issue the government attempted to breathe new life into the world role. Before discussing the specific variables which led British decision-makers to retrench, it is first necessary to analyze this government and the strains which became increasingly apparent in its overseas policy. Understanding the Labour government's stance on the east of Suez network underscores the gravity of the change which took place in British foreign policy in the late 1960s. More importantly, this context is crucial to comprehend fully the variables which dislodged the status quo.

HOLDING THE LINE: THE LABOUR GOVERNMENT OF 1964–6

Interestingly, the last years of the Conservative governments of Macmillan and Douglas-Home were marked by little more than a general public concern over the extent and the costs of Britain's defense responsibilities overseas. Only months after the Labour government came to office in October 1964, opposition to the east of Suez role became more visible and persistent. Attacks on the overseas role only grew more savage during the government's tenure. In part, this was a consequence of critics in the Labour movement finally being able to voice their opinions to a government of their own. A shift in popular attitudes which appeared to affect all Western polities at this time also appears to have contributed to the ensuing political storm. Whatever the cause, the Labour ministry did not flinch in the face of rising pressures to retrench.

There are a number of reasons why the Labour government which took office in 1964 chose to maintain Britain's military presence in the east of Suez area. The perceived need to provide the country with a post-imperial sense of national purpose seems to have influenced the new Labour Cabinet as much as any of its predecessors. Access to oil and the need to guarantee American financial backing also figured into the Labour government's calculations on the overseas military role, and the problem of how to disentangle existing obligations remained daunting.[54] One obligation in particular seemed to prevent any immediate withdrawal from the Indian Ocean area. When Labour took power in 1964 Britain was involved in an ongoing low-intensity struggle in Borneo against Indonesia, called 'confrontation.' To cut troops significantly in the area would have undermined this operation, sapping the morale of British forces and perhaps emboldening their opponents.

A foreign policy fiasco would have been particularly damaging since this was a Labour regime with a left-wing premier. Wilson and his ministerial colleagues felt that given their political pedigree they had to remain beyond reproach on foreign policy issues. Even the mildest lapse might be seized upon and given untoward interpretations.[55] In addition, the Labour Party had won a bare majority of just four in Parliament and a snap defeat remained a possibility. With such a frail parliamentary underpinning, the first Wilson government was a consciously temporary one, obliged to steer carefully and to attempt to protect the country's brittle economy from shocks. The government's first aim was to maintain its popularity until the opportunity to secure a fuller endorsement at the polls presented itself. Radical policy change was not on the political agenda.

Yet, at the same time, the government was not simply compelled by political circumstances to maintain the east of Suez commitments.

The nucleus of the new Labour Cabinet consisted of men from the old Labour right who fervently supported the overseas military role.[56] The core of this grouping included James Callaghan, the Chancellor; Denis Healey, the Defence Minister; Patrick Gordon Walker, the Foreign Secretary; Michael Stewart, who would replace Gordon Walker after only three months in office; and George Brown, the Minister of Economic Affairs.[57] In the pages which follow, such champions of the east of Suez network in the Labour Cabinet will be labelled 'Bevinites,' both because the term offers a useful shorthand and because they represented a sizable contingent in the PLP, which espoused the type of traditional foreign policy course charted in the late 1940s by the forceful Foreign Secretary.[58] Although from the left of the party, Prime Minister Harold Wilson was perhaps the staunchest supporter of the east of Suez role in government. To understand why the Labour Cabinet clung so tenaciously to east of Suez commitments as pressures for withdrawal mounted in the late 1960s, particular attention must be given to Wilson's romantic conception of the world role and his governing style. For, as Alan Sked and Chris Cook note, 'it is difficult to exaggerate the degree to which the new Labour government was dominated by Harold Wilson.'[59] It was only after the Prime Minister's perception of Britain's place in the world altered and his standing in the nation began to wane that progress was made by those calling for withdrawal.

Harold Wilson is often characterized as a person who had few, if any, firmly held political beliefs. He is said to be a man who succeeded in politics largely because of his skill at short-term political tactics and stratagems, not because he had a coherent vision for Britain's future. This image of Wilson is not merely a legacy of his premiership, it was apparent throughout his political career. Before Wilson assumed the party leadership in 1963, Michael Foot, from the left-wing of the party, observed that he was widely thought to be 'tricky, untrustworthy, an addict of political infighting...' and, perhaps worse still, that 'he sits on the fence.'[60] This characterization of Wilson's political style is largely accurate, as maneuvering for short-term political advantage was a skill in which he was particularly adept.[61]

Yet, Wilson adhered to one overriding belief perhaps too rigidly: he was convinced that Britain was and must remain a great power. The Labour Prime Minister's political philosophy centered on a dirigiste economic policy which he felt would cure the nation's economic woes. The resulting economic revival would ensure Britain's place at the top table in world politics.

Because of his high opinion of Britain's weight in the world, Wilson felt that two areas of foreign policy were sacrosanct: sterling's parity and the east of Suez role. When considering parity, Wilson ardently wanted to maintain sterling as a major reserve currency and to preserve London's position as a world banker. He recognized the international prestige which could flow from these roles. He also appreciated that Labour had been linked in the public mind with devaluation since the time of Cripps in 1949. Considering this, it would have been political suicide to devalue with the wafer-thin parliamentary majority his party held in 1964 and 1965.[62]

Once Wilson had staked his reputation on sterling's parity early in his term, it became a primary end of governmental policy. In Wilson's mind, to devalue in the face of economic pressures would have been an ignominious retreat. Although it demonstrated that Labour was as concerned as the Conservatives to protect Britain's international reputation, a serious political danger arose from the position taken by the Prime Minister. As he repeatedly pronounced his determination to defend sterling, the possibility of his own credibility being devalued along with the pound grew.[63]

Yet, it was with regard to the country's east of Suez role that the Prime Minister diverged most sharply from his pragmatic political instincts. Wilson's speeches on the overseas role were filled with both emotion and romantic imagery. He was not alone in this regard, for many senior Labour ministers in the mid-1960s reverted to phrases akin to the later imperialists in their efforts to defend the country's overseas role.[64] In the Prime Minister's case, this tendency to portray the east of Suez role as inviolate may stem partly from his proclivity for using extravagant phrases and partly from his longstanding personal interest in the Commonwealth. Wilson had a distinct streak of romantic conservatism in his outlook on world politics, and the Commonwealth and the east of Suez role provided outlets for his vision of a Britain which would once again shape international affairs. As late as the 1964 election, Wilson claimed that it would still be possible to mold the Commonwealth into a vast economic and political power bloc capable of rivalling the United States and the USSR for world leadership.[65] Such a notion was out of step with the reality of the time. By the mid-1960s, most commentators on world affairs and even the Foreign Office had accepted that the Commonwealth was little more than a hollow edifice.

Wilson's governing style ensured that what he saw as the two pillars of Britain's world role remained central components of the country's foreign policy. The new Prime Minister was determined to take decisions on everything that mattered instead of letting events wash over him.[66] He summarized his views to the American political scientist Richard Neustadt before the 1964 election, with Neustadt reporting that:

> He means to take all decisions into his own hands. He wants not only to make ultimate decisions but to pass issues through his own mind early, sitting at the centre of a brains-trust, with himself as the first brains-truster, on the model he says, of J.F.K. . . . 'I shall be Chairman of the Board, not President,' he says, but 'Managing Director too, and very active at it.'[67]

Once in office, the Labour Prime Minister placed a very firm hand on the tiller of state and was reluctant to delegate authority. A Number 10 official at the time recalls that Wilson thought open discussion in Cabinet was a risk to be avoided; Wilson 'held to the principle that you should never have a meeting in which the conclusions had not been established in advance.'[68] Such an activist governing style would later cause many of his Cabinet colleagues to accuse him of being presidential.[69]

Not surprisingly, then, given the Prime Minister's convictions and his style of government, the first Wilson government implemented a foreign policy very similar to its Conservative predecessors. In a Commons debate on 16 December 1964, shortly after he had taken power, Wilson confirmed that continuity was the order of the day in overseas policy:

> I want to make it clear that whatever we may do in the field of cost effectiveness, value for money, and a stringent review of expenditure, we cannot afford to relinquish our world role, our role which, for shorthand purposes, is sometimes called our 'east of Suez' role . . .[70]

No other country could make the contribution Britain made to the world outside of Europe, as Wilson went on to explain with regard to American attitudes:

> Our American allies are not so impressed with our claims to be a world power or to have a seat at the Top Table if we base our claims on matching our nuclear policy with theirs. They are perfectly capable of doing the arithmetic of megatons. What does impress them is our ability to mount peacekeeping operations that no one else can mount.[71]

Wilson also argued in this speech that the balance among Britain's overseas commitments required re-evaluation, with the implication being that Britain's military role in Europe needed trimming. He declared that in weapons manufacture unsophisticated weapons needed for small-scale warfare would henceforth be given emphasis over costly, high-tech weapons which were appropriate only for Europe. Thus, the east of Suez role was undeniably the Labour government's first foreign policy priority.

Yet, this early speech illuminates a tension that would persist in the Labour government's overseas policy. The Wilson government was determined to reduce what they saw as runaway defense expenditures while at the same time preserving Britain's status as a world power. The contradictions in these two goals would soon pull Britain's overseas policy in divergent directions, producing notable policy contortions. Moreover, this inherent tension would over the coming years prove to be yet another millstone around decision-makers' necks which justified withdrawal.

In an effort to contain defense expenditure, the Labour government placed a straight cap on spending. As the National Economic Plan, the policy program based on Wilson's dirigiste economic policies, took shape, Treasury suggestions that the planned defense budget for 1969 of £2400 million be trimmed to £2000 million became an immutable ceiling. Throughout the late 1960s defense efficiency was measured both publicly and privately by this somewhat arbitrary figure, which had no reference to specific weapon programs or defense policies.[72] The cap would result in significant reductions in the forces deployed in the east of Suez area over the coming years. All the while, the country's commitments in the area remained stable. Subsequently, the gap between Britain's economic and military capabilities and its overseas commitments, which was already of considerable size before Labour took power, grew alarmingly over the life of the government.

The Labour government's first two Defence White Papers, in 1965 and in 1966, reflected the tension which existed in overseas policy. Both of these White Papers underscored the government's desire to maintain the east of Suez role. Britain had treaty obligations in the area and a significant interest in promoting stability and economic prosperity there. Considering this, paragraph 20 of the 1965 White Paper concluded that it would be 'politically irresponsible and economically wasteful' for British leaders to contemplate withdrawal from any part of the overseas role.[73]

At the same time, it was imperative that defense spending be reduced to free up resources for investment in the industrial base, the overriding goal of the Labour government's economic plan and an economic necessity.[74] Certain weapons programs were cut immediately by the government, such as the HS681 medium transport aircraft and the fifth Polaris submarine. The 1966 White Paper went furthest in making defense spending cuts and in placing operational limitations on Britain's east of Suez role. The 1966 statement canceled the new aircraft carriers which had been planned for the Navy. Existing carriers, already very old, would be decommissioned by the mid-1970s. An island base staging scheme, using aircraft mobility and small bases throughout the area, was deemed sufficient to allow Britain to retain the east of Suez role at considerable savings. Because of the limitations of the island base scheme on purely military grounds, many analysts at the time felt that the abandonment of the carrier force – what Philip Darby terms 'at once the hub and the symbol of British power east of Suez' – was a decisive step away from world power.[75] Both the Chief of the Naval Staff, Sir David Luce, and the Minister of Defence for the Navy, Christopher Mayhew, resigned over this decision and what they felt to be the unacceptable overstretching of British forces which would result.

Britain could afford a more limited presence in the Indian Ocean area, the 1966 White Paper argued, because the country would no longer attempt to undertake major military operations without allied assistance. What constituted a major operation and what degree of allied support would be required were never fully specified. Hence, this supposed limitation on Britain's east of Suez role essentially was a call for greater allied burden-sharing, and as such, it was a relatively uninspiring attempt to reduce Britain's overseas burdens. The British had tried to compel their allies to provide further assistance prior to this. Such appeals for assistance stood little chance of success at a time when all of Britain's major allies, including the US, were striving to reduce defence spending at all costs.

The 1966 statement pledged further limitations on the east of Suez role. Britain would henceforth only accept a defense obligation in another country when the appropriate facilities were supplied and, furthermore, there would be no attempt to maintain defense facilities in a nation if its presence was opposed by either the government or the populace.[76] This was also a rather superficial restriction of Britain's east of Suez role, for without the naval power provided by the carrier, Britain was incapable of providing military support to a country without the host government's acquiescence. One fairly major reduction in overseas commitments was announced in the 1966 statement. Britain was going to abandon the base in Aden in 1967 or 1968, with additional troops stationed in Persian Gulf outposts to compensate.[77]

Nevertheless, Britain's world role remained largely intact despite the restrictions which the Labour government placed on it during its first two years in office. Labour government decision-makers had no intention of surrendering the international influence which the possession of an overseas military network seemed to bestow upon Britain.[78] The Prime Minister's chimerical image of the country's world role and his activist governing style were especially important in maintaining the status quo in Britain's overseas policy.

Yet, the military network east of Suez was not maintained without considerable exertion by Labour leaders. Economic constraint bore down upon the government ever more, and as appreciation of Britain's declining status in the world steadily grew in the public, calls for significant reductions in the overseas role intensified. In fact, despite his immense influence within the government, throughout his tenure the Prime Minister was compelled to perform a delicate balancing act among multiple pressures over the east of Suez issue. To understand why the Labour government eventually succumbed to the calls for retrenchment, the character of this balancing act must be described. Moreover, the full range of the pressures on the government both at home and abroad must be analyzed.

MANAGING COUNTERVAILING PRESSURES ON THE WORLD ROLE: THE INCHOATE COALITION AGAINST EAST OF SUEZ

Other than minor adjustments, then, the first Wilson government made no concessions to those calling for reductions in Britain's overseas military role, despite the debate which raged on this subject from 1965 on. Yet, from the time that the Labour government took office a potentially powerful coalition existed which favored major change in the country's foreign policy. This dormant coalition consisted of three groups in the government: those who wanted to economize, which included practically everyone in Cabinet; those who hoped to focus the government's energies on Europe, such as George Brown and rising Cabinet ministers Roy Jenkins and Anthony Crosland;

and left-wingers who were suspicious of the past imperial role, such as Richard Crossman, Barbara Castle, and Tony Benn.[79]

There are two main reasons why this coalition never gelled during the first three years of the Labour government, overturning the status quo in Britain's overseas policy. The first has to do with the nature of Cabinet government itself and the time constraints involved in managing a Cabinet level portfolio. Typically, ministers exhaust all of their energies attempting to keep up with the swift flow of events in their own ministries. Rarely can they give anything more than partial consideration to policies in other departments.[80] The chief minister without portfolio is the Prime Minister, and he alone is empowered to draw up general policy guidelines and oversee policies in disparate areas. Yet, Wilson had no desire to alter the path of policy with regard to the east of Suez role. One can suspect that ministers opposing the east of Suez role did not act because they were both too busy with matters in their own departments and they feared appearing uninformed or even foolish when speaking out on matters outside of their ministerial purview. Denis Healey confirms this view when he recalls that, during his first years as Defence Minister, he was unchallenged by other ministers on the course of the country's overseas policy.[81]

The second reason the inchoate coalition against the east of Suez role did not solidify has to do, again, with Harold Wilson's governing style. Beyond manipulating the Cabinet's agenda, Wilson skillfully introduced two tensions into his politics. He placed political heavyweights in his Cabinet in perpetual rivalry by shifting ministerial posts, and he assiduously balanced the left and right wings of his party. Wilson was particularly adept at judging the way that the political winds within his government were blowing, and he adjusted his policies and reconfigured his Cabinet accordingly.[82] In doing so, he was able to fend off challenges to his position as leader. More importantly, though, his Cabinet reshuffles purposely created pockets of tension within his government which hindered the development of a coalition opposing his core policies.

Although Wilson attempted to create rivalry and tension at all levels of his government, he was most concerned to balance out what he termed his 'crown princes,' or the two or three ministers most likely to challenge his position as premier. During the first three years of his premiership this involved checking two men, James Callaghan and George Brown. Wilson placed these two leaders of the old Labour right in the government's most powerful positions to, in the words of Wilson biographer Ben Pimlott, 'placate, occupy, [and] neutralize' them.[83] Callaghan was made Chancellor while Brown headed the Department of Economic Affairs (DEA), a newly formed institutional competitor to the Treasury. Since the two were distrustful of one another, if one of them dared to challenge sterling's parity or the overseas role, for example, the other could be counted on to side with Wilson, effectively thwarting policy change.[84]

The second tension that Wilson maintained in his politics was that between his old leftist entourage and the rightist political heavyweights, such as Callaghan and Brown, whom he felt obliged to put in his Cabinet. In balancing left and right, Wilson assuaged the suspicions of the right by following rightist foreign and domestic policies, and he satisfied the left by simply being their man, for no other politician of the left had either the stature or the following to become the party leader, much less Prime Minister. Although they might bitterly criticize his policies and rebel in parliament, left-wing MPs would fall in behind their leader if his political position was challenged. And if a left-wing backbencher proved to be consistently troublesome, he or she would be swept into government, effectively silencing them.[85]

Although Wilson was successful at perpetuating these tensions on the government benches of the House of Commons, the government's policies were not made in a political vacuum. As the east of Suez debate developed, mounting pressures outside of the government affected decision-makers as well. The foremost example is the Labour Party, for a party as fraction-ridden as Labour was in the late 1960s could not be appeased solely by the Prime Minister's juggling act, no matter how adept he and his Cabinet colleagues might have been. As has already been intimated, pressure for withdrawal from the overseas role continued to grow rapidly among the Labour Party's rank and file after 1965. Despite the government's attempts to the contrary, backbench revolts over the government's foreign policy became both frequent and of a scale never before seen in postwar British politics.[86] Nevertheless, because he was their only viable leader, Wilson was able to stand up to left-wing criticism of his foreign policy and, in essence, to remain the master of his party.

Opposition to the overseas commitments grew outside of the Labour Party from 1965 on as well, especially in pro-Europe circles. The Liberal Party leader Jo Grimond attacked the east of Suez peacekeeping role at the Liberal Party Conference in 1965, although the Liberals had been less than enthusiastic about Britain's world role for some time. In addition, Enoch Powell, the shadow Defence Minister, took a somewhat surprising stance for a senior Conservative politician at the 1965 Party Conference, calling for the United Kingdom to withdraw from all overseas commitments in the next decade, allowing local forces in the Indian Ocean area to reach their own balances. Attitudes also turned more consistently sour in the press. By early 1967 it seemed that only the *Daily Express* and the *Daily Telegraph*, those last bastions of British imperialism, refrained from taking the government to task for excessive spending overseas.[87] *The Times* had again switched back to opposing the overseas role by this time.

The position of the Conservative Opposition is of particular note, for Powell's stance on the issue was deeply unsettling to many of his colleagues.[88] The divisions within the Conservative ranks on the east of Suez issue, though never gaining wide visibility, underscore the increasing volatility of attitudes toward the overseas military role during this period. That such a senior shadow minister in the party of empire would consistently assert that Britain had to 'free herself from the long servitude of her 70 year old dreams' and disengage from overseas positions demonstrates that attitudes, and indeed the times, were changing.[89] Admittedly, Powell was something of a maverick in the Conservative Party and he struck a very individualistic chord while a shadow minister. But he was not without supporters in the party on this issue. He felt sure that the Leader of the Opposition, Ted Heath, was among them. The shadow Defence Minister sincerely believed he had been chosen to articulate Conservative views on defense matters because the party leader agreed that the overseas military network had become anachronistic. Heath's ardent support for the east of Suez role, especially in later years as the Wilson government began to dismantle it, was a central cause of the rift which would open up between these two Conservative political heavyweights, with Powell eventually being dismissed from the shadow Cabinet following his infamous April 1968 speech on immigration.[90]

Before this point, Powell had been allowed to follow his own logic on the east of Suez issue and many others because the Conservative Party was clearly in a period of transition, adjusting to the Opposition benches after 13 years of power. The party was actively groping for a new governing philosophy. The consensus politics of the 1950s, which emphasized economics and materialism, now appeared worn and shallow, and the Conservative Party had not produced a political or an electoral formula which was as vibrant as Labour's message of harnessing technology for economic growth. In this quest to refurbish their image and their philosophy the Conservatives were largely unsuccessful in the late 1960s, as large portions of the electorate had trouble identifying exactly what the party represented throughout the period. Nonetheless, one of the principal goals of the Conservative leadership was to draw clear distinctions between themselves and their Labour opponents, decisively discarding with the consensus politics of the past.[91] So long as the Labour government staunchly defended the east of Suez role, Powell's criticism offered a point of difference which potentially could be expanded upon. This option was, perhaps not surprisingly, never exercised. The broad outline of the Opposition's foreign policy throughout this period supported the status quo in the Indian Ocean area, rather than radical change. No better example of this can be found than the statement made by Sir Alec Douglas-Home following Powell's speech at the 1965 Conservative Party Conference. Sir Alec, who as shadow Foreign Secretary had general responsibility for the party's overseas policies, quickly and reassuringly declared that the Conservatives would never withdraw British forces from the east of Suez network if it would create a strategic vacuum in the area (which it almost certainly would).

Controversy thus swirled outside the government over the east of Suez issue in the mid-1960s, as was discussed previously. Sharply divergent opinions existed within both major parties, and they were increasingly and at times passionately vocalized. At the same time, the pressures which first manifest themselves in the foreign policy bureaucracy in the late 1950s were, by the mid-1960s, taking more tangible forms. The Treasury axe was wielded with increasing force as the 1960s wore on. As is customary, the senior department took no specific policy positions, although some of its senior staff may have done so in inter-departmental forums as they had in the secret reviews of the 1950s.[92] Instead, the Treasury consistently held the line against defense spending increases and eventually began to push for lower expenditure levels, effectively cutting the substance out of the east of Suez policy. The Foreign Office was by the late 1960s leaning decisively toward Europe in its policy proposals, although the department still desired a limited military presence in the Middle East to maintain its diplomatic presence there and to keep oil flowing freely to Britain.[93] Also, military attitudes on reductions in the overseas role were softening somewhat. Military men quite legitimately feared being drawn into a conflict which was beyond Britain's capability to win, as appeared to be happening to the United States in Southeast Asia.[94] Perhaps the only department providing unfailing support to the overseas role was the Commonwealth Relations Office, which felt that the rapidly rotting political hulk of the Commonwealth was propped up by the overseas military network. But the CRO was a weak department which had only been further emasculated by the Plowden Report of 1964. These diverging perspectives in the foreign policy bureaucracy hardly amounted to a ringing endorsement of the world role. To the contrary, support for the east of Suez role seemed to be waning by the late 1960s throughout Britain's foreign policy apparatus.[95]

Yet, as prominent as rising pressure to reduce overseas commitments within Britain was, especially in the Labour Party, there was also countervailing pressure from abroad. Britain's allies in the area, particularly Singapore, Malaysia, and Australia, all rushed to lobby in London on behalf of the world role whenever word spread that commitment reductions were being contemplated. More consistent and perhaps more influential pressure came from the United States, which sought all of the assistance it could muster in global policing as it became further embroiled in revolutionary struggle in Southeast Asia.

Washington's attitude toward Britain's overseas military role underwent dramatic transformation after the Suez crisis in 1956. Before this time American policymakers shared either ambivalence or outright disdain for Britain's world role, in part because of the anti-imperialist ideals which were so common in American foreign policy circles. By the late 1950s, however, US leaders were, in Michael Carver's words, 'only too eager to find partners to share the White Man's burden in containing the spread of communism in the developing world.'[96] Transformations in American grand strategy partly explain this changed outlook. American policymakers by 1960 had come to realize that a massive nuclear arsenal had limited applicability in the small-scale conflicts of the developing world, increasingly the locale of the fight against communism. They also recognized that the costs of policing the world with conventional weapons was beyond even the United States' considerable capabilities. Allies had thus become more necessary in the global struggle against communism, and in Washington's new strategic outlook, Britain's role in the Indian Ocean area suddenly appeared vital.[97]

The first meetings between the leaders of the new Labour government and American officials underscored the importance that the US government attached to Britain's role east of Suez. George Thomson, who became the Commonwealth Secretary in 1967, provides a vivid example when recalling the lobbying efforts of Averell Harriman, the

American Ambassador at large in London. According to Thomson, Harriman 'descended from a great height upon us immediately after the new government was formed and a number of us were brainwashed, by him, about the British need to support the United States in terms of global commitments.'[98] Yet, it was the first meeting between Wilson and US President Lyndon Johnson in Washington in December 1964 which was crucial in consolidating the Labour government's view on the east of Suez role, a view which would remain relatively steadfast over the next three years. At this meeting, Wilson pledged to preserve Britain's overseas military role and Johnson vowed to back sterling and to provide diplomatic support to British policies in Southern Rhodesia, where a rebel colonial regime was preparing to declare its independence from the United Kingdom.

While important in setting the tone for Labour's foreign policy, this early meeting merely confirmed an implicit arrangement which had existed between London and Washington for some time. In this arrangement, Britain kept a watchful eye over subSaharan Africa, battled communist revolutionaries in Southern Arabia and South Asia, and maintained a military presence in the Indian Ocean area. In return, the United States shared nuclear secrets, elevated Britain's international status by treating Britain as its closest ally, and rescued Britain during financial crises.[99] This largely implicit understanding illustrates how, in many ways, the two countries were bound together by international political necessity. Britain required financial and diplomatic assistance from the United States to maintain its world role and the US felt that it was vitally important to have at least one major ally in its global undertaking. The most visible sign of Anglo-American cooperation in global policing at this time was the construction of the US military facility on the island of Diego Garcia in the Indian Ocean, which began immediately after the Labour government took office.

American pressure on Britain increased in 1965 as domestic dissent rose in Britain and the American commitment in Vietnam escalated. The tacit arrangement soon took a more concrete form. A secret pact was arranged which underscored the essence of the Anglo-American relationship in this period: the United States would provide massive aid to prop up the pound so long as Britain did not devalue or withdraw from east of Suez commitments.[100] The US administration also made it known that future purchases of British military hardware, which were critical for the balance of payments, would depend upon Britain staying east of Suez.[101]

For obvious political reasons, the connection between US financial support and Britain's position in the Far East was vigorously denied by Wilson and other Labour leaders both during and after the events of the late 1960s.[102] It would have been politically self-destructive to stress such a link in speeches at home, and Wilson even went so far as to deny its existence in Cabinet.[103] Richard Crossman records a Cabinet meeting in early 1966 when the Prime Minister insisted that there was no connection between American aid and the overseas role. Yet, without so much as a pause, he reminded his colleagues that US financial assistance 'is not unrelated to the way we behave in the Far East; any direct announcement of our withdrawal for example, could not fail to have a profound effect on my personal relations with LBJ and the way the Americans treat us.'[104]

It is clear in hindsight that British decision-makers by this time had, as Ben Pimlott claims, 'become conscious as never before that the special relationship was actually a client one, at a time when the Americans had something specific to ask of their client.'[105] Yet, the pressure placed on London by the United States caused little discomfort in the Labour Cabinet. The senior ministers responsible for the country's foreign policy, especially the Prime Minister, championed precisely what the United States was asking: for Britain to remain a global power.

In this climate of countervailing pressures at home and abroad a coalition opposing the east of Suez role never materialized. Not surprisingly, Wilson, the master political strategist, effected a delicate balance between the financial strings being pulled by Washington and the growing anti-east of Suez lobby among Labour MPs: pleading American pressure to backbenchers and party constraints to the Americans. His tactical skills and the support of senior ministers in Cabinet ensured that the issue of withdrawal from the world role never saw the political light of day.[106] Yet, given Britain's frail economy and the swelling ranks of those dissatisfied with the overseas military role at home, it is not surprising that the reservoir of political skill possessed by the Prime Minister and his senior colleagues eventually ran dry. The reason that this occurred and its phasing are important for understanding Britain's retrenchment.

7 Relinquishing World Power: Britain's Financial Crises of 1966–7

By early 1966 the main arguments for and against the east of Suez role had been introduced into the debate over withdrawal. As the controversy wore on, it gradually came to be accepted that the maintenance of stability in the Indian Ocean area during a transitional period was the core issue. The economic and political viability of former colonies had to be ensured, and strong ties with Britain continued. In this context, some type of withdrawal seemed certain. The main question that remained was how substantial the withdrawal would be and what, if any, role Britain should play in the area in the future. Even so, the writing was far from on the wall for the world role. Numerous policy options remained. Staunch advocates of the world role were confident that any withdrawals made in the late 1960s, a period of severe economic duress, could be reversed in better times.

Advocates were buoyed by the government's position. As the controversy over the overseas role intensified, the Labour government firmly held to a policy of continuity. Yet, repeated external shocks in the form of financial crises would eventually drain the Labour Cabinet of its momentum, while also causing a shift in the Cabinet's delicate balance of political power. These crises and the political transformations that followed proved to be of enormous import for the world role, because government calculations on the east of Suez network were radically reversed in their wake. Other factors, of course, were also significant in the eventual decision for complete disengagement. Strategic ideas were transformed and the institutional machinery necessary for change was created. The end of confrontation in Borneo allowed greater reductions in the forces overseas. The movement of opinion within Cabinet toward Europe gradually altered perceptions on Britain's overseas commitments. And, perhaps a little less significant, the easing of American pressure on Britain provided yet more room for maneuver. Nonetheless, while such considerations provided the foundations for withdrawal, it was the financial crises and the resulting political upheaval which struck the decisive blows.

CRISIS AND CHANGE

The Labour government had reached what in hindsight can be regarded as its political apex in early 1966. The economy appeared healthy and an election was called for March, which resulted in a convincing victory for the Labour Party. There could be no question, moreover, to whom the victory belonged. The campaign concentrated on Wilson's leadership credentials rather than any broader Labour policy platform and victory at the polls only served to underscore his immense popularity at that time.[1] When the polls closed, a slim parliamentary majority of three was converted into a majority of 97. It was a remarkable triumph for a leader who had governed for nearly a year and a half with a precarious parliamentary undergirding. Yet, within weeks of this electoral feat, a crisis developed which undermined the popular standing of both the Prime Minister and his government.

The issue was sterling, which had long been in a fragile position. The fundamental reason for the pound's weakness was, as Chancellor James Callaghan would later explain, 'the world's opinion that Britain was not competitive with other trading nations, and [the fact that] our sterling reserves were never large enough to permit us to withstand that opinion.'[2] Although economists at the time worried that sterling was vulnerable to a sudden shock, the Labour leadership was convinced that this danger could be avoided by skillful macroeconomic management. The government had proved dexterous enough to avoid an economic débâcle, after all, during the first Wilson government.[3]

Yet, sterling's precarious position, only one jolt away from catastrophe, could not last forever. The requisite jar was provided by a seamen's strike in the summer of 1966. The currency markets anticipated considerable dislocation in British industry as exports languished on closed docks or, worse still, that the country's export capacity might be permanently damaged.[4] Relentless selling of sterling began in July 1966 and it was further encouraged by untimely remarks by the French President, Georges Pompidou, who suggested that Britain would have to devalue before it could be seriously considered for entry in the Common Market. The first major rift in the government only made matters worse. Frank Cousins, Minister of Technology, and former head of one of the country's most powerful unions, the Transport and General Workers Union, resigned over the government's prices and incomes policy and returned to his union, leading to expectations of a further deterioration of government–labor relations and perhaps more industrial unrest.

It was evident that action had to be taken by the government. A large and hardening coalition in the Cabinet favored devaluation as a way to resolve the seemingly intractable problem of the currency, although many in this group failed to recognize that drastic budgetary cuts would still be required to take full advantage of the change in parity. Contrarily, the Prime Minister remained unshakable in defence of sterling throughout the crisis. He argued that since harsh measures would have to be taken with or without devaluation, it seemed politically wise to wait and devalue when the government was in a position of economic strength. He eventually convinced a wavering Callaghan, who was a tyro in economic matters in comparison to the Prime Minister, that parity could not be sacrificed, and the two pushed through the most severe deflationary package imposed on the British economy since the Second World War.[5]

The Prime Minister's stubbornness on this issue sheds light on his self-image. His ally Richard Crossman best captures this when he states that Wilson's 'image of himself is as a gritty, practical, Yorkshireman, a fighter, a Britisher who does not switch, who hangs on.'[6] Such tenacity staved off devaluation in 1966, and with the support of the Chancellor and other vacillating ministers, Wilson made the subject once again strictly taboo in Cabinet. Wilson's determination and his political stamina also, of course, provide at least a partial explanation of why the country's foreign policy course did not waver as domestic dissension escalated in the late 1960s.

The east of Suez role was not questioned during the July 1966 sterling crisis, although this shock would in time spark a critical reappraisal of Britain's overseas commitments. The military role overseas was, in fact, probably a significant factor considered by the Wilson cabinet which weighed in against devaluation. Not only was the value of sterling widely seen as a symbol of national pride; parity was an integral part of both the special relationship with the US and the country's east of Suez role. A devaluation would require sharp reductions in overseas expenditures. Since Labour Party backbenchers would inevitably insist that defense spending bear the brunt of any such cuts, the potential for some form of contraction of the world role and a serious rift with the United States seemed very real. Small wonder, then, that the Prime Minister firmly opposed such a potentially hazardous policy course.

The deflationary measures taken in July, although ultimately only a stopgap measure, worked to stabilize the pound. The economy picked up and by early 1967 seemed back on course. Yet, there was a price to be paid. The Labour government's past policy of economic growth through planning, which was encapsulated in the National Economic Plan, was sacrificed on the altar of sterling's parity. The deflationary measures implemented discouraged productivity and cut government spending, effectively ending the government's attempts to inject new life into the British economy.[7] Also, along with the National Economic Plan went much of the ideological core of the Labour Party which Wilson had so carefully crafted since 1964 around the themes of technological innovation and government-led growth. As the government's self-defined rationale in domestic politics evaporated, the Cabinet had little alternative but to turn its attention to overseas affairs.

This shift of attention in the autumn and winter of 1966 did not occur on an upnote. Labour Party morale sunk after the July 1966 crisis, with the episode even being described in the corridors of the House of Commons as Labour's 'Suez crisis.' Despite his successful stand against devaluation, the Prime Minister was perhaps hardest hit. He had convinced himself that he was the one man with the answer to Britain's economic troubles, and the 1966 sterling crisis proved this belief false. Wilson suddenly lost one of his most prized assets, his self-assurance, and from this point on he appeared to be a man under siege.[8] The abrupt change in the Prime Minister was readily apparent both at home and abroad. Crossman thought it 'the most dramatic decline any modern PM has suffered.'[9] In the United States, Secretary of State Rusk told Johnson that Wilson no longer seemed the same nimble tactician that had mastered the House of Commons in 1964 and 1965. Rather, Rusk observed, 'events seem to have become his master and he is rushing from one fire to another without ever really putting any of them out.'[10] Worse still, as Wilson's standing slumped in the polls, he became consumed by worry over largely accurate rumors of a plot to remove him from the leadership. Although the effect was delayed, the Prime Minister's fading political capital and his blurring political vision eventually would have ramifications for the world role.

The overseas issue which emerged to divert the government's attention from its domestic problems was the European Economic Community (EEC). Tony Benn, who had just been appointed the Minister of Technology, concisely summarizes the motivation behind the turn to Europe: 'Those of us who favored application [to the EEC] were not too worried about the conditions because we were a defeated Cabinet. We were now looking for solutions to our problems from the outside and somehow we were persuaded that the Common Market was the way of making progress.'[11] There was an economic rationale for entry as well. Benn, for example, wanted to replace 'imperial Britain' with 'industrial Britain' and by joining the EEC he felt Britain could finally 'cut Queen Victoria's umbilical cord.'[12] Yet, by this time, no one argued that entry offered a swift or even a sure remedy for the country's economic woes. Even Home Secretary Roy Jenkins, one of the most ardent advocates of entry in the Cabinet, admitted that 'in the first three or four years we shall lose but not gain.'[13]

The real reason for joining Europe was, as Benn suggests, political. The various factions of the inchoate anti-world role coalition were prone to see Europe as a viable alternative to an increasingly overstretched overseas military role and the perpetual fragility of sterling – the twin pillars of Britain's globalist framework. Moreover, the Common Market was one area of foreign policy where the Prime Minister's views were pliant. Wilson had long followed the prevailing wind behind ministerial and public opinion on Europe, and he shifted in favor of applying for entry into the EEC as his Cabinet drifted in that direction.[14]

The majority of Wilson's Cabinet was actually pro-Europe by the time of the 1966 election, but it was only after the July sterling crisis that Cabinet attention became fixated on entry.[15] Soon after the crisis the Prime Minister announced that he and his recently appointed Foreign Secretary, George Brown, would tour Common Market capitals in early 1967 in order to determine the prospects for British entry. Because he was a vocal advocate of closer relations with Europe, Brown's promotion was itself widely interpreted at the time as a decisive move toward the Common Market. Yet, the move more likely reflected the Prime Minister's continuing attempt to balance his rivals in Cabinet. Promoting Brown to the Foreign Office would place him on an equal institutional footing with the other principal 'crown prince,' Callaghan. Wilson thought this change necessary after Brown's previous department, the DEA, lost its *raison d'être* in the deflationary package of summer 1966.[16] A veiled political rationale underlay the tour of EEC capitals as well: to demonstrate that the government's political momentum was still rolling forward.

The tour thus was mainly planned as a matter of practical politics, but by its end the Prime Minister was converted into a champion of British entry in the Common Market. Motivated by his enthusiasm, the Cabinet agreed to apply and with three-line whips on both major parties, the proposal passed in the Commons in early May 1967, 488 votes to 62. The initiative came to nothing, however, as the French President, Charles de Gaulle, gave his infamous 'not yet' response just weeks later on 16 May. French coolness to any enlargement of the EEC that might upset its political hegemony over the organization was well known, but the rebuff still was a deep disappointment for a Labour government desperately searching for propitious policy paths.[17]

This attempt to steer a new foreign policy course had serious ramifications for Britain's overseas military role nonetheless. The movement of opinion in Cabinet toward Europe, which waned only temporarily after de Gaulle's veto, marked a simultaneous trend away from support for the east of Suez role. With the bid to enter the Common Market, ministers were beginning, at some level, to accept that Britain was a European and not a world power. Yet, the connection between these two trends was not immediately obvious to participants. One minister present, Patrick Gordon Walker, reports that the move toward Europe and the possibility of contraction in the overseas military role were not treated as being 'directly or intellectually related' by the Cabinet at this time.[18] The Labour government's foreign policy pronouncements in late 1966 and much of 1967, which resolutely backed the east of Suez role, lend considerable support to this view.[19]

Better evidence of the analytical separation between Europe and the overseas role made by senior ministers, and the Prime Minister especially, can be found in the increasingly acrid relationship between the Parliamentary Labour Party (PLP) and the government. During the run-up to the 1966 election only one backbencher openly attacked the government's defense policy. William Warbey resigned his seat because the government, he felt, was 'not carrying out... a Socialist [defense] policy, let alone a Labour [defense] policy.'[20] Yet, when the constraints of a slim parliamentary majority were lifted from the PLP in March 1966, it soon became apparent that Warbey's sentiment was not uncommon. As many as 62 backbenchers abstained from the vote on the 1967 Defence White Paper, the first official government pronouncement on defense policy since the election, largely because of their unhappiness over the government's position on the east of Suez commitments. This was the largest demonstration of dissent since the Labour government had come to power in 1964. Beyond the problems that a large parliamentary majority held for the government, this rebellion also illustrates that the Wilson government preferred to maintain fairly loose control over their backbench colleagues. Not long after, the screws of party discipline began to be tightened.[21]

Instead of setting any embryonic ideas that the Prime Minister may have had about where Britain's future lay, in Europe or the east of Suez area, the parliamentary revolt only infuriated him. He immediately addressed a full meeting of the PLP. As *The Times* reported, he 'turned savagely on the rebels,' implicitly threatening expulsion from the party in a speech which underscored his steadfast support for the east of Suez role.[22] It is evident, then, that in the Prime Minister's mind any moves the government made toward Europe did not equate with a simultaneous desire to abandon Britain's commitments in the wider world. Neither does it appear that other senior ministers made a connection between entry into the Common Market and an alteration in Britain's overseas role. Healey, Brown, and Callaghan, the core of the Cabinet with respect to foreign policy formulation, had unambiguously Bevinite roots and, as later events would verify, continued to stand resolutely behind the east of Suez role.

Thus, as many in the Labour Party began to rail against the government's conservative foreign policy, the government refused to flinch. This was, moreover, not the first sign of the rapidly growing dissatisfaction in the Labour movement since the election. The government had been on the run over the east of Suez issue during the party conference of the previous year. The highlight of the conference, and the low point for the government, was the enthusiastic applause given to Christopher Mayhew when he dismissed the east of Suez role as a 'sure road to bankruptcy.'[23] Other foreign policy issues, of course, caused acrimony between large sections of the Labour Party and its leadership. Strong opposition developed in almost every corner of the party to the government's backing of American policy in Vietnam, which was interwoven with east of Suez policy. Fortunately for the government, on this issue it was largely able to ignore the increasingly vocal opposition in the party by appeasing left-wing 'peace-horses' in Parliament.[24]

In addition, as pressure against the Vietnam War and the east of Suez role intensified in the Labour Party, countervailing pressures from the US began to ease. The 1966 sterling crisis brought increased appreciation of Britain's economic vulnerability in US foreign policy circles, and subsequently the signals coming from Washington became less adamant. This did not mean that American communiqués to London were necessarily consistent. How pressure was to be eased upon Britain in large part depended upon where you sat in the American administration. The Secretary of the Treasury, Joseph Fowler, thought that the United States could no longer both block devaluation and insist that

Britain maintain a military presence east of Suez. If a choice had to be made he would favor retrenchment from the east of Suez role, and Under-Secretary of State George Ball and the administration's elder statesman Dean Acheson agreed. Rusk and Secretary of Defense McNamara felt that devaluation would be the lesser of the two evils. Nonetheless, all of the principal architects of American foreign policy agreed that the intense pressure applied to their closest ally over the past few years was becoming increasingly inappropriate.[25]

In the midst of such rapidly changing conditions in their domestic and international political arenas, British decision-makers not surprisingly took a cautious approach to defence policy. The 1967 Defence White Paper, which had sparked a revolt in the PLP, was called a 'progress report on a policy...of wait and see' by the *Economist*.[26] Although the statement illuminated a shift in governmental emphasis away from the east of Suez role, there was to be no basic change in defence policy. Just as before, Britain would retain an overseas military role and an ongoing scrutiny of defense expenditure would ensure, in Denis Healey's words, that 'we are doing it as cheaply as we can.'[27]

This guarded document concealed the fact that the 1966 sterling crisis and the various domestic and international pressures which followed were beginning to cause key figures within the government to question the viability of the east of Suez role. Wilson claims that three months after the July crisis both he and Healey had accepted the fact that abandoning the overseas military role had to be considered a serious policy option given Britain's financial predicament.[28] Further economies would have to be found in defense, and a new review of Britain's defense policy was set in motion with a committee of officials called the 'Defence and Overseas Policy Working Party.' The basis of the review was the lowering of the £2000 million spending limit previously enshrined by the Labour government. Part of the reason a lowered spending limit was thought to be attainable was that confrontation with Indonesia had drawn to a close in early 1966, providing the Labour government with its first real opportunity for considerable reductions in overseas forces.

During this new, intense round of defense scrutiny, one could again overhear many of the lingering issues first raised during the secret reviews of the 1950s in Whitehall discussions. Patrick Gordon Walker summarizes the questions which suddenly reappeared in the corridors of power about the benefits that Britain accrued from the overseas military role:

How could we ever get out of our balance of payments problem whilst we spent so much across the exchanges on defence? Why should Britain pursue policies so different from those of other equivalent European powers and so much more costly? Why should we not, like other European countries, obtain oil from the Persian Gulf by paying for it instead of maintaining forces there?[29]

Just as after the Suez crisis in 1956, an external shock sparked earnest debate in the government on the foundations of Britain's grand strategy, after nearly seven years of quixotic acceptance.

The official level committee completed its review by late March 1967, when its conclusions were forwarded to the Defence and Overseas Policy Committee under the Prime Minister's chairmanship. By April the basic framework of the revised defense program had been agreed upon by this Cabinet committee, which essentially entailed halving British forces in the Far East by 1970–1 and pulling out altogether sometime during the 1970s. Although details of the new policy course still had to be filled in, officials in the Ministry of Defence began to work almost immediately on the phasing of reductions and possible solutions to the local problems which might follow.

Three months of vigorous diplomacy followed as the news was broken to Britain's allies. George Brown was dispatched to Washington to find the Johnson administration disturbed that such a policy might be announced while the war in Vietnam continued. Healey went to the Far East to disclose the provisional plan, where leaders in Australia, Singapore, and Malaysia also urged that no date be announced for Britain's withdrawal. Tunku Abdul Rahman, the Malaysian leader, and Lee Kuan Yew of Singapore visited London separately that spring to make this plea, and both found favorable audiences in the Foreign Office and the MoD. Politicians in all three countries and in various parts of Britain's foreign policy bureaucracy seemed convinced that if conditions changed, Britain might at some later point be persuaded to stay.[30]

The Cabinet was divided over the proposed changes, most particularly over whether a firm date for withdrawal should be announced and how it would be worded. Although the evidence remains far from complete, it appears that the Home Secretary, Roy Jenkins, was supported by left-wingers such as Barbara Castle and Richard Crossman in insisting that a firm date be fixed and publicly announced.[31] The overseas departments and the Bevinite heart of the Cabinet eventually won on this issue. No firm date was set. Advocates of the east of Suez role no doubt felt that this would allow the flexibility of reconsidering, and possibly reversing, the decision of limited withdrawal at a later interval.

The government's decisions were announced in the *Supplemental White Paper on Defence* (Cmnd. 3357)[32] on 18 July 1967. It echoed the words of the February 1967 White Paper in its claim that the principal aim of British policy outside of Europe was to foster developments which would allow local peoples to coexist peacefully without the presence of outside forces. Given this purpose, Britain would be free to withdraw its military personnel from the east of Suez area as soon as regional stability was achieved in the Middle East and the Far East. In the latter region, the level of stability achieved thus far allowed Britain to halve British forces in Singapore and Malaysia in 1970-1 and then to withdraw them completely by the mid-1970s. Yet, this did not amount to a complete abandonment of the area, as these reductions would be tied to policies on aid, training, and most importantly, a special military capability for use in the area. The thrust of the new program was to get immediate balance of payments benefits by reducing the overall size of the armed forces overseas. Alternative force structures, particularly mobile forces, would yield economies while also maintaining the capacity to contribute to security in the Indian Ocean area.[33] Perhaps most importantly, the *Supplemental White Paper* of July 1967 was claimed to mark the end of a long series of defense reviews.[34] It seemed that a balance had finally been reached between economic constraint and a permanent, and more modest and sustainable, overseas military role.

There was, however, no mention of the commitment to the Persian Gulf in the revised defense program and nothing to indicate that the government was planning a future withdrawal from that area. Despite condemnation from *The Times* and searching backbench questions, the parliamentary debate on the *Supplemental White Paper* ended without clarification on this issue.[35] The government evidently had no intention of retreating from the Middle East. Add to this the special military capability in the Far East, which was far from superficial as debate in the House of Commons revealed, and what in hindsight appears to be a relatively abrupt redirection of British foreign policy was actually characterized by significant elements of continuity. Repeated statements asserting Britain's determination to fulfill its east of Suez obligations in the *Supplemental White Paper* underscore this point.

Consequently, the abandonment of bases in Singapore and Malaysia, so long the underpinning of British power in the Far East, was not at the time seen to mark a major shift in policy. 'It is significant,' David Greenwood observes, 'that ministers saw (or presented) the prescriptions of Cmnd. 3357 as *modifications* in the composition and location of forces for east of Suez contingencies, and nothing more.'[36] This point was not missed by contemporaries. One academic commentator of the time, Neville Brown, called the July 1967 announcement 'a streamlining of dispositions rather than a revision of commitments.'[37]

The political community received the defense revisions as though they were simply more of the same. The direct lineage of the 1967 announcement from the government's previous cost-cutting measures was emphasized by most politically relevant actors, particularly in the House of Commons. A good example is the Liberal Party's defense spokesman, Emlyn Hooson, who castigated the government for once again cutting 'down the commitment or the ability to carry out the obligation while still retaining that obligation.'[38] This emphasis on continuity may be partially explained by the heated domestic political atmosphere on this issue, in that only very dramatic policy reversals, such as complete disengagement, may have been able to satisfy opponents of the overseas military role. Also, the government undoubtedly preferred to stress policy consistency to calm any anxieties felt by its overseas allies.

The east of Suez role thus was widely perceived to remain much as it was before, although British forces would cut a new, more modest figure in the area. Best of all for the Labour government, the world role presumably would be maintained at considerably less expense. Shedding Far Eastern forces held the promise of reducing Britain's defence expenditure below the £2000 million barrier: to £1900 million by 1970–1, at 1964 prices, and to £1800 million by the mid-1970s.[39] The search for economies following the 1966 sterling crisis had, it seemed, drawn to a close.

Yet, economic considerations were not the only, or perhaps even the most significant, variables driving the policy changes of early 1967. As can be expected, political considerations figured prominently in decision-makers' calculations as well. Most notably, as Patrick Gordon Walker suggests above, there was increasing concern in the Cabinet over the utility of Britain's overseas military role. The United States', experience in Vietnam was slowly altering perceptions of what western military power could hope to accomplish in the area and Britain's inability to have any impact whatsoever on the course of the Six-Day Arab-Israeli war in June underscored such concerns. Equally relevant was the continuing movement of opinion in Cabinet in favor of redefining Britain as a European rather than a world power. Although senior ministers both then and later have minimized its relevance, the swelling ranks of those critical of the government's foreign policy in the Labour Party most likely magnified such newfound doubts about the world role. It is not difficult to see how political considerations such as these, along with the tremors still working their way through the political system after the 1966 financial crisis, combined to produce a potent force for change.

On the political level, the formula developed by the Labour government in July 1967 was in large part successful. The government navigated a middle course between internal and external pressure, avoiding a direct collision with either. Allied leaders communicated their disappointment, but in moderate tones. The backbench assault on the government's foreign policy continued, but much of the air had been lifted out from behind the rebels' sails. Fifty-seven left-wing Labour MPs presented an amendment calling for a more rapid withdrawal from all commitments in the Indian Ocean area, but only 19 actually abstained in the vote on the July White Paper.[40] No doubt backbenchers recalled the heavy-handed response of the party hierarchy after the rebellion just a few months prior. The Conservatives criticized the new policy in the Commons, but so long as Enoch Powell remained shadow Defence Minister, their condemnation rang hollow.

Thus, although it might be argued in retrospect that the first critical steps toward withdrawal were taken in the defence restructuring of July 1967, it was not perceived as such at the time. The commitments in the east of Suez area remained and numerous policy options remained open for the future.[41] Patrick Gordon Walker, Minister without Portfolio and then Minister of Education at this time, claims that the decision to fully withdraw from Britain's military role outside of Europe may have 'subconsciously been reached' with the decision to abandon permanent facilities in the Far East. But, Gordon Walker continues, at the time 'the Cabinet as a whole and the PM...flinched from recognizing' that the changes they had made pushed Britain one step closer to being a regional, and not a world, power.[42]

Instead, the architects of Labour's foreign policy underscored the fact that the east of Suez role had been preserved. They felt that they had finally reached a lasting solution to the strains which were continually placed on the country's defense apparatus by relative economic decline. Overseas military deployments were now so streamlined that the world role could be maintained even if the British economy continued to falter. Thus, at least with regard to the east of Suez role, decision-makers believed that policy had finally been steered away from the cliff's edge. Unfortunately for the Labour government's leaders, this belief proved to be an illusion.

THE FINAL SETTLEMENT

When the government was planning the country's reformulated defence posture in the spring of 1967, the economy was on an upswing. Standard measures indicated that the economy had recovered from the sterling crisis of the previous year. Unemployment stood at a mere 1.5 per cent. A balance of payments surplus had been achieved by the end of 1966, and manufacturing employment and output reached an all-time high, which has never been surpassed.[43] The Labour government's confidence that the east of Suez role could be maintained indefinitely given its new, sleeker dimensions seemed in many respects justified.

In this climate, opponents of devaluation felt that the deflationary policies of the previous summer had proven successful, perhaps so much so that devaluation could be avoided altogether. Yet, sterling was still considered overvalued by many in the financial community.[44] And, as long as the argument that sterling was overvalued remained convincing, the possibility of another dislocating financial crisis continued to exist. Ironically, the government's attempts to provide a boost to the economy and to maintain positive political momentum by applying to enter the EEC only further weakened sterling. The move toward Europe raised new fears in the ever-sensitive financial world, making the pound's position more tenuous, because it was assumed that British entry would create an additional strain on the balance of payments.[45]

The direction of policy since July 1966 thus did not stabilize Britain's financial situation to the extent that many opponents of devaluation had thought. Nevertheless, improvement in the economy and the continued inability of the Conservatives to capitalize on Labour's political vacillation combined to push the Prime Minister and his party back into popular favor, at least in the polls. Wilson slowly began to regain his confidence and by September he was able to pronounce that his government had reached an economic 'turning point.' Defense reductions and other reforms had placed overseas payments in rough balance, the Prime Minister claimed, providing the country with an excellent opportunity to advance in production.[46]

Yet, events would soon undermine this optimism, as well as the confident assertion that the *Supplemental White Paper* of 1967 was the last in a long series of reforms to the country's overseas position. Less than six months after the July statement on Britain's overseas role was announced the program was abandoned, replaced by a shorter timetable for withdrawal and a policy of complete retrenchment. The crossroads was reached in November, and by January 1968 the July position had been officially discarded. The key to understanding this abrupt *volte-face* lies in a rapid erosion of Britain's economic position and the increasing political efficacy of those who argued for total withdrawal.

Economic problems loomed even as Wilson sanguinely announced that the economy was positioned to leap forward. The Arab-Israeli war in June resulted in a temporary closure of the Suez Canal, which held up Britain's usual flow of oil at the source. Civil war in Nigeria only added to Britain's difficulties in acquiring oil and the country soon was forced to buy alternative supplies from the Western Hemisphere at higher prices. Worse still, the government's optimism was given another jolt by the October trade figures, which recorded the worst monthly trade deficit in British history, £107 million higher than the previous record set in January 1964 under the Tories.[47] An indefinite dock strike announced in September in Liverpool and London was the last shock that the country's already precarious financial position could withstand. The strike hit exports much as the seamen's strike had done in 1966, and it had a similar effect on the pound.[48] By late October the government found it increasingly difficult to hold the line on sterling, and the country was soon engulfed in a second sterling crisis.

The economic situation deteriorated so rapidly that the devaluation that Wilson had fought so hard to avoid the previous year, sacrificing his reputation in the process, now seemed imminent. The Prime Minister's instincts remained as opposed to devaluation as ever, and he managed to rally his two most powerful rivals in government, Callaghan and Brown, to his side. All three men were convinced that devaluation should only be undertaken from a position of strength, not forced upon the government. Yet, the situation was much too desperate for such a postponement; the currency markets were in flux and a considerable number of those who had wavered in Cabinet during the first crisis were, by this time, convinced that a change in parity was unavoidable. The momentum toward Europe only hardened Cabinet opinion in favor of devaluation.

In such a situation, the only hope of salvation for the Prime Minister and his senior ministers was a substantial American loan. When it became apparent that the United States could not prop up the pound, in part because it was increasingly coming under economic strain itself, a change in the level of parity was inescapable. The shock of enforced devaluation initiated a process which would eventually bring Britain's overseas military role to an ignominious end. The change in sterling's parity, from being exchanged at $2.80 to $2.40, instantly added £50 million to defense costs annually, which meant that further defense reductions were once again necessary.[49] Moreover, as the Prime Minister and others opposing devaluation consistently warned, a 'ghoulish package' of economic measures would be required to take advantage of the opportunity offered by devaluation and to maintain the confidence of the world's financial markets.[50] A substantial diversion of resources to exports and investment was necessary, and domestic demand had to be suppressed, as the entire purpose of devaluation was to provide a sizable enough boost to British exporters to improve the balance of payments.

In the immediate aftermath of devaluation the Chancellor was confident that the necessary cuts, while severe, could be made without significant alterations to existing policy. With regard to the overseas role, this resulted in a range of limited expenditure cuts being announced after the change in parity. The most notable of these were the phasing out of the carrier HMS *Victorious* more rapidly and the abandonment of plans to build an air staging-post on Aldabra, an uninhabited island off the coast of eastern Africa. Aldabra was unique because it was the only planned staging-post which would have allowed Britain to bypass both the Middle East and northern Africa and, in doing so, to circumvent those countries that would be most likely to deny overflight rights. The loss of this staging-post severely limited Britain's strategic flexibility, and would make it difficult to guarantee a special military capacity in the Far East after the withdrawal from the bases in Singapore and Malaysia in the mid-1970s.[51]

Still, such reductions in Britain's military capabilities were not accompanied by reductions in the scope of the country's overseas commitments. The Defence Minister, Healey, confirmed this point in late November when he insisted that 'we can have no reversal of the July decision' on the overseas role.[52] The purely economic considerations arising after devaluation did not, it seems, necessitate a withdrawal from Britain's military role abroad. Much depended on how the events of November 1967 were interpreted and how they were utilized to shape the political agenda.

In other words, the political transformations set in motion by devaluation had a much greater impact on the east of Suez role than economic concerns, either immediate or long-term. Two such transformations were crucial in determining the future path of Britain's foreign policy. First, devaluation eroded the credibility and the confidence of the most influential and the most steadfast political actor supporting the east of Suez role, the Prime Minister. Second, this external shock finally upset the Bevinite consensus at the heart of the Cabinet. The effect that devaluation had upon Wilson can be outlined briefly, but the Cabinet shift was a more complicated and lengthier process and hence it must be analyzed in greater detail. It was this Cabinet shift which in the end proved decisive.

With regard to the Prime Minister, Wilson was politically and perhaps even psychologically scarred by devaluation. He had staked his political reputation and his career on parity and when the pound was undermined so, it seems, were some of his political sensibilities. Ministers noted that his behavior became somewhat bizarre after November 1967.[53] Most peculiar was his cheerful, almost euphoric reaction to the change in parity. Instead of behaving as if his government had suffered a setback when this core policy goal was discarded, Wilson both publicly and privately presented the decision as a hard-won political victory. This behavior may have merely been a symptom of the battle fatigue he suffered after the long, punishing struggle to maintain parity, but it was nonetheless perceived as inappropriate and disingenuous both in the public and in the Commons. It caused what was already a growing credibility gap for the Prime Minister, which extended back at least to the scrapping of the National Plan, to widen into a large schism. If it was not increasingly the case before, Wilson was simply no longer believed after devaluation.[54] 'He has only to hint at such grand concepts as "the national interest" or "Britain's honour" or as much as whisper "promise" or "pledge",' one hostile commentator observed, 'for the whole House to break into embarrassed blushing on the Labour side or guffaws from the Opposition.'[55] Although this characterization was not entirely fair, it was accurate. The Prime Minister's political capital seemed to be severely depleted by devaluation and his subsequent attempts to repackage the decision. For some period after this, Wilson seemed to retreat from the tribulations of political leadership, taking a less than active role in Cabinet.[56]

Although the Prime Minister seemed to recede politically, he remained active enough to oversee the most dramatic shift in the balance of Cabinet power in his government's tenure. This shift overturned the coalition which had dominated the foreign policy process in Britain for almost three years, staunchly supporting the east of Suez role all the while. The political transformations in the aftermath of devaluation allowed a new winning coalition to gel on this issue, one that would call for an end to Britain's world role. The creation of this new winning coalition involved more, of course, than the relative passivity of a humbled Prime Minister. In fact, what would prove to be a profound transformation with regard to the east of Suez role was not consciously planned or debated by leading members of the Cabinet; it was largely an indirect result of the scramble for political survival in the wake of a severe external shock.

The reformulation of the nucleus of the Cabinet originated from the humiliation of a failed Chancellor and the short-term political calculations the Prime Minister used to fill the vacancy. Although Wilson urged Callaghan to stay on, both men recognized that the position of a Chancellor who had done what he consistently pledged not to do – devalue – was untenable in the long run. Reluctantly accepting Callaghan's resignation, Wilson nevertheless knew he could not allow such a prominent politician of the old right to join the ranks of Labour's always troublesome backbenchers. The two men had been locked in dispute often enough over the past three years for the Prime Minister to realize that his Chancellor could be a considerable source of trouble if he were freed from the shackles of collective government.

Astutely calculating that Callaghan's political fortunes would again rise, Wilson engineered a Cabinet reshuffle which would keep Callaghan under his watchful supervision while also promoting a powerful rival to check his ambitions. The Prime Minister also needed to breathe new life into his beleaguered government when making these changes. Both goals could be accomplished, Wilson concluded, by a direct switch between Callaghan and Roy Jenkins, the Home Secretary, with the two postings to take effect at the end of November. Jenkins was popular and had succeeded at the Home Office, a post where most men fail, and it seemed he could provide a much needed new look to the Treasury during a relatively dire moment.[57]

It is improbable that Wilson calculated the potential impact that this Cabinet swap would have on the overseas military role, the last of his core policies. He was attempting first and foremost to ensure that his presence on the political scene would not fade, for his political standing was low enough that a palace coup was a distinct possibility.[58] To do so, he reverted to the instinctual strategizing he used to keep his rivals within the government at bay, and such strategizing provides the most convincing explanation of the November 1967 reshuffle. It is likely that Jenkins' promotion had less to do with his popularity or his past ministerial successes than with the fact that he and Callaghan were bitter political adversaries. Neither man would ever contemplate supporting the other in a bid for the leadership, which could not be said of other candidates for the Chancellorship. Thus, the Prime Minister felt that by promoting Jenkins he had perpetuated the galaxy of jealous rivals in his Cabinet which he had toiled so hard to maintain since taking office.

This time, however, the Prime Minister's usually adroit balancing act among potential challengers faltered. His strategy up to this point had been to always multiply, rather than reduce, the number of would-be challengers. Carefully balancing several conceivable potentates would, the Prime Minister thought, make them wary enough of each other to fear any dislocation at the center of the government. After all, if an adversary ascended to the premiership, unsuccessful challengers might find their own ministerial careers abruptly coming to an end. The best explication that Wilson provided of his Cabinet-balancing strategy was that given to his ally Richard Crossman after the first sterling crisis in 1966: 'I managed to increase my own crown princes from two to six. That was the point of my reshuffle... Now I've got seven potential Chancellors and I've knocked out the situation where Jenkins is the only alternative to Callaghan.'[59] The Prime Minister was convinced, it seems, that 'safety was in numbers.'[60]

Yet, probably unwittingly, in his post-devaluation switch the Prime Minister had reversed his previous formula for political survival. Instead of expanding the number of would-be successors, placing them in posts where they would check each other's political rapacity, the Cabinet switch in November 1967 had the opposite effect. The number of potential challengers contracted alarmingly to just one. At a time when the Prime Minister's own political standing and his personal confidence were reeling and his government was foundering politically, it was inevitable that this reversal would have serious policy ramifications.

As Ben Pimlott observes, 'the resolution of the Chancellorship in Jenkins' favour upset the equilibrium' in the Cabinet which Wilson had so conscientiously tried to foster.[61] All of the crown princes were by this point politically damaged: Callaghan was weakened for nearly a year after devaluation; Brown, after a series of public and private outbursts, was considered too temperamental and unstable for the premiership; Barbara Castle, Minister for Transport, too far to the left; Crossman, the Lord President, too erratic; Stewart, at the DEA, too colorless; Healey too associated with high defense spending; and Crosland too detached from the party rank and file.[62] All were political vulnerable, that is, except for Jenkins, whose political capital was rapidly ascending. The new Chancellor was at this moment the only serious challenger to the throne and the only senior minister who was untarnished by the government's policy capitulations of the past year and a half.

Cabinet politics were transformed rapidly in this context. The Chancellor soon became the most influential minister in Cabinet, often seeming to overshadow even the Prime Minister. In his biography of Jenkins, John Campbell claims that at this time 'the PM was effectively in his [that is, Jenkins'] power.'[63] Crossman simply records that Jenkins was the 'dominant force in the Cabinet.'[64] It would have been impossible for Wilson to circumvent Jenkins at this point, so the Prime Minister tried to tie himself, in Jenkins' words, 'if not by hoops of steel, at least by bonds of mutual self-interest' to his rising Chancellor.[65] Their asymmetrical political relationship was evident to even the most casual observer. In newspapers at this time, for example, the Prime Minister was regularly caricatured as Jenkins' poodle.

The altered dynamics of Cabinet politics had serious repercussions for the east of Suez role. In essence, Jenkins' promotion had overturned the Bevinite consensus at the heart of the Cabinet. The new Chancellor had long advocated a closer relationship with Europe and was highly critical of what he saw as outdated imperialist pretensions embodied in the east of Suez role.[66] This was the first time since the late 1940s, in Attlee's government, that a senior minister intimately involved in the foreign policy process adamantly opposed the world role. The long-standing and seemingly impregnable wall of senior ministerial support for Britain's east of Suez commitments now had a gaping hole in it, and soon it began to crumble. It was this incidental political transformation, initiated for purely political motives with little or no contemplation of the impact on the east of Suez commitments, that as much and probably more than economic constraint spelt the end of Britain's world role.

Timing was crucial in this political upheaval. Jenkins gained prominence during a unique historical juncture in the evolution of post-1945 British foreign policy. In the aftermath of repeated external shocks the political system was more fluid than at any point since the Second World War in late 1967 and early 1968 and, consequently, it was more susceptible to dramatic new policy initiatives. The new Chancellor thus found himself in an unanticipated and enviable position which is rare within the confines of Cabinet government: that of a policy entrepreneur, able almost single-handedly to shape a radical new policy agenda within a 'policy window.'[67] This transformation did not, of course, occur in the absence of political opposition, but the opposition encountered was unusually feeble and ultimately surmountable. In sum, the period after devaluation was a rare historical moment when a single actor was able to stand in between cross-cutting historical trends, upsetting the status quo and guiding policy in a new direction.

On becoming Chancellor, Jenkins found that the economic situation had not improved after devaluation. Sterling remained under pressure, and many in the financial world thought that a second devaluation was imminent. Jenkins later recalled that even after the change in parity in 1967, 'we were... always near the edge of the cliff [when trying to maintain sterling], with any gust of wind, or sudden stone in the path, or inattention to steering, liable to send us over.'[68] More severe expenditure cuts were necessary, and it was apparent that significant policy changes were inevitable. Consequently, the Prime Minister announced on 18 December that a stringent review of all areas of governmental spending, including defense, would begin immediately.[69]

The Chancellor set about determining which policy programs would fall under the budgetary axe using only his own political instincts as a guide. While officials in the Treasury were at this time making him sufficiently aware of the economic perils that lay ahead without swift action, they were, as he notes, 'less good at suggesting constructive action.'[70] Such dormancy in a department well known for its competent advice may have been at least partly due to the exhaustion and demoralization that set in following the Treasury's long and unsuccessful struggle against devaluation. Treasury officials were not alone in this regard, as a degree of disillusionment was common among opponents of devaluation in both the official and the political layers of government.[71]

Although Jenkins had little help from subordinates, at the same time he had few restraints placed on him from above. Worn down by repeated external shocks and policy failures, the Prime Minister by this time had lost his drive and his vision in matters of policy. Any thoughts of economic planning at home or grandiose roles abroad were abruptly discarded. By late 1967 Wilson was content to agree with his Chancellor that, at this stage in his government, only one policy calculation was truly important: what was good for the balance of payments was good for Labour and, by extension, Britain as a whole.[72] Political survival overrode all other policy goals for the Prime Minister at this time, for he recognized that some type of solution, even a partial one, to Britain's economic troubles was necessary to regain his political credibility and to give Labour a chance at victory in the next election.

In this relatively unobstructed political environment, Jenkins was free to rely on his own internal map of Britain's domestic and foreign priorities in planning expenditure cuts. He proposed a 'controversial quadrilateral' of cuts to help shore up the economy, the four corners of which were: postponing for four years the raising of the school leaving age to 16; a restoration of prescription charges; the early and complete withdrawal of British forces from the east of Suez area, with a handful of exceptions like Hong Kong, and the renouncement of British commitments in the area; and finally the cancellation of an order of 50 US F-111A strike aircraft which were needed if the overseas role was maintained. Given his views of Britain's overseas role, it is not surprising that the elimination of the east of Suez network was at the heart of Jenkins' plan. Crossman pithily described the proposed reductions as the 'slaughter [of] some sacred cows in order to appease the bankers.'[73] None was more sacred than the overseas military role, particularly to the Prime Minister. Wilson nevertheless accepted the reductions with little contestation in mid-December 1967. Thereafter, he helped to guide the policy changes through Cabinet, providing unfailing support.

The Prime Minister chose to consider the cuts in a gruelling series of eight Cabinet meetings from 4 January to 15 January, a tactic that he thought would wear down the opposition to the proposed reductions. The Chancellor did most of the advocacy for the cuts in these sessions, with Wilson providing silent, but steady, support for the package. As Tony Benn recollects, as the Cabinet debate wore on the Prime Minister was 'never quite equal to the occasion.'[74] Wilson's tacit support was nevertheless crucial. When debate ended on the overseas military role, only a wafer-thin majority backed retrenchment. Stalwart senior ministers who had ensured Britain's military presence east of Suez since Labour had taken office – instinctive world role men such as Brown, Callaghan, Healey, Thomson, and Stewart – fought vigorously against complete disengagement. It was the Prime Minister's 'tail' of relatively loyal followers in Cabinet that carried the day, allowing the Chancellor to push through his cuts successfully. Thus, despite his immense influence at the time, Jenkins depended on the Prime Minister's coterie to override his old friends on the right in the Cabinet.[75]

Among other things, the slender majority supporting retrenchment in the Cabinet illuminates the complexities of policy entrepreneurship in collective forms of government. Cabinet government can almost never be a one-person production, and hence policy entrepreneurship in this setting requires the acquiescence, reluctant or otherwise, of important ministers, particularly the Prime Minister. At the end of the day, although Jenkins in large part molded the policy path that Britain took after devaluation, it was the quiet advocacy of the Prime Minister which ensured its implementation.

Moreover, even with the Prime Minister's support a majority in Cabinet was far from assured.[76] An episode recorded by the Chancellor epitomizes the tenacity of those who opposed retrenchment. It also underscores how narrow was the margin of victory for the reformers. Being relatively green, the Chancellor mistakingly agreed to meet some of his colleagues from Labour's old right in George Brown's room in the House of Commons. When he arrived he found the three principal ministers from overseas departments – Brown at the Foreign Office, Healey at the MoD, and George Thomson at the CRO – and a handful of officials waiting for him. In Jenkins' words, 'they all proceeded to defend Britain's world-wide role with an attachment to imperial commitments worthy of a conclave of Joseph Chamberlain, Kitchener of Khartoum, and George Nathaniel Curzon.' Although the overseas ministers knocked him 'around like a squash ball' that afternoon, Jenkins managed to escape and eventually carried the day in Cabinet.[77] A particularly telling moment came during the penultimate session on the proposed cuts, on 12 January, when the Foreign Secretary began to turn the tide of Cabinet opinion by arguing that the Americans were extremely concerned about the possibility of a British withdrawal from the east of Suez area. Jenkins took this opportunity to extract revenge on his former assailant by forcefully reaffirming the dire need for a major redirection of the country's foreign policy.[78]

Resistance also came from Whitehall, although by this time formerly powerful voices opposing retrenchment in the foreign policy apparatus, while not muted, grew increasingly muffled. Both the FO and the CRO called for a continuation of Britain's military presence in the east of Suez area, even if this would entail a substantial reduction of British force levels overseas.[79] The MoD and the Chiefs of Staff also staunchly opposed complete withdrawal, but in a distinctive way. The services and their institutional reflection, the MoD, argued that the gap between Britain's commitments in the east of Suez area and the forces committed there had been stretched too far, and consequently commitments would have to be curtailed if there were to be any further budget reductions.[80] Ironically, although few in the military services anticipated or wanted such an outcome, because defense cuts were unavoidable this stance was tantamount to saying that Britain would have to abandon some or all of its overseas role.

The Defence Minister complied with this position, and hence he appeared at times to be an adamant defender of the overseas role to those favoring retrenchment. Yet, it seems that by this time Healey believed that retrenchment was unavoidable and perhaps even a preferable option.[81] He may have conveyed this opinion to the Chancellor during a series of lunches the two men had together before the Cabinet meetings on the cuts, further buoying the coalition which was forming in support of retrenchment.[82] Yet, more than any tacit support by the Defence Minister, it was Wilson's skillful management of Cabinet that was critical in overcoming bureaucratic opposition. He guided the Cabinet through the east of Suez debate swiftly, thwarting a counter-attack by the overseas departments, who were bolstered by the US and Britain's erstwhile allies in the Far East and the Persian Gulf.[83]

It was, in fact, among Britain's overseas allies that those favoring retrenchment discovered the most stubborn resistance. While the status quo position adopted by the overseas ministries resonated little with domestic political actors at the time, it found considerable support abroad. Persian Gulf states repeatedly offered to underwrite Britain's presence in that part of the world.[84] In addition, Singapore's Prime Minister Lee Kuan Yew flew to London in the middle of the heated Cabinet debates over Britain's overseas commitments to lobby for the continuation of the east of Suez role, making the situation that much more difficult for the newly constituted coalition favoring retrenchment. Even more consequential was the anger expressed by the United States over the possibility of retrenchment.

Despite the fact that the US had taken an increasingly conciliatory position on Britain's financial and military overstretch over the past year, once the decision was upon them, the Johnson administration recoiled from the thought of Britain withdrawing completely from the east of Suez role. For an American administration facing increasing difficulties in Vietnam, retrenchment by their closest ally and their only partner in global policing was considered the ultimate betrayal. The President sent a sharply worded letter to the Prime Minister on 14 January, which stated that if Britain abandoned east of Suez commitments and rescinded the F-111A order, the United States would no longer consider Britain a valuable ally in any strategic theater, including Europe. For a Labour government which had clung for so long to notions of Britain's greatness, the possibility of such a diplomatic relegation by their closest, and most powerful, ally stung.[85]

The Prime Minister's reply was predictably distressed, but he did not shrink from the challenge. His reply underscores how agonizing the decisions of early January 1968 were for all involved. It also illuminates the fact he and many of colleagues felt that Britain had finally, after repeated economic crises, turned the corner with regard to the world role. Wilson cabled President Johnson that the British were 'sick and tired of being thought willing to eke out a comfortable existence on borrowed money.' Sacrifices at home were tolerable, but 'we must no longer overstrain our real resources and capabilities in the military field abroad.' The Labour government was simply trying to find a military role which would be commensurate with Britain's means; they had no intention, as might be suspected in some corners of the US administration, of carving out a new neutralist foreign policy. Wilson concluded:

> Believe me, Lyndon, the decisions that we are having to take now have been the most difficult and the heaviest that I, and I think all of my colleagues, can remember in our public life... we are taking them because we are convinced that, in the longer term, only thus can Britain find the new place on the world stage that, I firmly believe, the British people ardently desire.[86]

The point of no return for Britain's overseas military role had thus finally been reached. As the Cabinet's thinking drifted toward withdrawal, the skeleton military force in the east of Suez area advocated by the Foreign Office and the Commonwealth Relations Office was never given full consideration. A forceful new Chancellor and a reticent, but nevertheless effectual, Prime Minister were committed to steering British foreign policy in a new direction, and with great difficulties and over spirited opposition, they were able to craft a new winning coalition in the government on this issue.

The outcome was known as 'Black Tuesday' in the Ministry of Defence, as the government's decisions were announced on Tuesday, 16 January 1968. All of the Treasury's proposed reductions won support in Cabinet. Consequently, nearly all British forces would be withdrawn from the Middle East and East Asia by the end of 1971 and thereafter Britain claimed no special capability to use force in the area. In short, Britain would, with this decision, cease to be a truly global military power. It would no longer maintain permanent military facilities overseas for the purpose of projecting British influence and shaping political outcomes in distant regions, in this case in the east of Suez area. With this announcement a critical threshold had been crossed for any declining power, that from global to regional power. Although historical watersheds such as this are rarely clean or definitive, it can be argued with confidence that Britain's military and diplomatic interests lay predominantly in Europe after the decisions of early 1968. The Labour government was finally, in Crossman's imagery, 'breaking through the status barrier,' laying down the old symbols of empire, wealth, and overseas military might.[87]

COMMENTARY ON THE PROCESS OF RETRENCHMENT

It must be emphasized that financial crises and economic constraint more generally cannot in and of themselves explain British policymakers' decision to retrench in 1968. Successive economic crises did weaken the arguments of the Bevinite wing in the Labour Party which felt that Britain was still capable of maintaining a world role, while they simultaneously strengthened the case of those calling for withdrawal. Yet, even after the extreme shock of devaluation policy options other than complete disengagement from the east of Suez role were available. One such option appeared at first to be the government's chosen policy course. In this regard, Roy Jenkins' unfortunate episode in the Foreign Secretary's room in the House of Commons illustrates an important point: if a different political mix had emerged within the Cabinet in November 1967, Britain's overseas military role would almost certainly have survived the second financial crisis and the post-devaluation budgetary cuts, although perhaps in a truncated form.

Thus, although it was a crucial variable in the decision to retrench, the external shock associated with repeated financial crises was not sufficient. The range of policy alternatives available to policymakers was transformed by these shocks, particularly after devaluation. For the purpose of illustrating this point, it is useful to depict decision-makers' policy options as resting along a continuum. One end of the continuum was narrowed by the policy failures and the economic constraints of the late 1960s, while the other end was simultaneously being broadened. Bold new policy paths now became conceivable options. In other words, repeated external shocks in the late 1960s and related policy failures can be characterized as providing a window of opportunity for policymakers, which allowed them to consider, and if they elected to do so, to chart a radical new policy course.

The most important repercussion of the external shocks of the late 1960s was the Cabinet reshuffle precipitated by devaluation, which transformed the dynamics of politics in the Cabinet. It was this transformation in Britain's highest policymaking institution which ultimately proved critical in determining the country's foreign policy path. The Bevinite consensus wavered slightly, but in the end remained firm, in the wake of the first sterling crisis in 1966. It was completely overturned following the second sterling crisis in 1967. When a new winning coalition formed in the Cabinet in the urgent atmosphere of late 1967 and early 1968, the country's overseas role was abruptly brought to an end. A single man, Roy Jenkins, played a key role in crafting this coalition. He can thus be labelled a policy entrepreneur, able almost single-handedly to shape a stark new policy course. Yet, despite the immense influence of Jenkins and other particulars involved, the general process at work remains that of a coalitional shift. When examining British retrenchment, the dynamic between external shock and coalitional change provides a convincing and relatively parsimonious explanation of Britain's withdrawal from the east of Suez commitments (as will be analyzed in detail in the concluding chapter).

It is the second half of this combination which has typically been overlooked in studies of Britain's retrenchment, and in studies of the foreign policy of declining powers more generally.[88] Economic constraint and related economic crises may make holding on to the overseas role steadily more difficult and, in this way, drive the retrenchment process. But before there can be any substantial reformulation of policy, the domestic political arena must be ripe for change. The domestic arena can be said to be primed for a policy revolution, as opposed to the standard evolution, when the political coalition supporting the status quo is discredited in key decision-making institutions. It is in such moments of flux that an inchoate coalition favoring a dramatic reversal of policy can gain ascendancy in the policymaking apparatus. As the alliance of groups calling for change gels, a new winning coalition is created in this issue area. The solid political foundation necessary to push a major redirection of policy through the policymaking process has thus been established, and the nation then embarks on a radical new policy course.

The processes at work in Britain's withdrawal from the east of Suez role are analyzed in detail in the concluding chapter. Variables beyond external shock and coalitional change were, of course, also necessary for retrenchment. Perhaps most important, institutional consolidation and a transformed conception of the world role among policymakers and analysts contributed to Britain's retreat from overseas commitments. As we shall see, other things being equal, the interaction of variables such as these can be expected to play a significant role in other cases of retrenchment, whether it be from a strategic military role, an imperial role, or otherwise.

8 Conclusions: Politics, History, and the East of Suez Decision

The decision to withdraw from the east of Suez role was, as one participant observes, 'epoch-making and revolutionary.'[1] From that point forward, Britain became principally a European rather than a global power, although the country was certainly still capable of significant, albeit intermittent, performances on the global stage. Conventional explanations of this momentous decision tend to emphasize its economic determinants. Alan Sked and Chris Cook, for example, claim that

> the most important single factor in seeing the end of Britain's 'world role' was... the harsh facts of economic life.... It was the German mark more than any socialist belief that brought the end of Britain's 'east of Suez' role, that caused the abandonment of expensive defence weaponry and finally caused Wilson to turn to the Common Market.[2]

It is true that Britain's economic power had been steadily waning in relation to her main trading competitors in the postwar period. By the late 1960s the United Kingdom's gross estimated resources were thought to be roughly $80 billion, well behind that possessed by either West Germany ($101 billion), France ($96 billion), or Japan ($113 billion).[3] Yet, Japan devoted less than 1 per cent of its GNP to defense at this time and Germany spent only 4.3 per cent.[4] The figure for Britain never stood below 5.8 per cent, even though the size of Britain's armed forces had been slashed from a level of nearly 700 000 in 1957, when Duncan Sandys announced the end of National Service, to slightly over 400 000 ten years later. Britain's military commitments east of Suez also remained remarkably steady in the two decades following the Second World War. British garrisons were still scattered across the Indian Ocean area, from the Persian Gulf to Singapore, in the late 1960s. Thus, in many ways, the tale of Britain's post-1945 east of Suez role is that of a country attempting to maintain world power while the resources it needed to do so slowly ebbed away.

The country's relative economic decline was, in fact, crucial in driving the decision to abandon the world role. But relative economic decline does not provide an exhaustive explanation of the country's withdrawal from east of Suez. Although victory in the two devastating world wars of the first half of the twentieth century distorted the trend to a degree, British policymakers had been acutely aware of their country's somewhat lackluster economic performance in comparison to trading rivals since at least the 1870s. Relative economic decline was thus a constant pressure on British policymakers throughout this century, particularly after 1945, and it is difficult to explain dramatic change with a constant. Other variables, notably domestic variables, had to work in combination with relative decline to convince British policymakers that it was no longer feasible to maintain a world role.

In other words, what was termed 'bounded' causes at the beginning of this study must be analyzed as well as 'constant' causes such as relative decline.[5] Constant causes are long-term, perhaps even permanent, phenomena which have deep social and political ramifications for the polity. Bounded causes are relatively abrupt political events which open or foreclose options for policymakers. They also tend to be important primarily for the policy issue under study. Since constant and bounded causes are inexorably intertwined as a policy unfolds historically, it can be expected that analysts must take account of both to explain major changes of policy, such as Britain's withdrawal from east of Suez.

As has been noted, the fundamental constant cause affecting British policymakers was the continual external pressure stemming from the country's relative decline. The most significant manifestations of this pressure were the foreign policy and economic crises which repeatedly pummelled postwar Britain. In fact, since Britain was so regularly racked by them, these crises can also be characterized as a constant cause. Such pressures and shocks affect the polity in countless ways. But with regard to policy change, crises are perhaps most crucial because they unsettle ingrained political routines and illuminate the flaws in current policies. In doing so, crises can introduce brief moments of fluidity in the policy process where the barriers to policy change are suddenly removed and dramatic policy change becomes conceivable. Of course, the opportunity provided by such fleeting junctures, often called 'policy windows,' must be exploited before any truly radical reversal of policy can take place. The most important ingredient necessary to capitalize on such opportunities is the creation of a firm domestic political base which advocates policy change. In other words, the crafting of winning coalition in key policymaking institutions is necessary for a dramatic reversal of policy. There can be no doubt that the coalitional shift which occurred in the Wilson Cabinet in 1968, when the political status quo was finally overturned and a new winning coalition gelled, was essential for the decision to retrench from east of Suez. This last, overlooked political variable is of a different type than either decline or crisis. In this instance, at least, the new winning coalition can be considered a bounded cause, since its effects were largely limited to the east of Suez issue.

Thus, as is so often the case when the opportunity for change presents itself, the willingness to break from well-worn practices must be present as well.[6] Britain suffered through a number of crises before the eventual decision to retrench in 1968. One such transition period can be found in the early postwar years, up to 1947, when the potential for a substantial redirection of overseas policy was clearly present. The domestic political landscape was radically reshaped at this time, and Attlee pushed for similar changes in British policy abroad. Moreover, a series of crises in 1947 – the convertibility crisis, the evacuation of Palestine and Greece, and most importantly the granting of Indian independence – all were severe shocks. In retrospect, it seems that the combined effects of these shocks could have, at a minimum, compelled British policymakers to reconsider the costs of the country's expansive overseas military role. Historians have, in fact, harshly criticized the postwar Labour government for not abandoning the world role when India, long the hub of the east of Suez network, gained its freedom.[7] Less than a decade later the Suez crisis was an even sharper blow which underscored Britain's economic and military weakness and the limitations of the country's overseas military network. Yet, substantial policy change never followed these crises of the late 1940s and late 1950s. Although Britain's force structures were streamlined, the country's extensive military commitments in the east of Suez area remained for the most part unaltered.

The willingness for change was simply not sufficiently widespread in these earlier crises, primarily because the assumption of British greatness continued to have a strong hold over policymakers and public alike. The convention which guided British politics in the postwar period, the consensus around the country's ability to maintain both 'greatness' abroad and 'welfare' at home, remained firm. There were other factors which helped to sustain the status quo as well, such as the vested interests of the foreign policy bureaucracy, fragmentation in the machinery of government which prevented policymakers from seeing Britain's overseas role as a whole, ongoing military operations overseas, and in the later part of this period, American economic and political pressure on Britain to stay east of Suez.

In short, the dominant political coalition in British foreign policy, centered around an overriding belief in 'greatness,' had not been overturned by the devastating crises of the 1940s and 1950s and the seemingly endless progression of Britain's relative decline in economic and military power. It was only in the late 1960s, after a series of severe financial crises, that faith in Britain's ability to maintain the world role eventually faltered and the political coalition supporting the status quo was undermined in the Cabinet. Even then, a political foundation conducive to change had to be molded in the Cabinet before the structural pressures associated with relative economic decline could be translated into retrenchment.

Thus, as anticipated, a troika of variables lies at the heart of Britain's withdrawal from east of Suez. The relationship between relative decline, external shock, and the eventual coalitional shift in the Cabinet provides a parsimonious and relatively powerful explanation of Britain's disengagement from its world role. But, we must also look beyond this triad of variables to provide an exhaustive explanation of this episode. While crucial, exogenous pressures such as relative decline and crises were not in and of themselves sufficient to forge the east of Suez winning coalition. For example, it has been shown that the financial crises of 1966 and 1967 and the constraints they imposed proved in many ways to be less important in the crafting of a winning coalition than the political maneuvering which followed. In fact, if it were not for Harold Wilson's failed attempt to check his 'crown princes' after devaluation, Britain's overseas military role may well have survived the financial crises of the late 1960s. Therefore, what is typically a constant in British politics, the politics of balancing both personalities and political power in the Cabinet, proved to be critically important in the decision to abandon east of Suez commitments.

A number of other bounded causes conceivably could have been important in the construction of a winning coalition favoring withdrawal as well. It must be emphasized that these influences rest at a different analytical level than the three variables which drove the retrenchment process: decline, crises, and the crafting of a new winning coalition. The bounded causes discussed below helped to facilitate the formation of the last, crucial variable in this triad. Hence, although they would not be expected to compel policymakers to dramatically redirect policy on their own, their impact could be considerable when refracted through the coalition-building process in the Cabinet.

Conclusions

One hypothesized bounded cause which does not add to our understanding of the east of Suez decision is patron pressure. Despite the consistent theme of anti-colonialism in postwar US foreign policy, Washington remained indifferent to Britain's east of Suez role throughout much of the period under study. In the late 1940s and 1950s, American diplomacy was primarily concerned with increasing the British contribution to NATO. But after the Kennedy administration took office in 1960, emphasis was increasingly given to the West's world-wide conventional strength and, subsequently, American policy toward Britain's east of Suez role shifted. But it shifted to support Britain's overseas military role, not to oppose it. From 1961 on, particularly as US involvement in the Vietnam morass grew deeper, the US exerted considerable political and economic pressure on Britain to keep the east of Suez commitments.[8] Such pressure did ease somewhat in the late 1960s, pushing the policy window opened by the sterling crises of 1966 and 1967 slightly wider than it would have been otherwise. Yet, given the immense strain they were coming under in other areas, this modest change of opinion in Washington seems to have been at best a marginal consideration for the policymakers who made the decision to abandon the overseas military role.

Changing attitudes within the Cabinet are another potential bounded cause which adds little to our explication of the east of Suez decision. While economic decline and blows to the national pride such as Suez led many in the press, the Parliament, and even in the foreign policy bureaucracy to begin questioning Britain's world role, ministerial support for the east of Suez role did not waver until 1968, at least among those key policymakers who had a say in the formulation of the country's foreign policy. Once in government, political leaders seemed unwilling to recognize Britain's diminished status in the world, and evidence of the country's relative decline was never greater than in the 1960s. Even then, the Wilson Cabinet staunchly supported the east of Suez role until the Bevinite heart of the Cabinet was overturned by the sterling crises and the attempt to limit the political fallout which followed. The east of Suez decision thus cannot be explained by a gradual transformation of ministerial attitudes. Rather, an abrupt shift which elevated key individuals to authority in the Cabinet, notably Roy Jenkins, inadvertently led to the creation of a new winning coalition on the east of Suez issue.

When considering the firm support given to the east of Suez role by successive postwar British Cabinets, the weight of history must be taken into account. History probably bore down upon ministers, particularly the Prime Minister, in a way which was very different from MPs, mandarins, or journalists. Just as Lyndon Johnson refused to be remembered as the first US President to lose a war, successive postwar Cabinets seemed to flinch from the idea of going down in history as the demolition crew responsible for dismantling the last vestiges of world power.[9] On an issue as central to the national consciousness as the east of Suez role, this should not be surprising. For centuries a military network abroad, and particularly sea power, had been both intertwined with the British national identity and assumed to be crucial for the national welfare. Taking the responsibility for shedding such a role, given the deep, emotional ties that many of the British had with it, was naturally not something decision-makers were eager to do. This was particularly the case since they themselves had matured during a period when Britain's overseas role was almost universally held to be an immutable feature of international affairs.

Another bounded cause with the potential to affect the coalition-building process is parliamentary opinion. MPs from the governing party clearly have the greatest ability to influence this process, and there can be little doubt that backbench opposition to the world role was a conspicuous pressure on policymakers in the late 1960s. But its impact on the east of Suez decision is somewhat suspect. Unlike the Attlee and Macmillan governments in the first two transition periods under study, each of which held a relatively firm grip over their supporters, the Wilson government was plagued by backbench revolts which were unprecedented in their size and their frequency. The main cause of such unrest was the widespread sentiment among Labour backbenchers, both from the left and the right, that the government was spending too much on defence, particularly on an overseas military role that many felt the nation could ill-afford to maintain. Yet Wilson's unique position within the Labour Party, being the standard-bearer for the left while at the same time assuaging much of the right by following orthodox policies, meant that backbench uprisings never seriously threatened to topple the government. More importantly, although they certainly grabbed much public attention, it does not appear that the rebels' criticisms had any direct impact on the east of Suez decision. Participants in the decision, such as Wilson, Jenkins, Gordon Walker, and numerous senior mandarins, confirm this fact.[10]

In this instance, the recollections of policymakers are probably close to the mark. The Wilson Cabinet rather easily withstood virulent backbench opposition to the east of Suez role for nearly three years before the decision to withdraw was taken. Had it not been for the sterling crises, which undermined the government's options and its credibility, it seems likely that the government would have continued to rebuff parliamentary critics. What's more, backbench opinion did not figure prominently in policymakers' calculations even after a policy window had been opened by financial crises in the late 1960s. In the urgent political atmosphere following the blow of devaluation, the Cabinet was preoccupied with more pressing matters, namely the looming economic troubles and, for the Prime Minister at least, the need to prevent a palace revolt. Thus, there can be no doubt that party management has been a crucial aspect of governance in postwar Britain. But when it comes to policy input, it seems that the gulf between the Cabinet on one hand and backbenchers and the party rank and file on the other is often too wide to breach, even in decisions as crucial as that on east of Suez.

If such a breach existed for the group upon whom the government depended to remain in power, their backbenchers, it was only wider for the opposition party and the articulate public. In the former, criticism of the overseas military role was common in the late 1950s while Labour was in opposition and was present, somewhat paradoxically, in the Conservative ranks in the late 1960s. Yet, such opposition seems to have made few inroads into government thinking during these periods. If anything, the stance that the shadow Defence Minister, Enoch Powell, took against east of Suez in the late 1960s helped to muffle the howl that might have been expected from the Conservative ranks as a Labour government dismantled the overseas military role. In the Fourth Estate and academic forums, censure of the world role was extremely rare before the Suez crisis, and it would be the early 1960s before consistent opposition to east of Suez emerged. By the late 1960s criticism of Britain's overseas military role was both impassioned and common, but opponents of the east of Suez network were by no means the dominant force in the press. Even if they had been, decision- makers tended to pay little heed to views expressed outside of Whitehall during this period. It seems that the decision to withdraw from the world role was no exception in this regard.

Although they did not influence decision-makers directly, the criticisms expressed in Parliament and in the articulate public, including those by well-informed military strategists such as Sir Basil Liddell Hart, were nevertheless important in the east of Suez decision. Opponents of the east of Suez role provided a tenable alternative vision of Britain's future for both policymakers and the public alike, a future based on commercial power and a regional role within Europe. As the traditional conception of Britain's role in the world was gradually discredited by Britain's postwar crises, especially the Suez episode and the sterling crises of the late 1960s, the potency of this alternative vision grew.

In many ways, the growing appeal of anti-east of Suez ideas provided a necessary underpinning for the decision to retrench. While it was a combination of external shock and Cabinet politics which eventually allowed these ideas to influence policy, the mere presence of valid and well-articulated policy alternatives helped to legitimize change. Thus, consistent calls for disengagement in this segment of elite opinion helped to create a political climate that accepted the abrupt end of Britain's world role as a feasible, and perhaps even a preferable, policy option. Such a political climate was not to be found in the late 1940s and late 1950s.

If press and parliamentary opinion figured into the east of Suez decision in a subtle and indirect way, the effect of changing attitudes in the foreign policy bureaucracy was perhaps even less palpable. Opinion in the overseas departments never reached the point where outright opposition to the world role was common, except perhaps in the savings-hungry Treasury. Criticism of the east of Suez network had been registered as early as the secret reviews of Britain's world role in the late 1950s. Yet it must be remembered that the secret reviews initiated by Macmillan were unusual forums. Whitehall of the late 1950s and early 1960s was more commonly characterized by emphatic support for Britain's overseas military role, as was the case in the late 1940s. But by the late 1960s, such ardent backing of the east of Suez network had evaporated. Even the military, which benefited tremendously from the large budgets needed to maintain an extensive array of troops and weapons overseas, adopted a position which condoned substantial cuts in Britain's overseas commitments. This acquiescent attitude in Whitehall certainly did not propel British policymakers toward the east of Suez decision. Yet, when the decision was being made during those fateful days in late December 1967 and early January 1968, neither did the foreign policy bureaucracy raise any real barriers to change. Given the fervent opposition to retrenchment in Whitehall, and particularly in the military, in the 1940s and 1950s, this in itself was a remarkable metamorphosis. And it adds to our explanation of the country's withdrawal from its overseas military role.

In addition, a subtle transformation in the way that overseas bases were viewed as a strategic concern helped to facilitate the decision to retrench as well. By the early 1960s, policymakers no longer quixotically accepted that Britain's chain of bases east of Suez was inherently valuable to British foreign policy or that it somehow buttressed the nation's greatness. Prior to this time, the intrinsic worth of overseas bases was virtually taken as an article of faith in Whitehall. Such outposts had, after all, formed the backbone of the country's overseas role since at least 1815.[11] But the Suez venture underscored the limitations of static bases in modern military operations, and by the late 1950s rising Third World nationalism made Britain's overseas possessions increasingly precarious. The foreign policy establishment soon realized that a network of bases abroad provided them with no guarantees; it was merely a means to an end. Once this modest change of outlook became widely accepted, it became much easier for many in the bureaucratic and political layers of government to consider abandoning the east of Suez role.

Thus, changing attitudes in Parliament, the articulate public, and Whitehall were not the only ancillary influences on the east of Suez decision. A fresh perspective on Britain's overseas garrisons by military strategists and policymakers alike would also facilitate the construction of a winning coalition favoring withdrawal. There was a more palpable, and perhaps the more important, bounded cause of the east of Suez decision however: institutional change.

As we have seen, throughout the postwar era a plethora of bureaucratic fiefdoms had vested interests in maintaining the east of Suez network. The potency of this bureaucratic barrier to change was clearly demonstrated to the first postwar Prime Minister, Clement Attlee. From 1945 to 1947, fierce opposition from the Chiefs of Staff and the Foreign Office frustrated his attempts to withdraw from Britain's military positions in the Middle East. Perhaps the most severe blow to Attlee's reforming drive was the Chiefs of Staff threat to resign *en masse*, which Attlee feared would confirm public suspicions that a Labour government was incapable of managing the country's overseas affairs. Such resistance eventually forced Attlee to capitulate, and talk of reducing the country's world role was never heard again in the 1945–51 Labour government. A threat of joint resignation by the Chiefs of Staff also undermined the Sandys Doctrine's attempt to reduce spending on the armed forces in the late 1950s. The importance of the military veto over changes in the overseas military role in the decades following the Second World War is thus evident. But the military was far from the only interest in the foreign policy bureaucracy which defended the east of Suez role in the

1940s and 1950s. During the first two transition periods, every department concerned with overseas affairs had a stake in the military role abroad. And as a result, the foreign policy bureaucracy as a whole strove to prevent any substantial diminution of the east of Suez network.

When consolidation in Britain's foreign policy apparatus in the early 1960s eliminated these bureaucratic barriers to change, it in effect laid the groundwork for the east of Suez decision. In many ways, it is to changes in the foreign policy machinery that we must look to understand Whitehall's growing indifference toward the world role in the late 1960s. The seemingly constant criticism of the foreign policy establishment in the press and in Parliament during this period also played some part in undermining senior mandarins' sang-froid.[12] More important, however, were the numerous administrative reforms which curtailed the foreign policy bureaucracy's political power.

First sparked by the Suez débâcle, the reorganization of Britain's foreign policy machinery in the early 1960s was designed to achieve economies and to rationalize policy by reducing the overlapping jurisdictions and rivalry among departments. But the institutional streamlining had an unintended result: as the foreign policy establishment contracted in the 1960s, so did the main constituency within the government which had a vested interest in maintaining overseas military commitments. Following the recommendations of the Plowden Report of 1964, two Cabinet-level departments intimately involved in overseas policies – the Colonial Office (1966) and the Commonwealth Relations Office (1968) – were abolished. Yet, it was in the defense apparatus that the centripetal thrust of the institutional reorganization was most marked. In 1964 the three separate service departments were merged into a unified Ministry of Defence. In one fell swoop, the armed services lost direct access to the political arena. The ability of the Chiefs of Staff to consult the Prime Minister either individually or alone remained, but when the service departments lost their autonomy, the Chiefs' influence dwindled rapidly. Subsequently, one of the most visible barriers to retrenchment was eliminated. From roughly the mid-1960s on, the military could not stand in the way of a decision to abandon the world role.

At the end of the day, the centralization of the foreign policy apparatus made it easier for opponents of the east of Suez role to overcome the extremely potent mix of inertia and tradition which buttressed the world role. In fact, it can be seriously questioned whether Jenkins' slim majority in Cabinet would have been capable of pushing withdrawal through in 1968 over the vehement military opposition which had characterized previous decades. The majority of the winning coalition was so slender that the presence of just one more minister representing an overseas department, such as the defunct Colonial Office, might have tilted the balance of power in the Cabinet against reformers in 1968. Thus the institutional changes of the mid- 1960s figure prominently in the east of Suez decision. A reorganization of foreign policy machinery designed to bolster the country's overseas military role actually facilitated its demise.

Explaining the various factors involved in the east of Suez decision is thus not simple or straightforward. Both constant and bounded causes must be included to provide an exhaustive explanation. Relative economic decline, backbench pressure, discarded strategic prescriptions, institutional change, external shock, and Cabinet politics all played some part in the events of January 1968. This is a lengthy list, and it provides little understanding of Britain's withdrawal from world power in and of itself. But it was not just the existence of these variables which was important; after all, many of these phenomena, such as relative decline, external shocks, and a transformed strategic outlook, had been present for years and even decades before the east of Suez decision. It was the juxtaposition of these forces at a particular time which produced such a radical break with the past.[13]

To provide a complete explanation of the east of Suez decision, then, we must consider how these variables interacted with one another over time. This interaction can be summarized succinctly. As has been noted, the constant cause of relative decline bore down on policymakers over decades. The pressures which built up as a result of Britain's dwindling international influence were revealed most forcefully in the form of economic and diplomatic crises. The repeated external hammer blows which Britain endured after 1945 did not in and of themselves produce retrenchment, but these crises would leave a distinct trail of adaptation which proved to be vitally important in the eventual decision to redirect policy. This is least apparent in the first transition period, 1945–7, where reform was effectively blocked and there were few institutional or policy transformations which seriously impacted the east of Suez decision. Nonetheless, the overseas military role was earnestly challenged at this juncture, and the multiple barriers to change came into view as perhaps never before. The second transition period was of greater consequence. Popular and governmental responses to the jolt of the Suez crisis and to the increased awareness of relative decline which followed this débâcle – namely, institutional transformation, changing attitudes in the press and Parliament, and the discarding of outdated strategic prescriptions – altered the political and institutional setting in which policymakers operated. Such changes would prove to be crucial after another severe shock upset the existing political balance within the Cabinet, opening a policy window. Along with incidental political maneuvering, these bounded causes played a major role in the construction of a winning coalition on the east of Suez issue in the wake of the sterling crises of the late 1960s. Following devaluation in November 1967 the political coalition at the heart of the Wilson Cabinet supporting the status quo was overturned. And when the inchoate factions opposing the world role gelled into a winning coalition, the firm political and institutional foundation necessary for a dramatic reversal of policy had been created.

This study began with the assumption that history had to be brought back into the study of foreign policy decision-making. Studies of foreign policy decisions usually examine only the weeks or months preceding a decision.[14] With such a short frame of reference, the decision-making arena and domestic political environment must of necessity be treated as static variables. But, as we have seen, such variables are rarely inert. The pliability of the decision-making arena and changes in the domestic political environment must be included in one's analysis to provide an adequate explanation of a decision-making episode, particularly when policy is dramatically redirected.

In other words, a grasp of the way in which the 'shadow of the past' weighs on any particular policy decision is crucial. Over 20 years ago, a participant in the east of Suez decision made an observation which seems obvious on the surface, but has not been sufficiently addressed in academic studies of foreign policymaking. Referring to the British context, Patrick Gordon Walker noted that 'each decision may have an impact upon party, Parliament, and public that may well affect expected reactions to later decisions.'[15] Policy thus can be thought of as a historical branching process, where decisions at one interval shape the policy options open at later intervals. In order to gain a satisfactory explanation of any particular decision-making episode, it is essential to analyze a policy's history.[16] Although there may be other ways to improve the historical accuracy of foreign policy studies, a longitudinal analysis of key junctures in the evolution of a policy, such as that employed here, captures the relevant bounded causes which can prove critical in a later decisions.

The east of Suez example also illustrates that we must sharpen our conceptualization of the shadow of the past. In the literature on foreign policymaking, the historical path a policy follows is often characterized in such a way that it seems as though a series of constraints are imposed upon policymakers over time. Policies made at earlier junctions are primarily thought to foreclose options at later points.[17] But, as the consolidation of Britain's foreign policy machinery illustrates in the east of Suez decision, earlier choices can also open up new policy paths. In this case, they removed one of the largest obstacles to change, military and bureaucratic resistance.

In the final analysis, then, Britain's decision to withdraw from an overseas military role can only be understood in the context of past crises and the policy changes and societal transformations which followed in their wake. Decisions to redirect policy are not made with a click. They are the result of pressures which have built up over time and earlier attempts to adapt to these pressures. Consequently, it would seem then that dramatic reversals of policy must be viewed through a broad analytical lens which incorporates the shadow of the past. Studies of foreign policy restructuring which are myopic with regard to a policy's history will provide only partial explanations of the decisions being examined. Hence, they will ultimately prove unsatisfactory.

BEYOND BRITAIN

Of course, longitudinal studies of foreign policy decisions do not, or should not, lessen generalizability. In this study, the most generalizable explanation of the east of Suez decision is found in the relationship between relative decline, external shock, and the eventual coalitional shift in the Cabinet. It can be expected, in fact, that the interaction among this triad of variables would be at the heart of any explanation of a declining power choosing to retrench from a military network abroad, whether it be a strategic or an imperial network. As has been demonstrated with regard to Britain's withdrawal from world power, relative decline provides the context and the incentive for decision-makers contemplating the withdrawal from overseas bases. Such structural change also precipitates crises, which open up policy windows and provide the opportunity for policy change. And finally, this opportunity must be exploited: a winning coalition must be crafted within key policymaking institutions, creating the political foundation necessary for a substantial redirection of policy. In fact, these three variables represent the essential layers of explanation one would expect to find when a state adapts to international change: first, the structural change in the international system itself (relative decline); second, the effect of such change on the state (crises); and, third, the eventual political response (a winning coalition).

One must also look beyond this triad to provide an exhaustive explanation of an episode of retrenchment. Most importantly, the bounded causes which help to facilitate the formation of a winning coalition, the crucial link between international pressures and policy change, must be delineated. Which bounded causes are anticipated to be important in this process will largely depend on the domestic political structure of the state in question. Hence, secondary influences which were pivotal in the crafting of a winning coalition on the east of Suez issue may not be so in other settings, where the layout of the domestic political terrain differs and access to the policy process is shaped along distinctive, but perhaps similarly well-worn, paths. Broader state–society relations and the values and norms ingrained in the political culture must be taken into consideration as well, for they also help to determine which actors have influence in the political arena and may either aid or impede the formation of a winning coalition.[18] Thus, as with all macro-theoretical frameworks applicable to different temporal domains and national settings, attention must be paid to the context.[19]

Taking such considerations into account, the relevance of this framework can be briefly sketched for two other prominent examples of retrenchment in the latter half of the twentieth century. The case with perhaps the greatest surface similarity is the French withdrawal from Africa, its last substantial imperial stronghold, in the late 1950s and early 1960s. To understand the liquidation of the French empire in Africa, one must first look to the country's declining international prestige in the early post-1945 period. The era of European primacy in world affairs had passed, and this affected French leaders as much as it did their British counterparts. Worse still, France's dwindling prominence on the global stage was dramatically underscored by defeat and occupation during the Second World War. It was in this context that French decision-makers began to face mounting difficulties in colonial possessions in Indochina and Northern Africa in the decade and a half after 1945.[20] The defeat at Dien Bien Phu in 1954 was a stunning blow, spelling the end of French colonial rule in Southeast Asia. Two years later an insurrection began in Algeria, long considered to be nearly an integral part of France itself. There can be little doubt that the tremors that French colonial officials were increasingly feeling in such lands reverberated in the metropole, precipitating crises which coincided with the political tumult commonly associated with the Fourth Republic. The eventual result of such shocks, particularly the Algerian crisis, was perhaps the most radical form of coalition shift: the complete dismantling of the old regime and the birth of the Fifth Republic in 1958. Not long after this momentous political shift, the country's new leadership, centered on President Charles de Gaulle, decided to depart from colonial possessions in Africa. By 1960 16 new African nations entered the United Nations, almost all of whom had ties with France. After this point, the French empire for all practical purposes ceased to exist. As can be expected, there are important differences between France's rapid colonial retrenchment and Britain's withdrawal from east of Suez. For one, the latter was principally a strategic and not a colonial network after 1947, and the process of withdrawal from these two different types of overseas holdings can be anticipated to diverge in certain respects. Also, France's relative economic decline was not nearly as acute as was Britain's during this period, for its economy grew rapidly in absolute terms from the early 1950s.[21] Yet, while the specific dynamics differ, the broad outline of international decline, crises, and domestic political shift is common to both examples of retrenchment.

The Soviet Union's withdrawal from overseas military positions fits this pattern as well. This example of retrenchment had wider ramifications for the international system and was only a small component of a much more significant historical transformation, the collapse of the Soviet state itself. Nonetheless, if one wants to understand the sharp redirection of Soviet foreign policy and the retreat from overseas outposts, the familiar triad of decline, crises, and coalitional shift offers a good starting point. With regard to the first of these, the Soviet command economy began to slip in competition with the West by the early 1970s. The stagnation which was a hallmark of the Brezhnev era was marked by inefficient agriculture, an inadequate supply of consumer goods, and a growing technological gap with the West. While shielded from the type of economic shocks which might beset a struggling nation fully integrated in the global economy, the country would nonetheless suffer through the bitter humiliation associated with the 'losing effort' in Afghanistan throughout the 1980s. Growing economic and diplomatic pressures would eventually result in what can be broadly characterized as a coalitional shift in Soviet politics, the ascension to power of Mikhail Gorbachev. As is well documented, Gorbachev, who was an uncommitted thinker in terms of foreign policy priorities, would soon accept many of the ideas of a cadre of reformers who were critical of existing conditions in the USSR, and his 'new thinking' resulted in a revolution in Soviet foreign policy which would come to include the shedding of commitments abroad.[22] Of course, as Matthew Evangelista, among others, has shown, before this transformation could take place Gorbachev first had to consolidate his power base in the Politburo and the Central Committee, in effect forging a winning coalition.[23]

The broad similarities in these cases are reassuring. Yet, specialists familiar with the historical complexities of these countries will surely give considerable more attention to these examples of retrenchment, perhaps even mapping out the connections among decline, crises, and coalitional shift more precisely. Until such detailed research is done, the outlines above should be considered to be, at the very least, suggestive.

One further case might be added to this list, that of US retrenchment in post-Cold War era. If the US continues to decline in relative terms, and the extent to which it has done so is the subject of sharp debate, traditional perspectives on great power decline suggest that the country will eventually abandon many of its overseas outposts. Britain's gradual withdrawal from the east of Suez role may offer considerable insight into this process. A number of scholars, such as Bruce Russett and Paul Kennedy, have noted the comparable trajectories of British and American decline in this century, and the similar policy adaptations both countries' leaders have made in response to such change.[24] In this regard, the US defense establishment's current attempt to streamline its military apparatus and to increase mobility in order to maintain a global military presence in an era of declining defence budgets is of interest, as is the fact that questions about the country's overseas role are beginning to be raised at roughly the same time. Of course, at this juncture, it cannot be speculated when, or even if, the US will abandon its most vital overseas outposts. But if the country were to do so, the analytical framework advanced here can be expected to facilitate explanation. The triad of variables which drove the British retrenchment process will almost surely play a prominent role. Taking the fragmentation and porousness of the American political system into consideration, it can also be anticipated that coalition-building will be more difficult in the American setting, and that the number of actors with the potential to influence this process will be greater than in Britain (or France or the Soviet Union).[25]

In sum, then, the relationship between decline, crisis, and coalitional shift plays a central role when nations withdraw from overseas military roles. Analysis of these three variables provides an understanding of the most basic elements of the retrenchment process. Yet, it does not, of course, provide a full explanation of such episodes. A bevy of bounded causes may also facilitate the crafting of a winning coalition and hence they must be studied as well.

In other words, the findings of this study suggest that great powers do not often abandon prominent overseas roles either easily or through cold, rational calculation of the state's interests. The symbolism associated with such overseas networks is often too intertwined with policymakers' own beliefs, and even the popular imagination, for a purely rational dénouement. Leaders' perceptions of their country's international ambitions must be shaken, even shattered, and a solid domestic political underpinning favoring change must be constructed, before such a dramatic redirection of policy can occur.

In the case of Britain's east of Suez role, a celebrated chapter in British history was closed when a winning coalition favoring withdrawal was forged in 1968. The extensive network of fueling stations, dockyards, and military complexes which had been a crucial underpinning for the country's growth as a world power from the late seventeenth century, and which had long since been assumed to be vital for the nation's wealth and security, was abandoned. After centuries of wider influence, Britain was reduced to the status of a European power.

Notes

1 INTRODUCTION: PERSPECTIVES ON THE WITHDRAWAL FROM WORLD POWER

1. See, for example, E. Nordlinger, *Isolationism Reconfigured: American Foreign Policy for a New Century* (Princeton: Princeton University Press, 1995).
2. J. Abu-lughod, *Before European Hegemony: The World System AD 1250–1350* (New York: Oxford University Press, 1989), pp. 12–13, 360.
3. See G. Modelski and W.R. Thompson, *Seapower in Global Politics, 1494–1993* (Seattle: University of Washington, 1993); G.A. Ballard, *Rulers of the Indian Ocean* (London: Duckworth, 1928).
4. P. Kennedy, *The Rise and Fall of British Naval Mastery* (Atlantic Highlands, NJ: Ashfield, 1983), p. 67.
5. G. Harries-Jenkins, 'The Collapse of the Imperial Role', in J. Simpson (ed.), *Perspectives Upon British Defence Policy* (Southampton: University of Southampton Press, 1974), p. 25.
6. D. Reynolds, *Britannia Overruled: British Policy and World Power in the Twentieth Century* (New York: Longman, 1991), p. 27.
7. Harries-Jenkins, p. 24. Imperialist objectives certainly remained after Indian independence. But after a failed attempt to increase the amount of wealth extracted from colonies, particularly in Africa, in the late 1940s, the east of Suez network essentially became a strategic and an economic entity. See Chapters 3 and 5.
8. P. Darby, *British Defence Policy East of Suez 1947–1968* (London: Oxford University Press, 1973), p. 10.
9. D.C. Armstrong, 'The Changing Strategy of British Bases', PhD Dissertation, Department of Politics (Princeton: Princeton University, 1960), p. 139.
10. Darby, pp. 22–5.
11. Ibid., p. 32
12. S.J. Ball, 'Macmillan and British Defence Policy', R. Aldous and S. Lee (eds), *Harold Macmillan and Britain's World Role* (London: Macmillan, 1996), pp. 82–3.
13. Policymakers, in fact, would come to use 'east of Suez' and 'world role' interchangeably. See especially P. Catterall, 'The East of Suez Decision', *Contemporary Record*, Vol. 7 (1993), p. 622. Scholars often do this as well. For an example, see A. Sked and C. Cook, *Post-war Britain: A Political History* (London: Penguin, 1993), p. 233.
14. See K.O. Morgan, *The Peoples Peace: British History 1945–1989* (New York: Oxford University Press, 1990), p. 283; R.F. Holland, *The Pursuit of Greatness: Britain and the World Role 1900–1970* (London: Fontana, 1991), p. 330. The concepts 'world power' and 'great power' are nebulous. In general, this study uses both terms in accordance with William T.R. Fox's notion of a world power: a state with the ability to project

power worldwide, an ability which is typically buttressed by a network of overseas military positions. Such positions grant the world power sustained political and military influence in regions outside of its own. After the east of Suez decision in 1968, Britain could no longer be considered, by Fox's definition, a world power. It was a regional power, with the primary locus of its influence in Europe. See W.T.R. Fox, *The Superpowers: The United States, Britain, and the Soviet Union* (New York: Harcourt Brace, 1944). Also, for the distinctions between concepts such as world power and great power, see especially G.R. Berridge and J.W. Young, 'What is a "Great Power"?', *Political Studies*, Vol. 36 (1988), pp. 224–34.

15. Of course, a nation's world role is often considered to be more encompassing than a strategic network, no matter how significant. A world role embodies cultural, political, economic as well as military influence abroad. Yet, it seems that few paused to reflect on this distinction in post–1945 Britain, for the country's east of Suez network was widely assumed to have broader relevance.
16. P. Kennedy, *The Rise and Fall of the Great Powers* (New York: Vintage, 1987).
17. S.P. Huntington, 'Coping with the Lippmann Gap', *Foreign Affairs*, Vol. 66 (1988), p. 477; C.A. Kupchan, 'Empire, Military Power, and Economic Decline', *International Security*, Vol. 13 (1989), p. 48.
18. Kennedy, *Rise and Fall*, p. 539; R. Gilpin, *War and Change in World Politics* (New York: Cambridge University Press, 1981).
19. W.R. Thompson and G. Zuk, 'World Power and the Strategic Trap of Territorial Commitments', *International Studies Quarterly*, Vol. 30 (1986), p. 264.
20. The literature on US international decline, or lack thereof, is immense. See especially Gilpin; M. Rupert and D. Rapkin, 'The Erosion of US Leadership Capabilities', in P.M. Johnson and W.R. Thompson (eds), *Rhythms in Politics and Economics* (New York: Praeger, 1985), pp. 155–80; and J.S. Nye, *Bound to Lead* (New York: Basic Books, 1990).
21. Kennedy, *Naval Mastery*, p. 180.
22. C.J. Bartlett, 'The Mid-Victorian Reappraisal of Naval Policy', in K. Bourne and D.C. Watt (eds), *Studies in International History* (London: Archon, 1967), pp. 101–2.
23. J. Morris, *Farewell the Trumpets: An Imperial Retreat* (London: Harcourt, Brace, Jovanovich, 1978), p. 316. Britain did cede domination of the waters in the Western Hemisphere and East Asia to the US and Japanese navies respectively in the first decade of the twentieth century, marking a limitation in Britain's strategic requirements. Still, British commitments through 1939 remained easily the world's largest, and world-wide naval policy remained remarkably similar to that in the mid–1800s. See Kennedy, *Naval Mastery*, pp. 279–84.
24. See A. Friedberg, *The Weary Titan: Britain and the Experience of Relative Decline 1895–1905* (Princeton: Princeton University Press, 1988).
25. Kupchan, 'Empire and Economic Decline', p. 49.
26. Ibid.

27. C. Barnett, *The Collapse of British Power* (London: Morrow, 1972), pp. 587–8.
28. Kennedy, *Naval Mastery*, p. 317; Sked and Cook, p. 26.
29. M. Dockrill, *British Defence since 1945* (New York: Basil Blackwell, 1989), p. 31.
30. B.L. Montgomery, *Memoirs* (London: Collins, 1958), p. 435.
31. N. Brown, *Arms Without Empire: British Defence in the Modern World* (Baltimore: Penguin, 1967), p. 26.
32. M. Chalmers, *Paying for Defence: Military Spending and British Decline* (London: Pluto, 1985); K. Rasler and W.R. Thompson, 'Political–Economic Tradeoffs and British Relative Decline', in S. Chan and A. Mintz (eds), *Defense, Welfare, and Growth* (London: Routledge, 1992), pp. 36–60.
33. See, for example, J. Darwin, *Britain and Decolonisation* (New York: St. Martin's Press, 1988), pp. 291–5.
34. See Armstrong.
35. C.F. Hermann, 'Changing Course: When Governments Choose to Redirect Foreign Policy', *International Studies Quarterly*, Vol. 34 (1990), pp. 5–6; R. Rose, *Lesson-Drawing in Public Policy* (Chatham, NJ: Chatham House, 1993), pp. 140–7.
36. Friedberg, *Weary Titan*.
37. J. Snyder, *Myths of Empire: Domestic Politics and International Ambition* (Ithaca: Cornell University Press, 1991).
38. J.R. Ferris, *Men, Money, and Diplomacy: The Evolution of British Strategic Policy, 1919–1926* (Ithaca: Cornell University Press, 1989).
39. B.R. Posen, *The Sources of Military Doctrine: Britain, France, and Germany Between the World Wars* (Ithaca: Cornell University Press, 1984).
40. C.A. Kuphcan, *The Vulnerability of Empire* (Ithaca: Cornell University Press, 1994).
41. Ibid.
42. R.N. Rosecrance, 'Overextension, Vulnerability, and Conflict', *International Security*, Vol. 19 (1995), pp. 145–63.
43. Reynolds, p. 43; W.P. Snyder, *The Politics of British Defense Policy 1945–1962* (Columbus: Ohio State University, 1964), p. 61.
44. Kupchan, *Vulnerability*, p. 53. Cain and Hopkins demonstrate the pervasive influence of financial and service industry elites, most notably in the City, on British imperial expansion. See P.J. Cain and A.G. Hopkins, *British Imperialism: Crisis and Deconstruction 1914–1990* (New York: Longman, 1993).
45. Brown, p. 39.
46. See D.R. Tahtinen, *Arms in the Indian Ocean* (Washington, DC: American Enterprise Institute, 1977); P. Wall, *The Southern Oceans and the Security of the Free World* (London: Stacey International, 1977). The US and the USSR did establish limited base facilities in the Indian Ocean area. The most notable examples are the Soviet base in Aden, constructed after Britain's departure, and the American base in Diego Garcia, built in the mid–1960s. Neither superpower, however, developed a military presence in the area comparable to Britain's east of Suez role.
47. Kupchan, *Vulnerability*.

48. D. Vital, 'The Making of British Foreign Policy', *The Political Quarterly*, Vol. 39 (1968), p. 265.
49. See Holland, *Pursuit of Greatness*, p. 292.
50. Rosecrance, 'Overextension'.
51. See Chapter 5.
52. R.L. Sivard, *World Military and Social Expenditures* (Washington, DC: World Priorities, 1991), p. 27.
53. Kennedy, *Rise and Fall*, pp. 438–46, 539–40.
54. The literature on post–1945 British foreign policy often adopts a nearly economically deterministic position (see Chapter 2). Studies of the rise and decline of world powers implicitly accept this view as well. Few, if any, analyze the factors that can cause a state to abandon global commitments. Once it is ascertained that a state is declining economically and militarily in comparison to its rivals it is assumed that it will have no choice, over the long run, but to abandon excessive overseas commitments. Yet, the specific factors which can bring a nation to accept the 'truth' of its declining world position are not explicated (as attention is usually focused on the new rising world powers, which will either uphold the existing international order or mold a new one). Prominent examples include: Gilpin; Modelski and Thompson; Kennedy, *Rise and Fall*; and I. Wallerstein, *Politics of the World Economy* (New York: Cambridge University Press, 1988).
55. Darby, p. 334.
56. To date, no work has systematically analyzed the political factors involved in the east of Suez decision. Other scholars have, however, suggested that political considerations may be as important as economic necessity in explaining this episode. David Greenwood argues that political choice has played a role in all seemingly economically-driven defence decisions, including the east of Suez decision. In broader treatments of British foreign and defence policy, John Baylis, John Darwin, and David Reynolds also intimate that political considerations were vital in this decision. See Reynolds, p. 231; Darwin, p. 294; D. Greenwood, *The Economics of 'the East of Suez Decision'*, Aberdeen Studies in Defence Economics, No. 2 (Aberdeen: University of Aberdeen, 1973); D. Greenwood 'Defence and National Priorities since 1945', in J. Baylis (ed.), *British Defence Policy in a Changing World* (London: Croom Helm, 1977), pp. 174–207; J. Baylis, '"Greenwoodery" and British Defence Policy', *International Affairs*, Vol. 62 (1986), p. 453.
57. Morgan, *People's Peace*, p. 283.
58. R. Crossman, *Diaries of a Cabinet Minister*, Vol. 2 (New York: Holt, Rinehart, and Winston, 1976), p. 639.

2 DECLINE AND THE POLITICS OF RETRENCHMENT

1. Kennedy, *Naval Mastery*, p. 325.

2. T. McGrew, 'Security and Order: The Military Dimension', in M. Smith, S. Smith, and B. White (eds), *British Foreign Policy: Tradition, Change and Transformation* (Boston: Unwin Hyman, 1988), p. 113.
3. Dockrill, *British Defence*, p. 125; G. Martel, 'The Meaning of Power: Rethinking the Decline and Fall of Great Britain', *International History Review*, Vol. 13 (1991), p. 665. Prominent works which use decline to understand twentieth-century British foreign and defence policy include: Darwin; Friedberg; Snyder, *British Defense*; Kennedy, *Naval Mastery*; Kennedy, *The Realities Behind Diplomacy: Background Influences on British Foreign Policy, 1865–1980* (Boston: Allen and Unwin, 1981); R.N. Rosecrance, *Defence of the Realm: British Strategy in the Nuclear Epoch* (New York: Columbia University Press, 1968); C.J. Bartlett, *The Long Retreat: A Short History of British Defence Policy 1945–70* (New York: St. Martin's Press, 1972); F.S. Northedge, *Descent from Power: British Foreign Policy 1945–1973* (London: Allen and Unwin, 1974); P. Calvocoressi, *The British Experience 1945–1975* (London: Bodley Head, 1978). See also Greenwood's critique of the conventional view of contraction in post–1945 British defense policy and Baylis' assessment of Greenwood's arguments. Greenwood, 'National Priorities'; Baylis, 'Greenwoodery'. A broader critique of the standard view of British international decline in the late nineteenth and the twentieth centuries is found in Cain and Hopkins.
4. Dockrill, *British Defence*, p. 126.
5. K. Hartley, 'Defence with Less Money? The British Experience', in Gwyn Harries-Jenkins (ed.), *Armed Forces and Welfare Societies* (New York: St. Martin's Press, 1983), p. 16.
6. See Catterall, 'East of Suez'; and P. Hennessy, 'The Whitehall Model: Career Staff Support for Cabinet in Foreign Affairs', in C. Campbell, S.J., and M.J. Wyszomirski (eds), *Executive Leadership in Anglo-American Systems* (Pittsburgh: University of Pittsburgh Press, 1991), pp. 295–316.
7. The observation is that of Sir Frank Cooper, a senior official in the MoD during the east of Suez decision. See Catterall, 'East of Suez', p. 619.
8. Kennedy, *Realities*, p. 334; W.D. McIntyre, *Commonwealth of Nations: Origins and Impact* (Minneapolis: University of Minnesota Press, 1977), p. 341.
9. On British pre-eminence until the late 1930s, see B.J.C. McKercher, 'Our Most Dangerous Enemy: Great Britain Preeminent in the 1930s', *International History Review*, Vol. 13 (1991), pp. 751–83.
10. Critics include Harries-Jenkins, p. 26.
11. The preceding description of Britain's post–1945 international position draws from the perceptive analysis of Darwin, pp. 20–2.
12. Gilpin, *War and Change*; Kennedy, *Rise and Fall*.
13. Kennedy, *Rise and Fall*, pp. xvi, xxii.
14. Friedberg, p. 30.
15. On the usefulness of this approach, see P. Gourevitch, *Politics in Hard Times: Comparative Responses to International Economic Crises* (Ithaca: Cornell University Press, 1986); J.D. Hagan and J.A. Rosati, 'Emerging

Issues in Research on Foreign Policy Restructuring', in J.A. Rosati, J.D. Hagan, and M.W. Sampson III (eds), *Foreign Policy Restructuring* (Columbia: University of South Carolina Press, 1994), pp. 265–79; T. Risse-Kappen, 'Ideas do not Float Freely: Transnational Coalitions, Domestic Structures, and the End of the Cold War', *International Organization*, Vol. 48 (1994), pp. 185–214.

16. R.D. Putnam, 'Diplomacy and Domestic Politics: The Logic of Two-Level Games', *International Organization*, Vol. 42, p. 437; Risse-Kappen, p. 187.
17. Reynolds, p. 43; Snyder, *British Defense*, p. 61.
18. Vital, p. 255.
19. B.M. Russett, *Controlling the Sword: The Democratic Governance of National Security* (Cambridge, Mass.: Harvard University Press, 1990), p. 8.
20. Some approaches to the study of foreign policy do, of course, explicitly take politics into consideration. One example is the bureaucratic politics approach, often utilized in analyses of American foreign policy. Scholars debate whether this approach has utility in the British setting, particularly given the oft-noted ethos in Whitehall emphasizing compromise. The bureaucratic politics approach is implicitly incorporated into this study. The positions that foreign policy departments took on the overseas military role are analyzed, but only as one consideration among many. Since bureaucratic politics is less likely to impact British decision-makers in the way that it does their American counterparts, it seems wise to look both to, but also beyond, the bureaucracy for an explanation of the east of Suez decision. See W. Wallace, *The Foreign Policy Process in Britain* (London: Allen and Unwin, 1976), p. 9; S. Smith, 'Foreign Policy Analysis and the Study of British Foreign Policy', in L. Freedman and M. Clarke (eds), *Britain the World* (New York: Cambridge University Press, 1991), pp. 68–9.
21. A.L. Stinchcombe, *Constructing Social Theories* (New York: Harcourt, Brace, and World, 1968), pp. 101–29.
22. It is useful to recall that such withdrawals, while important, do not fall under the conceptual rubric of retrenchment in this work. In this study, retrenchment is operationally defined as the complete abandonment of an overseas military network, not the numerous adjustments which may be taken over decades to either streamline or scale down the network.
23. The distinction between historic and constant causes may be ambiguous. For instance, relative economic decline was at one point in time (the late 1870s) a new phenomenon which reshaped the political landscape within which British decision-makers had to operate. Nevertheless, differences in scope and duration should allow analysts, with careful consideration of the case at hand, to distinguish these conceptually different types of causation. See Stinchcombe; R.B. Collier and D. Collier, *Shaping the Political Arena* (Princeton: Princeton University Press, 1991).
24. Putnam, p. 428.
25. Wallace, *Policy Process*, p. 48.

26. A. King, 'The British Prime Ministership in the Age of the Career Politician', *West European Politics*, Vol. 14 (1991), pp. 36–7. The Prime Minister is of course advised in the construction of this system by the Cabinet Secretary.
27. M. Clarke, 'The Policy-Making Process', in M. Smith, S. Smith, and B. White (eds), *British Foreign Policy: Tradition, Change, and Transformation* (Boston: Unwin Hyman, 1988), p. 73; J. Barber, *The Prime Minister since 1945* (Cambridge, Mass.: Basil Blackwell, 1991), p. 74.
28. Clarke, p. 74; D.C. Watt, *Personalities and Policies: Studies in the Formulation of British Foreign Policy* (South Bend: University of Notre Dame, 1965), p. 3.
29. A. Cairncross and B. Eichengreen, *Sterling in Decline: The Devaluations of 1931, 1949, and 1967* (Oxford: Basil Blackwell, 1983), pp. 166–80.
30. S. James, *British Cabinet Government* (New York: Routledge, 1992), p. 119. In defense policy, the key role of the Prime Minister has been acknowledged since at least the Esher Report of 1904. As the early years of the Attlee premiership demonstrate, however, even the Prime Minister's strongest desires in the realm of defense policy may be defeated by powerful interests within the government. See Chapter 4.
31. See King, pp. 42–3; P. Hennessy, *Cabinet* (New York: Basil Blackwell, 1986), p. 6.
32. J. Frankel, *British Foreign Policy 1945–1973* (New York: Oxford University Press 1975), pp. 203–4.
33. Kennedy, *Realities*, p. 334.
34. D.C. Watt, 'Demythologizing the Eisenhower Era', in W.R. Louis and H. Bull (eds), *The 'Special Relationship': Anglo-American Relations since 1945* (Oxford: Clarendon, 1986), p. 7.
35. R. Edmunds, *Setting the Mould: The United States and Britain 1945–50* (New York: Norton, 1986), p. 227.
36. See C.C. Shoemaker, *Patron–Client State Relationships* (New York: Praeger, 1984).
37. Darwin, p. 18.
38. This definition of strategic assumptions is derived from recent scholarship which emphasizes the importance of strategic prescriptions in foreign policy change. See Risse-Kappen; J. Checkel, 'Ideas, Institutions, and the Gorbachev Foreign Policy Revolution', *World Politics*, Vol. 45 (1994), pp. 242–70. Strategic prescriptions, such as common security or flexible response, are policy alternatives which are presented to policymakers, and which may eventually prove important in a decision to redirect foreign policy. In the case of Britain's east of Suez policy and the eventual decision to withdraw, strategic prescriptions which had become ingrained into policymakers' beliefs (in other words, assumptions) are as, and probably much more, important for understanding the course of policy.
39. Kupchan, *Vulnerability*.
40. Checkel, p. 281.
41. Armstrong, p. 168; R. Powell, 'The Evolution of British Defence Policy, 1945–59', in J. Simpson (ed.), *Perspectives on British Defence Policy* (Southampton: University of Southampton Press, 1974), p. 59.

42. Kennedy, *Naval Mastery*, pp. 4, 267.
43. Armstrong, p. 36.
44. An extensive literature exists on the role that national leaders play in policy change, with psychological variables often being the primary focus. This study analyzes the changing attitudes of key policymakers, but it looks beyond any single individual, such as the Prime Minister, to all elite groups with the potential to influence the coalition-building process. In addition, key actors' positions on the east of Suez role are studied in the context of the broader policymaking arena and the political environment. For a useful summary of the literature on psychological variables and foreign policy change, which also notes the advantages of placing individual level variables in a broader context, see J.S. Levy, 'Learning and Foreign Policy: Sweeping a Conceptual Minefield', *International Organization*, Vol. 48 (1994), pp. 279–312.
45. Clarke, pp. 72–7.
46. See Reynolds; Watt, *Personalities*.
47. G. Parry, *Political Elites* (New York: Praeger, 1969), p. 52.
48. Vital, p. 83.
49. J.B. Christoph, 'High Civil Servants and the Politics of Consensualism in Great Britain', in M. Dogan (ed.), *The Mandarins of Western Europe* (New York: John Wiley, 1975), pp. 32–6.
50. Z.S. Steiner, 'Decision-making in American and British Foreign Policy: an Open and Shut Case', *Review of International Studies*, Vol. 13 (1987), p. 15.
51. Wallace, *Policy Process*, pp. 95, 117.
52. Snyder, *British Defense*, p. 70.
53. Wallace, *Policy Process*, pp. 88, 101.
54. Snyder, *British Defense*, p. 79; C. Farrands, 'State, Society, Culture and British Foreign Policy', in M. Smith, S. Smith, and B. White (eds), *British Foreign Policy: Tradition, Change, and Transformation* (Boston: Unwin Hyman, 1988), p. 67.
55. See Putnam, p. 445.
56. Clarke, p. 77; Capitanchik, 'Public Opinion and Popular Attitudes toward British Defence', in J. Baylis (ed.), *British Defence Policy in a Changing World* (London: Croom Helm, 1977), p. 259.
57. J. Frankel, 'Defence, Public Opinion, and Parliament', in J. Simpson (ed.), *Perspectives upon British Defence Policy* (Southampton: University of Southampton Press, 1974), p. 270. As mentioned in Chapter 1, pressure groups should not be expected to have a substantial impact on foreign policy in the British case. Other than occasional exceptions in low-policy issues such as procurement and trade, the British foreign policy apparatus has proven to be too insulated and cohesive to provide points of access for societal groups. It is thus unlikely, perhaps even inconceivable, that pressure groups would have had a large impact on the east of Suez decision, given its perceived importance for national security. See Farrands, pp. 64–6.
58. G.J. Ikenberry, 'Conclusion: An Institutional Approach to American Foreign Economic Policy', in G.J. Ikenberry, D.A. Lake, and M. Mas-

tanduno (eds), *The State and American Foreign Economic Policy* (Ithaca: Cornell University Press, 1988), p. 220.
59. J.G. March and J.P. Olsen, *Rediscovering Institutions: the Organizational Basis of Politics* (New York: Free Press, 1989), pp. 16–19.
60. W. Carlsnaes, 'The Agency–Structure Problem in Foreign Policy Analysis', *International Studies Quarterly*, Vol. 36 (1992), pp. 245–6.
61. Hagan and Rosati, p. 274; C.F. Hermann, 'Reflections on Foreign Policy Theory Building', in L. Neack, P. Haney, and J.A.K. Hey (eds), *Foreign Policy Analysis: Continuity and Change in Its Second Generation* (Englewood Cliffs, NJ: Prentice-Hall, 1995), p. 250.
62. D.C. Watt, *Succeeding John Bull* (New York: Cambridge University Press, 1984), p. 113. Watt's three intervals – 1946–51, 1956–8, and 1967–70 – differ slightly from those analyzed in this work, a discrepancy explained by this study's explicit focus on the east of Suez role.
63. See Kennedy, *Realities*, p. 344.
64. See D. Sanders, *Losing an Empire, Finding a Role* (New York: St. Martin's Press, 1990), p. 113; also see Armstrong; Darby.
65. R.E. Robinson and J. Gallagher, with A. Denny, *Africa and the Victorians: The Official Mind of Imperialism* (London: Oxford University Press, 1961), p. 11.
66. See especially Darby; but also Harries-Jenkins; Powell; J.C. Garnett, 'British Strategic Thought', in J. Baylis (ed.), *British Defence Policy in a Changing World* (London: Croom Helm, 1977), pp. 156–73.
67. J.C. Hurewitz, 'The Historical Context', in W.R. Louis and R. Owen (eds), *Suez 1956: The Crisis and Its Consequences* (New York: Clarendon, 1989), p. 11.
68. See K. Kyle, *Suez* (New York: St. Martin's Press, 1991), p. 560.
69. M. Brenner, 'The Problem of Innovation in the Nixon–Kissinger Foreign Policy', *International Studies Quarterly*, Vol. 17 (1973), p. 267.
70. See S.D. Krasner, 'Approaches to the State: Alternative Conceptions and Historical Dynamics', *Comparative Politics*, Vol. 16 (1984). An extensive literature on organizational theory explores this point. See S.P. Huntington, *Political Order in Changing Societies* (New Haven: Yale University Press, 1968), pp. 15–17.
71. See Levy, p. 304.
72. See R. Ovendale, *British Defence Policy since 1945* (Manchester: Manchester University Press, 1994), pp. 97–102.
73. J.M. Rochester, 'Prospects for United Nations Reform', *Occasional Paper*, Center for International Studies, No. 9032 (St. Louis: University of Missouri-St. Louis, 1993), p. 12. The opportunity that crises provide for foreign policy innovation has been widely recognized. For instance, Barbara Tuchman argues in her grand history *March of Folly* that 'woodenheadedness' – or rigidly adhering to a policy until the evidence against it becomes overwhelming, such as in a crisis – has been a trait common to policymakers for centuries. Even widely read textbooks embrace this view. In one example, John Stoessinger concludes that 'people abandon their bad habits only when catastrophe is close at hand. The intellect alone is not

enough. We must be shaken, almost shattered, before we change.' B. Tuchman, *March of Folly* (New York: Knopf, 1984); J.G. Stoessinger, *Why Nations Go To War*, 6th edn (New York: St. Martin's Press, 1993), p. 210.

74. A.L. George, 'Case Studies and Theory Development: the Method of Structured, Focused Comparison', in P.G. Lauren (ed.), *Diplomacy: New Approaches in History, Theory, and Policy* (New York: Free Press, 1979).
75. See A. Lijphart, 'Comparative Politics and the Comparative Method', *American Political Science Review*, Vol. 65 (1971); G. King, R.O. Keohane, and S. Verba, *Designing Social Inquiry* (Princeton: Princeton University Press, 1994).
76. Ikenberry, p. 226.
77. Krasner, p. 240.
78. Three separate literatures in the study of foreign policy stress the importance of a policy's past evolution: that on learning and foreign policy, a summary of which is found in Levy; that on foreign policy cycles, a notable example of which is J.A. Rosati, 'Cycles in Foreign Policy Restructuring', in J.A. Rosati, J.D. Hagan, and M.W. Sampson (eds), *Foreign Policy Restructuring* (Columbia: University of South Carolina Press, 1994), pp. 221–61; and that on evolutionary models and foreign policy, a recent framework exemplified by A. Farkas, 'Evolutionary Models in Foreign Policy Analysis', *International Studies Quarterly*, Vol. 40 (1996), pp. 343–61. The longitudinal study provided here differs from such work in its focus on coalitional politics and also by offering a structured framework to analyze the interaction between three levels of analysis – international, domestic, and societal/individual – in foreign policy change.
79. K.J. Holsti, 'The Comparative Analysis of Foreign Policy: Some Notes', in K.J. Holsti (ed.), *Change in the International System* (Brookfield, VT: Edward Elgar, 1991), pp. 194–5.
80. See E.H. Carr, *What is History?* (New York: Vintage, 1961), pp. 113–43; C. Ragin, *Constructing Social Research* (Thousand Oaks, CA: Pine Forge, 1994), pp. 114–18.
81. See Collier and Collier, pp. 35–7.

3 THE RETURN TO NORMALCY: POSTWAR BRITISH STRATEGY

1. P.J. Taylor, *Britain and the Cold War: 1945 as Geopolitical Transition* (New York: Pinter, 1990).
2. There are extensive institutional and psychological literatures on the stimuli that crises such as war provide to policy change. It is typically in the aftermath of major emergencies that the policy arena becomes fluid enough to allow for dramatic redirections of policy, because standard policies and procedures have been called into question. See Chapter 2.

3. A. Adamthwaite, 'Britain and the World, 1945–49: The View from the Foreign Office', *International Affairs*, Vol. 61 (1985), pp. 225–6.
4. A. Bullock, *The Life and Times of Ernest Bevin*, Vol. 3 (London: Heinemann, 1983), p. 66; A.I. Singh, *The Limits of British Influence: South Asia and the Anglo-American Relationship, 1947–56* (New York: St. Martin's Press, 1993), p. 14.
5. H. Weigert, 'Strategic Bases', in H. Weigert, V. Stefansson, and R.E. Harrison (eds), *New Compass of the World* (London: Harrap, 1949), p. 222.
6. Reynolds, p. 158.
7. J. Lewis, *Changing Direction: British Military Planning for Postwar Strategic Defence, 1942–47* (London: Sherwood, 1988), p. 363.
8. P. Hennessy, *Never Again, Britain 1945–51* (London: Cape, 1992), pp. 253–5.
9. R.F. Holland, 'The Imperial Factor in British Strategies from Attlee to Macmillan, 1945–63', *The Journal of Imperial and Commonwealth History*, Vol. 12 (1984), p. 169.
10. K. Harris, *Attlee* (London: Weidenfeld and Nicolson, 1982), p. 293.
11. Singh, pp. 2–7.
12. T.H. Anderson, *The United States, Great Britain, and the Cold War, 1944–47* (Columbia: University of Missouri Press, 1981), p. 33; K.O. Morgan, *Labour in Power, 1945–51* (Oxford: Clarendon, 1984), p. 263.
13. The following discussion draws upon David Reynolds' excellent and concise summary of Anglo-American relations between 1945 and 1947. See Reynolds, pp. 159–63.
14. Anderson, p. 152.
15. These are the estimates used to negotiate the American loan in 1945. Bullock, *Bevin*, Vol. 3, p. 49.
16. Holland, *Pursuit of Greatness*, p. 202.
17. Reynolds, p. 160.
18. Holland, *Pursuit of Greatness*, p. 203; R.N. Gardner, *Sterling–Dollar Diplomacy in Current Perspective* (New York: Columbia University Press, 1980), p. 226.
19. V. Rothwell, *Britain and the Cold War 1941–47* (London: Cape, 1982), p. 425.
20. Reynolds, p. 163.
21. Bullock, *Bevin*, Vol. 3, p. 33.
22. See Hennessy, *Never Again*, pp. 216–44.
23. See especially M.J. Cohen, *Palestine and the Great Powers, 1945–1948* (Princeton: Princeton University Press, 1982); W.R. Louis, *The British Empire in the Middle East 1945–51* (New York: Oxford University Press, 1984), chapter 4.
24. F.S. Northedge, 'Britain and the Middle East', in R. Ovendale (ed.), *The Foreign Policy of the British Labour Governments, 1945–51* (Leicester: Leicester University Press, 1984), pp. 162–5.
25. Louis, p. 419.
26. Montgomery, p. 46; Armstrong, p. 164.
27. Rosecrance, *Defense of the Realm*, p. 53.
28. Darby, p. 43.

29. Darby, p. 17; A. Gorst, 'Facing Facts? The Labour Government and Defence Policy, 1945–50', in N. Tiratsoo (ed.), *The Attlee Years* (New York: Pinter, 1991), p. 192.
30. A. Sampson, *Macmillan: a Study in Ambiguity* (New York: Simon and Schuster, 1967), p. 101.
31. F.A. Johnson, *Defence by Ministry: The British Ministry of Defence 1944–1974* (London: Duckworth, 1980), pp. 14–34.
32. See F.A. Johnson, *Defence by Committee: The British Committee of Imperial Defence* (New York: Oxford University Press, 1960), for a discussion of the functions of the Committee of Imperial Defence.
33. Darby, p. 20; Johnson, *Defence by Ministry*, p. 19.
34. Adamthwaite, p. 233.
35. Ibid.
36. Ibid.
37. Armstrong, pp. 160–8; Northedge, 'Britain and the Middle East', p. 177.
38. See C.B. Fawcett, 'Life Lines of the British Empire', in H.W. Weigert, V. Stefansson, and R.E. Harrison (eds), *New Compass of the World* (London: Harrap, 1949), pp. 238–48.
39. Darby, p. 15.
40. Ibid., p. 22.
41. Singh, pp. 27, 43, 49.
42. Holland, *Pursuit of Greatness*, p. 14.
43. Bullock, *Bevin*, Vol. 3, p. 35.
44. E. Monroe, *Britain's Moment in the Middle East 1914–1971* (Baltimore: Johns Hopkins University Press, 1981), p. 95.
45. Northedge, 'Britain and the Middle East', p. 149.
46. Holland, *Pursuit of Greatness*, p. 225.
47. Singh, p. 26.
48. Sked and Cook, p. 81; J. Kent, 'Bevin's Imperialism and the Idea of Euro-Africa, 1945–49', in M. Dockrill and J.W. Young (eds), *British Foreign Policy 1945–56* (New York: St. Martin's Press, 1989), pp. 47–76.
49. Rothwell, p. 409; Hennessy, *Never Again*, p. 224.
50. Hennessy, *Never Again*, p. 238.
51. See in particular Holland, *Pursuit of Greatness*; M. Blackwell, *Clinging to Grandeur: British Attitudes and Foreign Policy in the Aftermath of the Second World War* (Westport, CT: Greenwood, 1993). This is the consistent and extremely well-documented theme of studies which address British foreign policy during the Labour government of 1945–51. See Darby; Monroe; Louis; Morgan, *Labour in Power*; Hennessy, *Never Again*; M.A. Fitzsimons, *The Foreign Policy of the British Labour Government 1945–51* (South Bend: University of Notre Dame Press, 1953).
52. *Listener*, 11 November 1952, quoted in Darby, p. 22.
53. See Holland, *Pursuit of Greatness*, p. 218.
54. Ministry of Defence, *Statement Relating to Defence*, Cmnd. 6743 (1946), pp. 2–3.
55. Louis, p. 10.
56. Hennessy, *Never Again*, p. 240.
57. See Kennedy, *Naval Mastery*, pp. xxviii–xxix, 256–7.
58. Fawcett, pp. 244–5; Armstrong, p. 168; Darby, p. 31.

4 HOLDING COURSE: THE LABOUR GOVERNMENT OF 1945–51 AND THE STRUGGLE OVER STRATEGY

1. P. Addison, *The Road to 1945: British Politics and the Second World War* (London: Cape, 1975), p. 134.
2. Morgan, *Labour in Power*, p. 42.
3. Ibid.
4. S. Fielding. 'Don't Know, Don't Care: Popular Attitudes in Labour's Britain, 1945–51', in N. Tiratsoo (ed.), *The Attlee Years* (New York: Pinter, 1991), p. 107.
5. J.P. MacKintosh, *The British Cabinet* (Toronto: University of Toronto Press, 1962), p. 430.
6. Hennessy, *Never Again*, p. 303. Alan Bullock notes that Sir Edward Bridges, who kept the Minutes of the Cabinet, remarked on one occasion that among those 'Also Present' should be included 'The ghost of 1931,' so palpable was its influence whenever the Cabinet threatened to become divided. See Bullock, *Bevin*, Vol. 3, p. 77.
7. H. Pelling, *The Labour Governments, 1945–51* (New York: St. Martin's Press, 1984), p. 37.
8. B. Pimlott, 'The Labour Left', in C. Cook and I. Taylor (eds), *The Labour Party: An Introduction to its Structure and Politics* (New York: Longman, 1980), p. 172.
9. Holland, *Pursuit of Greatness*, p. 200.
10. Harris, p. 268.
11. James, *Cabinet*, p. 188.
12. Morgan, *Labour in Power*, p. 50.
13. B. Carter, *The Office of the Prime Minister* (London: Faber and Faber, 1956), p. 210; Bullock, *Bevin*, Vol. 3, p. 55.
14. D. Dilks, *The Diaries of Sir Alexander Cadogan, 1838–1945* (London: Cassell, 1971), p. 176.
15. Harris, p. 301; Bullock, *Bevin*, Vol. 3, pp. 60–2.
16. James, *Cabinet*, p. 194; K. Jefferys, *The Labour Party since 1945* (New York: St. Martin's Press, 1993), p. 10.
17. M. Foot, *Aneurin Bevan*, Vol. 2 (London: Granada, 1973), p. 32.
18. Bullock, *Bevin*, Vol. 3, p. 56.
19. T. Burridge, *Clement Attlee* (London: Cape, 1985), p. 220. The following analysis of Attlee's challenge to Britain's global role from 1945 to 1947 draws heavily upon the article on the subject by Smith and Zametica. See R. Smith and J. Zametica, 'The Cold Warrior: Clement Attlee Reconsidered', *International Affairs*, Vol. 61 (1985), pp. 237–52.
20. L.D. Epstein, *Britain – Uneasy Ally* (Chicago: University of Chicago Press, 1954), p. 99.
21. Harris, p. 294.
22. Smith and Zametica, p. 240.
23. Lewis, p. 363; Hennessy, *Never Again*, p. 256.
24. R. Bullen and M.E. Pelly (eds), *Documents on British Policy Overseas. Vol. 1, The Conference at Potsdam, 1945* (London: HMSO, 1984), pp. 363–4.
25. Smith and Zametica, p. 241.

26. Bullen and Pelly, p. 574.
27. Smith and Zametica, p. 243.
28. Hennessy, *Never Again*, p. 233.
29. Bullock, *Bevin*, Vol. 3, p. 113. As early as October 1945 Bevin declared to the Soviet Foreign Secretary Molotov that to give Russia control over the Italian colonies was inconceivable, because it would sever 'the lifeline of Empire' in the Mediterranean and the Middle East. See Morgan, *Labour in Power*, p. 242.

    Moreover, although some have questioned whether Bevin may have been manipulated into accepting and then propagating the Foreign Office view, the consensus seems to be that Bevin was far too forceful a figure to allow his policy to be hijacked by his officials. Morgan states that Bevin was a 'dominant, transcendent, creative force' in the Foreign Office. See *Labour in Power*, pp. 235–6. Bevin's biographer, Alan Bullock, goes so far as to claim that Bevin was a policy initiator of a type not seen in Britain since Lords Palmerston and Salisbury. See also Epstein, *Uneasy Ally*, p. 141.
30. Morgan, *Labour in Power*, p. 55.
31. Smith and Zametica, p. 243.
32. See Lewis.
33. Hennessy, *Never Again*, p. 262.
34. Bullock, *Bevin*, Vol. 3, p. 240.
35. B. Pimlott, *The Political Diary of Hugh Dalton* (London: Cape, 1986), pp. 368–9. The diary entry is dated 22 March 1946.
36. See Rothwell, chapter 5.
37. Burridge, pp. 254–5.
38. Bullock, *Bevin*, Vol. 3, p. 156.
39. Morgan, *Labour in Power*, p. 273. A more emphatic example of Bevin's attitude toward the Soviet Union by mid-1946 is given by Christopher Mayhew, one of his junior ministers. According to Mayhew, the Foreign Minister brusquely told him at this time: 'Molotov, Stalin, they are evil men.' Quoted in Hennessy, *Never Again*, p. 245.
40. Smith and Zametica, p. 245.
41. Ibid.
42. Gorst, pp. 191–5.
43. Bullock, *Bevin*, Vol. 3, pp. 349–50.
44. Smith and Zametica, p. 249.
45. Ibid., 251.
46. Montgomery, p. 436.
47. Harris, p. 300.
48. Holland, *Pursuit of Greatness*, p. 206.
49. *House of Commons Debates* [henceforward *HC Debates*], vol. 437, col. 1965.
50. Morgan, *Labour in Power*, p. 48.
51. Hennessy, *Never Again*, pp. 261–2.
52. J.D. Hoffman, *The Conservative Party in Opposition, 1945–51* (London: MacGibbon and Kee, 1964), pp. 135–219; J. Charmley, *A History of Conservative Politics, 1900–1996* (New York: St. Martin's Press, 1996), pp. 124–8.

53. Bartlett, *Long Retreat*, p. 25.
54. Morgan, *Labour in Power*, p. 237.
55. M.R. Gordon, *Conflict and Consensus in Labour's Foreign Policy 1914–1965* (Stanford: Stanford University Press, 1969), p. 7.
56. See Gordon, pp. 38–9; D. Keohane, *Labour Party Defence Policy since 1945* (London: Leicester University Press, 1993), pp. 2–4.
57. Epstein, *Uneasy Ally*, pp. 99–112, 128–34.
58. Bullock, *Bevin*, Vol. 1, pp. 511–12.
59. Epstein, *Uneasy Ally*, pp. 113–27.
60. Sked and Cook, p. 50.
61. H. Pelling, *A Short History of the Labour Party* (New York: St. Martin's Press, 1972), p. 100.
62. Pimlott, 'Labour Left', p. 173.
63. Rothwell, p. 228.
64. Sked and Cook, p. 50.
65. Pelling, *Short History*, p. 95; Pimlott, 'Labour Left', pp. 172–3.
66. E.J. Meehan, *The British Left-Wing and Foreign Policy* (New Brunswick: Rutgers University Press, 1960), p. 73.
67. Morgan, *Labour in Power*, pp. 70, 239.
68. Sked and Cook, p. 84.
69. Even with the loss of India, the Cabinet, including Bevin and Attlee, and the military tried their best to secure the Indian Army for colonial policing and to acquire basing rights in India. Nehru, however, would accede to none of these proposals, and events soon undermined the British government's hopes of a security relationship with India. See Singh, pp. 16–20.
70. Bullock, *Bevin*, Vol. 3, pp. 72, 192, 222, 279, 322; Morgan, *Labour in Power*, pp. 91–2.
71. Gordon, pp. 105, 115.
72. Morgan, *Labour in Power*, p. 330.
73. See A. Robertson, *The Bleak Midwinter, 1947* (Manchester: Manchester University Press, 1987).
74. D. Marquand, 'Sir Stafford Cripps', in M. Sissons and P. French (eds), *Age of Austerity* (London: Hodder and Stoughton, 1963), p. 170; A. Cairncross, *Years of Recovery: British Economic Policy 1945–51* (New York: Methuen, 1985), ch. 6.
75. Reynolds, p. 168.
76. G.M. Alexander, *The Prelude to the Truman Doctrine: British Policy in Greece, 1944–47* (New York: Oxford University Press, 1982), pp. 240–3.
77. Louis, pp. 459–60; Holland, *Pursuit of Greatness*, p. 219.
78. See Hennessy, *Never Again*, p. 235. A brief, but good, summary of the various views on Indian independence can be found in Sked and Cook, pp. 59–62. Philip Darby provides a useful description of the lingering attachment to Indian affairs among many in Britain, and the subtle, perhaps even subconscious, blow that the transfer of power must have been to much of the populace and scores of policymakers. For example, he states: 'One million British graves across the subcontinent, and varied mementos of the days of the Raj on the walls and mantelshelves of countless British homes bore witness to the genera-

tions that had served in India and that it could not all be in vain.' See Darby, p. 12.
79. Harris, pp. 332–54.
80. J.R.C. Dow, *The Management of the British Economy 1945–1960* (Cambridge: Cambridge University Press, 1964), pp. 22–6.
81. Cairncross, p. 137.
82. H. Dalton, *Memoirs 1945–60: High Tide and After* (London: Muller, 1962), p. 187.
83. Morgan, *Labour in Power*, p. 394.
84. Harris, pp. 347–50.
85. Holland, *Pursuit of Greatness*, p. 206.
86. Marquand, p. 171.
87. Jefferys, p. 11; D. Jay, *Change and Fortune* (London: Hutchinson, 1980), pp. 170–214.
88. Morgan, *Labour in Power*, p. 363.
89. Marquand, p. 179.
90. J.L. Gaddis, *The United States and the Origins of the Cold War 1941–1947* (New York: Columbia University Press, 1972), pp. 296–304.
91. See Don Cook, *Forging the Alliance: NATO 1945 to 1950* (London: Secker and Warburg, 1989), p. 125.
92. P. Weiler, *Ernest Bevin* (Manchester: Manchester University Press, 1993), p. 185.
93. Hennessy, *Never Again*, p. 296.
94. Rosecrance, *Defence of the Realm*, p. 77.
95. Darby, pp. 44–5.
96. Blackwell, pp. 144–50.

5 REAPPRAISAL: THE SUEZ CRISIS AND ITS AFTERMATH, 1957–60

1. Perceptions of overseas bases did begin to change in Whitehall before the Suez crisis, albeit very gradually. The best example of the evolution of British strategic thought in the early 1950s is the 1952 Defence Policy and Global Strategy Paper, discussed in Chapter 2, which specifically addressed the proper balance between nuclear weapons and overseas conventional forces. In this sense, one reason the Suez crisis was important was because it threw a number of emerging trends in British defence policy into sharp relief.
2. Sked and Cook, p. 129.
3. Kyle, pp. 164–5.
4. M. Beloff, 'The Crisis and Its Consequences for the British Conservatives', in W.R. Louis and R. Owen (eds), *Suez 1956: The Crisis and its Consequences* (Oxford: Clarendon, 1989), p. 328.
5. R.R. Bowie, 'Eisenhower, Dulles, and the Suez Crisis', in W.R. Louis and R. Owen (eds), *Suez 1956: The Crisis and Its Consequences* (Oxford: Clarendon, 1989), p. 201.
6. Sked and Cook, p. 130.

7. L. Johnman, 'Defending the Pound: the Economics of the Suez Crisis, 1956', in A. Gorst, L. Johnman, and W.S. Lucas (eds), *Post-war Britain, 1945–64: Themes and Perspectives* (London: Pinter, 1989), pp. 171–8.
8. Reynolds, p. 205.
9. Rosecrance, *Defence of the Realm*, p. 228.
10. Darwin, p. 223; W.S. Lucas, *Divided We Stand: Britain, the US, and the Suez Crisis* (London: Hodder and Stoughton, 1991), pp. 316–23.
11. Kyle, p. 533.
12. A. Horne, *Harold Macmillan*, Vol. 2 (New York: Viking, 1989), p. 19.
13. J.P. MacKintosh, *The British Cabinet*, 3rd edn (London: Stevens, 1977), p. 507.
14. L.A. Siedentop, 'Mr. Macmillan and the Edwardian Style', in V. Bogdanor and R. Skidelsky (eds), *The Age of Affluence 1951–1964* (New York: Macmillan, 1970), p. 32.
15. Sampson, p. 121.
16. Barber, pp. 67, 118; Sked and Cook, pp. 140–1.
17. Sampson, p. 122.
18. Ibid.
19. Mackintosh, *Cabinet*, 3rd edn, p. 507.
20. Beloff, p. 331.
21. L.D. Epstein, *British Politics and the Suez Crisis* (Urbana: University of Illinois Press, 1964), p. 87.
22. Morgan, *People's Peace*, p. 127.
23. Sampson, p. 125.
24. Lucas, pp. 300, 315.
25. M. Dockrill, 'Restoring the "Special Relationship": The Bermuda and Washington Conferences, 1957', in D. Richardson and G. Stone (eds), *Decisions and Diplomacy* (London: Routledge, 1995), p. 218.
26. Holland, *Pursuit of Greatness*, p. 283.
27. Dow, p. 200; Morgan, *People's Peace*, p. 171.
28. J. Barnes, 'From Eden to Macmillan, 1955–1959', in P. Hennessy and A. Seldon (eds), *Ruling Performance: British Governments from Attlee to Thatcher* (New York: Basil Blackwell, 1987), p. 100.
29. Barber, pp. 98, 104.
30. J. Turner, *Macmillan* (New York: Longman, 1994), p. 234.
31. Horne, p. 148.
32. Morgan, *People's Peace*, p. 189.
33. See S. Blank, 'Britain: The Politics of Foreign Economic Policy', *International Organization*, Vol. 31 (1977), pp. 673–721.
34. Watt, 'Eisenhower Era', p. 68.
35. Sampson, p. 160.
36. Pelling, *Short History*, pp. 109–20.
37. Sked and Cook, pp. 155–8.
38. Morgan, *People's Peace*, p. 193.
39. Ibid., p. 117.
40. Public Record Office, Kew [henceforward PRO]: PREM 11/1326, Macmillan to Eden, 23 March 1956.

41. For example, L. Radice, MoD, admitted in a November 1958 note to the Treasury that 'there is no long-term defence programme in any real sense of the term.' See PRO: T 225/1087.
42. PRO: PREM 11/1778, Macmillan and Monckton to Eden, March 1956.
43. Horne, p. 46.
44. Ibid., p. 47.
45. W. Wallace, 'World Status Without Tears', in V. Bogdanor and R. Skidelsky (eds), *The Age of Affluence: 1951–1964* (New York: Macmillan, 1970), p. 208.
46. PRO: PREM 11/1773, Bishop to Macmillan, 1 August 1957.
47. See R.N. Rosecrance and A. Stein, *Domestic Bases of Grand Strategy* (Ithaca: Cornell University Press, 1994).
48. Bartlett, *Long Retreat*, pp. 120–6.
49. Dockrill, 'Special Relationship', p. 206.
50. Sked and Cook, p. 141.
51. See PRO: DEFE 4/95.
52. Darby, pp. 145, 165; Gordon, pp. 268–84; P. Catterall, 'Foreign and Commonwealth Policy in Opposition: The Labour Party 1955–64', in W. Kaiser and G. Staerck (eds), *In Search of A Role: British Foreign Policy 1955–64* (Basingstoke: Macmillan, 1998), passim.
53. Bartlett, *Long Retreat*, p. 129.
54. Horne, p. 49.
55. Holland, *Pursuit of Greatness*, p. 281.
56. Sked and Cook, p. 143.
57. Horne, p. 43.
58. Morgan, *People's Peace*, p. 163.
59. Beloff, p. 328. Note also that a US presence in the Middle East had grown slowly but steadily before the Suez crisis, particularly in the 'Northern Tier' and in Pakistan (which the State Department included in its definition of the Middle East, but the FO did not). Of course, the US had long had close relations with Saudi Arabia as well. See Lucas; Singh.
60. PRO: CAB 134/2338, Official Committee on the Middle East, December 1957.
61. Dockrill, 'Special Relationship', p. 211.
62. See PRO: CAB 134/2338, Official Committee on the Middle East, 2 May 1957; Horne, p. 44. The only issue which the US and Britain consistently disagreed upon was Buraimi, a swath of land spanning the territories of British ally Oman and US client Saudi Arabia. See PRO: CAB 134/2338, Official Committee on the Middle East meetings, spring 1957 for the US–UK row over this issue, which did not strain the relatively firm bonds of Anglo-American cooperation more generally.
63. R.D. Shulzinger, 'The Impact of Suez on the United States Middle East Policy, 1957–58', in S.I. Troen and M. Shemesh (eds), *The Suez–Sinai Crisis 1956* (London: Frank Cass, 1990), pp. 251–65.
64. H. Beeley, 'The Middle East', in W.R. Louis and H. Bull (eds), *The 'Special Relationship': Anglo-American Relations since 1945* (Oxford: Clarendon, 1986), p. 286. For example, the Official Committee on the

Middle East concluded on 2 May 1957 that 'the U.S. and not Britain is now the predominant Western power in the Middle East.' Nevertheless, the 'further decline in our conventional military strength need not be locally reflected in the Gulf.' For, 'it is common ground that our position in the Gulf has hitherto enabled us to secure our interests...' in the Middle East, and'... the Gulf is the one area of the world where we may still hope to retain control relying on our resources alone.' PRO: CAB 134/2338.
65. Singh, pp. 193–226.
66. M. Carver, *Tightrope Walking: British Defence Policy since 1945* (London: Hutchinson, 1992), p. 50.
67. Darby, pp. 58, 114.
68. Holland, *Pursuit of Greatness*, p. 291.
69. Horne, p. 49.
70. Ibid., p. 51.
71. See PRO: PREM 11/2639, Brook, Cabinet Secretary, to Prime Minister, 5 May 1959 and Chancellor Heathcoat Amory to PM in May 1959 in particular on the upswing in defense spending in the late 1950s. On Macmillan's acquiescence to rising defense expenditure, see PRO: PREM 11/2639, Macmillan to Chancellor Heathcoat Amory, 9 May 1959.
72. Holland, *Pursuit of Greatness*, p. 293. The problems Britain encountered in trying to develop a missile capability, most notably with the cancellation of Blue Streak, have been well documented. See Bartlett, *Long Retreat*, pp. 174–80.
73. Darby, p. 163.
74. J.L. Gaddis, *Strategies of Containment: a Critical Reappraisal of Postwar American National Security Policy* (New York: Oxford University Press, 1982), pp. 205–14.
75. Wallace, 'World Status', p. 217.
76. See Catterall, 'Foreign and Commonwealth Policy'.
77. These reviews are discussed on elsewhere, although in limited detail. Brief summaries are provided by Darby, pp. 143–4, and by a participant, M. Carver, *Out of Step* (London: Hutchinson, 1989), pp. 288–9. Other works present a synopsis of the perspectives of Darby and Carver, such as Barnes; Ball. The review process is also briefly mentioned in Cain and Hopkins, p. 290; and P. Hennessy, 'The Intellectual Consequences of the Peace: British Foreign and Defence Policymaking', *Strathclyde Papers on Government and Foreign Policy*, No. 70 (1990), pp. 27–28.
78. Darby appropriately stresses that the post-Suez 'secret reviews' were of a different magnitude than previous defence reviews. Instead of merely searching for economies, they scrutinized the fundamental principles of British foreign policy. See Darby, p. 143.
79. D. Goldsworthy, *The Conservative Government and the End of Empire, 1951–57* (London: HMSO, 1994), p. 67.
80. PRO: FO 371/143702, Dean to H. Caccia, Ambassador to US, 24 June 1959.
81. Bartlett, *Long Retreat*, p. 190.
82. PRO: PREM 11/1778, Brook to Eden, 17 December 1956.

83. Darby, pp. 100–3.
84. *British Interests in the Mediterranean and the Middle East* (London: Royal Institute of International Affairs/Oxford University Press, 1958).
85. It is unclear which ministers were aware of the secret reviews of Britain's role in the world in the late 1950s. But, since Macmillan dominated the process of foreign policy formulation and the entire Cabinet knew of them when they were completed, it may be a moot point.
86. The international relations literature notes how statesmen consistently tend to believe that foreign governments make judgements on their resolve. There is, however, little systemic evidence to show that governments actually make such judgements, or that they view all of a nation's commitments abroad as equally important or credible. See G.H. Snyder and P. Diesing, *Conflict Among Nations* (Princeton: Princeton University Press, 1978).
87. PRO: PREM 11/2321, 'The Position of the United Kingdom in World Affairs,' report by officials, June 1958.
88. PRO: CAB 130/139, Future Policy Committee, 4 February 1958.
89. PRO: PREM 11/2321, 'United Kingdom in World Affairs', June 1958.
90. PRO: CAB 130/139, 'External Economic Aims,' Treasury memorandum prepared for the Future Policy Working Group, 12 January 1958. This memorandum states that maintaining the value of sterling is a 'matter of life and death to us as a country.' See also PRO: T225/1222, jkt on 'Defence Expenditure and Overseas Policy,' beginning 1 January 1956 and ending 22 March 1960.
91. PRO: CAB 130/153, Cabinet meetings on the Future Policy Cabinet Committee report 'The Position of the United Kingdom in World Affairs,' 9 June 1958, 7 July 1958.
92. PRO: FO 371/143702–143709, Cabinet Committee on 'Future Policy 1960–1970'.
93. Darby, p. 143.
94. PRO: FO 371/143706, draft of the working group's final report, 'Future Policy 1960–1970', September 1959, emphasis in original.
95. Carver, *Out of Step*, p. 288. Also, see PRO: FO 371/143705, R.W.B. Clarke, Treasury, to Patrick Dean, 15 August 1959 on the great difficulty participants had in trying to ascertain what theatre Britain should emphasize in the future.
96. Darby, p. 144; Carver, *Out of Step*, p. 289.
97. Darby, p. 144.
98. V. Bogdanor and R. Skidelsky, 'Introduction' to V. Bogdanor and R. Skidelsky, *The Age of Affluence: 1951–1964* (New York: Macmillan, 1970), pp. 10, 15.
99. Sampson, p. 133; Turner, pp. 137, 146.
100. Bogdanor and Skidelsky, p. 11.
101. Wallace, 'World Status', pp. 213, 219.
102. PRO: CAB 134/2340, 'United Kingdom's Interest in the Middle East', 15 June 1957.
103. Ibid.

104. Singh, pp. 193–226.
105. Senior Treasury mandarins argued that the view that some lower officials were pressing, that overseas military expenditures stifled exports, was overly simplistic. They claimed that wide qualitative judgements were necessary to determine the relationship between defence spending and exports, and this rendered such calculations too vague to be of value. See PRO: T 225/1087, notes from J.M. Forsyth, Principal, Overseas Finance and Planning Division, Treasury, to A.H. Ross, Assistant Under-Secretary, Foreign Office, 19 July 1959; and C.W. Fogarty, Principal, Treasury, to J.M. Forsyth, 21 July 1959. For a broad sample of documents which illustrate that while the Treasury was concerned with the excessive costs of defence spending, they did not specifically call for reductions in Britain's overseas commitments, see PRO: T 225/831, 'The Future Size and Shape of the Armed Forces'. In addition, examine PRO: T 225/1087, note from D.R. Serpell, Deputy Under-Secretary at the Treasury, to A. Fraser, also of the Treasury, 29 April 1959. In this note, Serpell states that the Treasury should continue to push for more overseas economies, but 'this does not necessarily mean that proposals for overseas military expenditure ought to be treated more severely than proposals for the same sources of expenditure at home – that would be short-sighted indeed.'
106. PRO: T 225/1087, D.R. Serpell, Deputy Under-Secretary at the Treasury, to A.W. France, also of the Treasury, 2 October 1959.
107. Epstein, *Suez*, p. 200.
108. Darby, pp. 203–8; Dockrill, *British Defence*, p. 78.
109. See Darwin, p. 222.
110. *Chicago Tribune*, 25 May 1995, Sec. B, p. 10 (Harold Wilson Obituary).

6 SETTING THE STAGE: LONGER-TERM IMPLICATIONS OF SUEZ

1. Morgan, *People's Peace*, p. 210.
2. Rosecrance, *Defence of the Realm*, p. 6, and Sanders, p. 89, provide concise examples of the turning point that the Suez episode represented in British foreign policy and the frustration and disillusionment that it engendered.
3. Armstrong, pp. 234–6.
4. It should be noted that General Glubb was dismissed from his command over the Jordanian Arab Legion around this time as well. Although this was done before the Suez crisis, in early 1956, it was still motivated by Arab nationalist sentiment. The Jordanian Arab Legion was largely officered and financed by Britain and hence it was a potent source of British influence. See Reynolds, p. 203.
5. Bartlett, *Long Retreat*, p. 127.
6. Darby, p. 280.
7. Carver, *Tightrope*, pp. 54–5.
8. Armstrong, p. 190.

9. A.P. Thornton, *The Imperial Idea and Its Enemies* (London: Macmillan, 1959), p. 334.
10. Reynolds, p. 231.
11. Darby, p. 330.
12. Ibid., p. 329.
13. Dockrill, *British Defence*, pp. 68, 81.
14. See H. Sprout and M. Sprout, 'The Dilemma of Rising Demands and Insufficient Resources', *World Politics*, Vol. 20 (1968), pp. 660–93.
15. Darby, p. 327.
16. Brown, p. 30.
17. Ibid., p. 14.
18. Huntington, 'Lippmann Gap', p. 477. In a classic study of overextension, Walter Lippmann argues that the United States began to suffer overstretch as soon as the nation began to meddle consistently in Latin American affairs in the early twentieth century. W. Lippmann, *US Foreign Policy: Shield of the Republic* (Boston: Little, Brown, 1943). Also, on American overstretch after 1945, see J. Lepgold, *The Declining Hegemon: The United States and European Defense, 1960–1990* (New York: Praeger, 1990), p. 61.
19. P. Hennessy, *Whitehall* (New York: Free Press, 1989), pp. 171–5.
20. Carver, *Tightrope*, p. 68; Johnson, *Defence by Ministry*, pp. 116, 124.
21. Dockrill, *British Defence*, p. 88.
22. Hennessy, 'Whitehall Model', p. 299.
23. Prime Minister, *Central Organization for Defence*, Cmnd. 2097 (1963), p. 1. For reasons of simplicity, the Secretary of State for Defence will still be called the Defence Minister in the remainder of this work, despite the change in official title.
24. Johnson, *Defence by Ministry*, pp. 118–20; Hennessy, *Whitehall*, p. 417.
25. F.M.G. Willson, *The Organization of British Central Government* (London: Allen and Unwin, 1968), p. 387.
26. Johnson, *Defence by Ministry*, p. 102.
27. Dockrill, *British Defence*, p. 89.
28. Bartlett, *Long Retreat*, p. 191.
29. Hennessy, 'Whitehall Model', p. 299.
30. Lord Plowden, *Report of the Committee on Representational Services Overseas*, Cmnd. 2276 (1964).
31. Reynolds, p. 46.
32. One observer at this time, Michael Howard, presciently grasps the importance of this institutional consolidation. He states that there was a '...total absence, within the loose confederation of ministries responsible for defence and overseas policy, of any machinery capable of formulating such a [limited retrenchment] policy effectively even if it had been required. No such excuses can any longer be made. Mr. Peter Thorneycroft and Lord Mountbatten have provided the necessary machinery, and Mr. Healey has the will and ability to use it.' M. Howard, 'Britain's Strategic Problem East of Suez', *International Affairs*, Vol. 42 (1966), p. 181.
33. Questions on the utility of static overseas bases had been slowly growing since the late 1940s. A notable juncture in this regard was the 1952

Defence Policy and Global Strategy Paper, discussed in Chapter 2. But a dramatic shift in British strategy on overseas bases took place only after the shock of Suez.
34. Holland, *Pursuit of Greatness*, p. 325.
35. See Darby, p. 243.
36. See Armstrong; Howard.
37. Bartlett, *Long Retreat*, p. 137.
38. Darby, p. 248.
39. Ibid., p. 276.
40. Armstrong, pp. 36, 187, 219, 334; Garnett, p. 168.
41. Armstrong, p. 83.
42. See R. Jervis, *Perception and Misperception in World Politics* (Princeton: Princeton University Press, 1976).
43. See Holland, *Pursuit of Greatness*, pp. 329, 337.
44. Brown, p. 39.
45. Sir B. Liddell Hart, *Deterrent or Defence* (New York: Praeger, 1960).
46. Bartlett, *Long Retreat*, p.164; Darby, pp. 164, 212.
47. Darby, p. 222.
48. Bartlett, *Long Retreat*, p. 226.
49. Holland, *Pursuit of Greatness*, p. 325. Referring to the cultural changes often termed the 'permissive society,' Kenneth Morgan states that 'Britain certainly changed in spectacular fashion, visually and morally, during the mid–1960s...It made a curious backdrop to Harold Wilson's reply of Victorian values and his attempt to revive an older patriotism in defence of the pound and an iron Britannia.' See Morgan, *People's Peace*, pp. 235, 259. For a perceptive analysis of the tenuous relationship between the national mood and formal politics during the first Wilson governments, see D. Walker, 'The First Wilson Governments, 1964–1970', in P. Hennessy and A. Seldon (eds), *Ruling Performance: British Governments from Attlee to Thatcher* (New York: Basil Blackwell, 1987), pp. 186–215.
50. Bartlett, *Long Retreat*, p. 216.
51. A.F. Havighurst, *Britain in Transition* (Chicago: University of Chicago Press, 1979), p. 523.
52. Bartlett, *Long Retreat*, pp. 217–19; D.C. Watt, 'The Decision to Withdraw from the Gulf', *Political Quarterly*, Vol. 39 (1968), pp. 311–18.
53. Ibid.
54. Darwin, pp. 289–91. Patrick Gordon Walker, Foreign Secretary until 1965, confirms these general reasons for staying east of Suez. He contends, however, that American pressure, financial or otherwise, did not significantly impact the Cabinet at this time. The preponderance of the evidence available at this time seems to say that American financial influence was in fact important. P. Gordon Walker, *The Cabinet* (London: Fontana, 1972), p. 123.
55. Keohane, p. 4.
56. Holland, *Pursuit of Greatness*, p. 332; Carver, *Tightrope*, p. 76.
57. The Minister of Economic Affairs was the title given for the minister heading the newly created Department of Economic Affairs, which was planned to be an institutional rival to the Treasury.

58. Others have used the term 'Bevinite' similarly, see in particular: Darwin, p. 290; Reynolds, p. 230; and Holland, *Pursuit of Greatness*, p. 332.
59. Sked and Cook, p. 201.
60. P. Foot, *The Politics of Harold Wilson* (London: Penguin, 1968), p. 302.
61. R.W. James, *Ambitions and Realities: British Politics 1964–70* (London: Weidenfeld and Nicolson, 1972), p. 22; Walker, p. 187.
62. Cairncross and Eichengreen, p. 166.
63. C. Wrigley, 'Now You See It, Now You Don't: Harold Wilson and Labour's Foreign Policy 1964–1970', in R. Coopey, S. Fielding, and N. Tiratsoo (eds), *The Wilson Governments 1964–1970* (New York: Pinter, 1993), p. 130.
64. Brown, p. 27.
65. Foot, *Wilson*, p. 24.
66. The phrase is Ben Pimlott's. See B. Pimlott, *Harold Wilson* (London: Harper Collins, 1992), p. 284.
67. D. Healey, *Time of My Life* (London: Michael Joseph, 1989), p. 330.
68. Pimlott, *Wilson*, p. 521.
69. George Brown made this claim in 1968 when he resigned as Foreign Minister. Barbara Castle and Richard Crossman, two Wilson allies, felt it to be a particularly damning accusation because 'everybody knows it is near the bone.' See B. Castle, *The Castle Diaries* (London: Weidenfeld and Nicolson, 1984), p. 202.

 Yet, it may have been because he lacked an authoritative persona in the Cabinet that Wilson became adroit in keeping issues from that body. Although the evidence is incomplete, it seems that Wilson suffered through verbal barrages in Cabinet which would have been unimaginable for his post–1945 predecessors, particularly after his confidence and his popularity began to ebb. See, for example, R. Jenkins, *A Life at the Center* (New York: Random House, 1991), p. 212.
70. *HC Debates*, vol. 704, cols. 423–4.
71. Ibid., cols. 425–6.
72. Holland, *Pursuit of Greatness*, p. 330.
73. Darby, p. 288.
74. Rosecrance, *Defence of the Realm*, p. 251.
75. Darby, p. 298.
76. This notion was not new. The 1965 Defence White Paper pledged much the same thing – not to maintain facilities in a country against its the government's wishes. Denis Healey later explained that the 1966 White Paper went further by implicitly stating that Britain would not remain in areas where the indigenous population opposed the UK's presence.
77. See Ovendale, pp. 136–41.
78. See Darwin, p. 290.
79. Gordon Walker, p. 122; Wrigley, p. 131.
80. Hennessy, *Cabinet*, p. 190.
81. Healey, p. 326. Debate exists on whether and how far British Cabinet government has moved away from the ideal of collective government since 1945, toward either a ministerial government type of system or a more presidential-style system. Elements of all three of these idealtypes obviously coexist during any period of time, but greater emphasis

is given to one of the models depending both on the Prime Minister's governing style and various historical trends. Healey implies that, at least from the vantage of defense policymaking, the ministerial government view more accurately captures the decision-making process in the first Wilson government. He claims his Cabinet colleagues were 'content in the main to let me get on with my job, so long as I did not interfere with theirs.' He goes on to say that the Prime Minister interfered in defense policy-making only during crisis situations, and even then Wilson was not excessively intrusive in this area of policy. See Healey, pp. 326, 331.

82. Gordon, p. 268.
83. Pimlott, *Wilson*, p. 329.
84. Ibid.
85. Walker, p. 187; H. Wilson, *The Labour Government 1964–1970* (London: Weidenfeld and Nicolson, 1971), p. 470.
86. Sked and Cook, p. 209.
87. Watt, 'Decision to Withdraw', p. 317.
88. Charmley, p. 187.
89. James, *Ambitions*, p. 180.
90. Ibid.
91. L. Johnman, 'The Conservative Party in Opposition, 1964–70', in R. Coopey, S. Fielding, and N. Tiratsoo (eds), *The Wilson Governments 1964–1970* (New York: Pinter, 1993), pp. 197–9.
92. Confidential information. Interview, high ranking MoD mandarin during the 1960s. See also Chapter 5.
93. Darby, p. 283; Ovendale, p. 14.
94. Carver, *Tightrope*, p. 76.
95. See Catterall, 'East of Suez', passim.
96. Carver, *Tightrope*, p. 65.
97. G.K. Tanham, 'A United States View', *International Affairs*, Vol. 42 (1966), pp. 194–206.
98. Catterall, 'East of Suez', p. 625.
99. Pimlott, *Wilson*, p. 383; Holland, *Pursuit of Greatness*, p. 324.
100. C. Ponting, *Breach of Promise* (London: Hamilton, 1989), pp. 43–55.
101. Darby, p. 296.
102. Wilson, pp. 187, 264; Gordon Walker, p. 124.
103. B. Lapping, *The Labour Government 1964–1970* (Harmondsworth: Penguin, 1970), pp. 86–9.
104. Crossman, *Diaries*, Vol. 2, p. 418.
105. Pimlott, *Wilson*, p. 384. See also Morgan, *People's Peace*, p. 269.
106. The phrase 'light of political day' is Darby's, p. 329.

7 RELINQUISHING WORLD POWER: BRITAIN'S FINANCIAL CRISES OF 1966–7

1. James, *Ambitions*, p. 27.
2. J. Callaghan, *Time and Chance* (London: Collins, 1987), p. 223.

3. Pimlott, *Wilson*, p. 404; F.T. Blackaby, 'Narrative 1960–74', in F.T. Blackaby (ed.), *British Economic Policy 1960–1974* (New York: Cambridge University Press, 1979), pp. 28–37. Contrary to what was commonly thought at the time, the underlying weakness of sterling was not caused by balance of payments deficits. At the time of the July 1966 financial crisis there was a small current account surplus for the year of £84 million. Sterling's dilemma was a result of the perception in the financial markets that Britain's economy was uncompetitive. See Blackaby, p. 37.
4. See H. Brandon, *In the Red: The Struggle for Sterling 1964–66* (Boston: Houghton Mifflin, 1967).
5. Cairncross and Eichengreen, p. 181.
6. Crossman, *Diaries*, Vol. 1, p. 332.
7. R. Opie, 'Economic Planning and Growth', in W. Beckerman (ed.), *The Labour Government's Economic Record 1964–1970* (London: Duckworth, 1972), p. 177.
8. Pimlott, *Wilson*, p. 429; Havighurst, p. 519.
9. Crossman, *Diaries*, Vol. 1, p. 587. See also Castle, p. 152; T. Benn, *Out of the Wilderness: Diaries, 1963–1967* (London: Hutchinson, 1987), p. 466.
10. P. Ziegler, *Wilson: The Authorized Life of Lord Wilson of Rievaulx* (London: Weidenfeld and Nicolson, 1993), p. 256.
11. Benn, *Wilderness*, p. 296.
12. Ibid., pp. 464, 496.
13. Reynolds, p. 232.
14. Foot, *Wilson*, p. 222.
15. Morgan, *People's Peace*, p. 272.
16. Pimlott, *Wilson*, p. 436; Ziegler, p. 260.
17. S. George, *Britain and European Integration* (Oxford: Basil Blackwell, 1991), p. 45; Sked and Cook, p. 236.
18. Gordon Walker, p. 129.
19. See especially R.G. Hepburn, 'Defence Policy and Parliament 1964 to 1968', M.Litt. Dissertation, Department of Strategic Studies (Aberdeen: University of Aberdeen, 1974), pp. 44–80.
20. *HC Debates*, vol. 725, col. 1805.
21. Wilson, pp. 377–8; D. Childs, *Britain since 1945* (New York: St. Martin's Press, 1979), p. 195.
22. *The Times*, 3 March 1967. See also Castle, p. 232; Benn, *Wilderness*, p. 490.
23. Darby, p. 314. This type of reaction was not altogether new in Labour Party Conferences in the late 1960s. Although it was not as animated as the 1966 Party Conference, 77 left-wing MPs succeeded in getting a resolution calling for drastic defense reductions passed at the 1965 conference. The resolution drew particular attention to the 'heavy burden of the national income involved in...outmoded bases abroad.' See Darby, p. 291.
24. Pimlott, *Wilson*, p. 393. It was only later, after the decision to retrench had been taken, that anti-Vietnam protests within the Labour movement had any serious impact on the government.
25. Ziegler, p. 254.

26. Darby, p. 315.
27. Hepburn, p. 40.
28. Wilson, p. 297.
29. Gordon Walker, p. 26. The question of the benefits that Britain accrued from the east of Suez role relative to other advanced industrial countries was an important one. For instance, John K. Wright, the MoD's Chief Economist in the late 1960s, claims that the main pressure that the government was under at the time 'was the argument over benefits – which became more and more difficult to sustain.' Quoted in Catterall, 'East of Suez', p. 628.
30. Darby, p. 319; Carver *Tightrope*, p. 81.
31. Carver, *Tightrope*, p. 81.
32. Ministry of Defence, *Supplemental Statement on Defence Policy 1967*, Cmnd. 3357.
33. Bartlett, *Long Retreat*, p. 221.
34. MoD, Cmnd. 3357, p. 12.
35. Darby, p. 320.
36. Catterall, 'East of Suez', p. 613, emphasis in original.
37. Brown, p. 157.
38. *HC Debates*, vol. 751, col. 1044.
39. Carver, *Tightrope*, p. 83.
40. Darby, p. 321; Hepburn, p. 67.
41. Most analysts of Britain's east of Suez policy agree that the writing was not, so to speak, on the wall for Britain's east of Suez role after the July 1967 Supplemental White Paper. See in particular Darby; Dockrill; Greenwood, *The 'East of Suez' Decision*; and also Greenwood's lengthy comments in Catterall, 'East of Suez'.
42. Gordon Walker, p. 129.
43. W. Beckerman, 'Objectives and Performance', in W. Beckerman (ed.), *The Labour Government's Economic Record: 1964–1970* (London: Duckworth, 1972), p. 62; Pimlott, *Wilson*, p. 466.
44. L. Stone, 'Britain and the World', in D. McKie and C. Cook (eds), *The Decade of Disillusion: British Politics in the 1960s* (New York: St. Martin's Press, 1972), p. 132.
45. L. Pliatzky, *Getting and Spending* (Oxford: Basil Blackwell, 1982), p. 86.
46. Foot, *Wilson*, p. 168.
47. Morgan, *People's Peace*, p. 274.
48. M. Stewart, *The Jekyll and Hyde Years: Politics and Economic Policy since 1964* (London: André Deutsch, 1977), p. 82.
49. Wilson, pp. 451–4; Gordon Walker, p. 129.
50. Blackaby, p. 44; Ziegler, p. 284.
51. Bartlett, *Long Retreat*, p. 223.
52. Darby, p. 322.
53. See Crossman, *Diaries*, Vol. 2, pp. 564, 657; Healey, p. 336; Pimlott, *Wilson*, p. 483.
54. Childs, p. 193; A. Morgan, *Harold Wilson* (London: Pluto, 1992), p. 315.
55. P. Worsthorne, *Sunday Telegraph*, 21 January 1968, cited in Pimlott, *Wilson*, p. 484.

56. On the Prime Minister's relative docility in Cabinet meetings following devaluation, particularly those dealing with the abandonment of Britain's military commitments in the Middle and Far East, see in particular Jenkins, pp. 212, 216, and T. Benn, *Office Without Power: Diaries 1968–1972* (London: Hutchinson, 1988), p. 13. Denis Healey implicitly makes the same point when contending that Wilson was very much a prime minister 'in trouble' after devaluation. See Healey, pp. 338, 344. Richard Crossman, on the other hand, maintains that Wilson recovered fairly quickly from the clout he had received from devaluation, emphasizing the Prime Minister's 'resilience, his bounce, his india-rubber quality which are a tremendous strength.' But in nearly the same breath, Crossman records Wilson's rapidly depreciating influence in Cabinet, noting that 'Prime Ministerial government is out for the moment.' 'Six months ago he would take the voices [in Cabinet] and interpret the voices as he liked,' but now, the Lord President emphasized '... the Prime Minister was being hoist in his own petard by having to count the votes each time.' See Crossman, *Diaries*, Vol. 2, pp. 592, 628, 640, 650. In his own account, Wilson consciously refrains from 'drawing back the veil' which covers Cabinet deliberations, but he nevertheless admits that he was compelled to count heads in Cabinet during the post-devaluation debates over spending cuts, intimating that such an act was only undertaken because of his considerably weakened power base. And, as one would expect, Wilson does not provide insight on the impact that devaluation had on him personally in his memoirs, but he does acknowledge that it was a 'drastic and distasteful step' as well as a 'shock to morale, and to Cabinet cohesion'. See Wilson, pp. 458, 473, 480–1.
57. See Morgan, *People's Peace*, p. 275; Ziegler, p. 282.
58. Sked and Cook, p. 225.
59. Crossman, *Diaries*, Vol. 1, pp. 462–3.
60. Pimlott, *Wilson*, p. 489.
61. Ibid.
62. See ibid.; Crossman, *Diaries*, Vol. 2, pp. 592, 614.
63. J. Campbell, *Roy Jenkins, A Biography* (New York: St. Martin's Press, 1983), p. 111.
64. Crossman, *Diaries*, Vol. 2, p. 639.
65. Jenkins, p. 207.
66. See Campbell; Jenkins; Crossman, *Diaries*, Vol. 2, p. 639.
67. A number of recent studies of foreign policy change have focused on the centrality of individuals or small groups in redirecting policy during particularly fluid moments in history. See in particular Ikenberry; Checkel; P.M. Haas, 'Epistemic Communities and International Policy Coordination', *International Organization*, Vol. 46 (1992), pp. 1–36; J.G. Stein, 'Political Learning by Doing: Gorbachev as an Uncommitted Thinker and Motivated Learner', *International Organization*, Vol. 48 (1994), pp. 155–83. For more detail on the concept of 'policy entrepreneur,' see especially D.B. Robertson, 'Policy Entrepreneurs and Policy Divergence', *Social Science Review*, Vol. 11 (1988), pp. 504–31 and M. Evangelista, 'Sources of Moderation in Soviet Security Policy', in P.E. Tetlock and R. Jervis (eds), *Behavior, Society, and Nuclear War* (New

York: Oxford University Press, 1991), pp. 254–354. On the concept of 'policy window,' see J.W. Kingdon, *Agendas, Alternatives, and Public Policies* (Boston: Little, Brown, 1984).

Also, such entrepreneurs were important in earlier cases of British strategic adjustment. Aaron Friedberg accords much significance to policy entrepreneurs in his study of British decline and adjustment from 1895 to 1905. He labels such actors 'change agents,' which he defines as 'middle- and upper-level officials whose views begin to deviate from the norm and who are able to receive a wider hearing only at moments of intense crisis.' See Friedberg, p. 18.

On Roy Jenkins' unique position in Wilson's post-devaluation Cabinet, see in particular Campbell, p. 111; Darwin, p. 293; Morgan, *Wilson*, pp. 310–42; Pimlott, *Wilson*, pp. 466–92; and Ziegler, pp. 262–86.

68. Jenkins, p. 209.
69. Darby, p. 323.
70. Jenkins, p. 209.
71. James, *Ambitions*, p. 45.
72. Foot, *Wilson*, p 195; Morgan, *Wilson*, p. 310.
73. Crossman, *Diaries*, Vol. 2, p. 619.
74. Benn, *Office Without Power*, p. 13.
75. Jenkins, p. 214; Reynolds, p. 230. While noting the importance of ministers loyal to the Prime Minister (which he termed 'Haroldites') in the post-devaluation cuts, Richard Crossman, in a less than magnanimous mood, exalted in the fact that the 'four pygmies...who had been running our foreign policy for the last three years' – Stewart, Brown, Callaghan, and Healey – had finally been overridden in Cabinet. See Crossman, *Diaries*, Vol. 2, p. 635.
76. As the Prime Minister himself acknowledged. Wilson, p. 479.
77. Jenkins, p. 213.
78. Crossman, *Diaries*, Vol. 2, pp. 646–7; Morgan, *Wilson*, p. 344.
79. Ovendale, p. 14; Catterall, 'East of Suez', p. 638.
80. Carver, *Tightrope*, p. 84.
81. Sir Ewen Broadbent, Denis Healey's Principal Private Secretary from 1967 to 1969, claims that devaluation was a real symbol in Defence Minister's mind, and that it began the 'switch in his mind towards Europe.' Sir Frank Cooper, Deputy Under- Secretary at the MoD at the time, concurs. He claims that Healey's sudden conversion to a pro-Europe stance had much to do with the special relationship with the US, and with the US Defense Secretary in particular: 'Part of it was his relationship with McNamara and how they had a sort of two men on the European stage act and the rest are bit-players; he loved that.' See Catterall, 'East of Suez', pp. 642, 636.
82. Healey, p. 335; Jenkins, p. 211.
83. Reynolds, p. 231.
84. Ibid.
85. Watt, *Succeeding John Bull*, p. 149; Ziegler, p. 285.
86. Wilson papers, box 72, Wilson to Johnson, 15 January 1968, Lyndon Johnson Library. Cited in Ziegler, p. 285.

87. Crossman, *Diaries*, Vol. 2, p. 639.
88. See T.J. McKeown, 'The Foreign Policy of a Declining Power', *International Organization*, Vol. 45 (1991), pp. 257–79.

8 CONCLUSIONS: POLITICS, HISTORY, AND THE EAST OF SUEZ DECISION

1. Gordon Walker, p. 134.
2. Sked and Cook, p. 233.
3. *United Nations Statistical Yearbook* (New York: United Nations, 1970), pp. 557–62.
4. Sked and Cook, p. 234.
5. Stinchcombe, pp. 101–29.
6. See B.A. Most and H.A. Starr, *Inquiry, Logic, and International Politics* (Columbia: University of South Carolina Press, 1989).
7. See, for example, Darby; Harries-Jenkins; Powell; Garnett.
8. Darby, p. 222.
9. See Cain and Hopkins, p. 311.
10. See Wilson; Jenkins; Gordon Walker; and Catterall, 'East of Suez'.
11. Reynolds, p. 8.
12. Snyder, *British Defense*, p. 75.
13. Charles Ragin, among others, notes that determining the configuration of causes behind a particular event rests at the heart of understanding in the social sciences. This work ascertains the factors which caused the east of Suez decision and places them in a logical analytical framework. See Ragin, *Constructing Social Research*.
14. Holsti, pp. 194–5.
15. Gordon Walker, p. 132.
16. Among others, G.J. Ikenberry and Charles Hermann have begun to recognize this point. See Ikenberry, pp. 223–6; Hermann, 'Reflections', p. 256.
17. See Ikenberry, p. 225.
18. See especially Risse-Kappen, p. 187.
19. On this point, see especially Hermann, 'Reflections', pp. 252–3; C. Tilly, *Big Structures, Large Processes, Huge Comparisons* (New York: Russell Sage, 1984), p. 79.
20. Singh, p. 49.
21. Kennedy, *Rise and Fall*, pp. 424–8.
22. Checkel, pp. 291–4; Stein, pp. 155–83.
23. Evangelista, pp. 254–354.
24. See Russett, p. 15; McKeown, pp. 257–79; P. Kennedy, 'American Grand Strategy: Learning from European Experience', in P. Kennedy (ed.), *Grand Strategies in War and Peace* (New Haven: Yale University Press, 1991), pp. 167–84.
25. All three countries have more insulated and autonomous foreign policy apparatuses than the US. On the British and American cases in particular, see Steiner.

Index

Acheson, Dean 157
Aden 4, 121, 130, 142
Afghanistan 191
Africa 4, 7, 9, 44, 46, 56, 57, 67, 68, 86, 90, 117, 120, 148, 164, 190–1
Alanbrooke, Viscount 67
Alaska 47
Aldabra 164
Aleutian Islands 47
Alexander, Albert Victor 67
Algeria 190–1
Amery, Julian 94
Amory, Sir Derick Heathcoat 111
Arab-Israeli War
 1948–9 50
 1967 160, 163
Armstrong, DeWitt 4, 31, 121, 131
Army, British 53, 103, 127, 130
Articulate public
 defined 34
 see also east of Suez winning coalition
Attlee, Clement 48, 50, 53, 74, 77, 79, 98, 102, 127, 168, 179, 182
 and attempted palace coup 81
 and Cabinet government 28, 61–5, 81–3
 challenge to the overseas military role 44, 59, 65–73, 86–7, 185
 declining political clout 71, 81–2
 election of 1945 67
 foreign policy views 65–6
 relationship with Bevin 28, 63–5, 72, 81
 see also Labour government(s) 1945–51
Australia 30, 52, 68, 86, 127, 147, 158

Bahrain 5
Ball, George 157
Bartlett, C.J. 7, 133
Benn, Tony 143, 153–4, 170

Berlin, 1948 blockade of 76, 84
Bermuda 95, 105
Bevan, Aneurin 62, 72, 92
Bevin, Ernest 37, 49, 56, 62, 67, 74, 76, 77, 79, 85
 and creation of NATO 82, 83–4
 attitude toward Soviet Union 46, 69
 disagreement with Attlee over east of Suez 67–71
 relationship with Attlee 28, 63–5, 72, 81
Bevinites 137, 156, 158, 165, 168, 174–5
Bishop, Frederick 100
Bogdanor, Vernon 114
Boothby, Robert 49
Borneo 4, 136, 150
Boulding, Kenneth 39
Bounded causes 25, 29, 41, 178–9, 187–8, 190, 193
Brenner, Michael 38
Brezhnev, Leonid 191
British Empire 3, 8, 12, 20, 37, 43, 46, 55, 56, 57, 66, 122
British foreign policy institutions
 fragmentation 44, 52–4, 109, 179
 insularity 12, 23, 28
 postwar exhaustion 54
 reorganization 41, 88, 118, 124–9, 186–7
British Honduras 10
Brook, Sir Norman 109, 110, 112
Brown, George 137, 142, 143–4, 154, 156, 158, 163, 168, 171
Brown, Neville 160
Bullock, Alan 64, 68, 70
Burma 55
Butler, R.A. 73, 93

Cabinet
 and British foreign policy 22–3, 27–8

Index

Cabinet (*contd*)
  see also East of Suez winning coalition, Cabinet politics *and* individual premiers
Cadogan, Sir Alexander 63
Callaghan, James 117, 137, 143–4, 151, 152, 156, 163, 164, 166–7, 168, 171
Campaign for Nuclear Disarmament 34
Campbell, John 168
Canada 52, 125, 127
Carlsnaes, Walter 35
Carver, Michael 113, 147
Castle, Barbara 143, 158, 168
Ceylon 4, 55, 117, 120
Chamberlain, Joseph 171
Chiefs of Staff, British 38, 46, 51, 53, 79, 106, 112–13, 126, 172, 186
  conflict with Attlee over the east of Suez role 67–72, 86, 185
China 3, 122
Churchill, Randolph 104
Churchill, Sir Winston 45, 48, 53, 66, 67, 72, 73, 90, 91, 92, 104, 125, 127
  and Attlee regime's foreign policy 77–8
Churchill government (1951–5) 37, 38, 93
Cobden, Richard 74
Colonial Office 12, 53, 109, 113, 127, 128, 186, 187
Committee on Defence and Overseas Policy 126
Common Market
  see European Economic Community (EEC)
Commonwealth 12, 55, 68, 80, 91, 116, 138, 147
Commonwealth Relations Office 12, 53, 107, 109, 127, 128, 146–7, 171–3, 186
Conservative Government(s) 1957–63
  and Anglo-American relations 90, 96, 103, 110, 112, 114–15

  and British press 103, 109–10, 125, 133
  and economy 88, 96, 97–8, 101, 111–13, 114–15, 118
  and election of 1959 98
  and 'guns versus butter' debate 98–103
  and nuclear weapons 94–5, 103–5, 107–8
  and popularity 92, 98, 118, 135
  and 'secret' reviews of Britain's global role (1957–60) 89, 108–16, 129, 184
  and shadow of Suez crisis 92
Conservative Party 91, 138, 162, 163
  and Attlee regime's foreign policy 73–4, 77–8
  and Macmillan government 94, 103–4
  and Wilson regime's foreign policy 139, 144–6, 161, 183
  morale after the Suez crisis 92
Constant causes 25, 41, 178, 187
Convertibility crisis of 1947 78, 80
Cook, Chris 137, 177
Cousins, Frank 151
Crimean War 7
Cripps, Sir Stafford 62, 81, 82, 83, 138
Crosland, Anthony 115, 142, 168
Crossman, Richard 17, 75, 76, 102, 122, 143, 149, 152, 153, 158, 167–8, 170, 174
Curzon, George Nathaniel 171
Cyprus 52, 104, 122
Czechoslovakia 13, 76, 84

Dalton, Hugh 62, 67, 68, 69, 72, 74, 79, 81, 82
Darby, Phillip 5, 16, 55, 107, 123, 141
Dardanelles 46
Dean, Sir Patrick 109, 112
Defence Committee 53, 68, 69, 72, 126
Defence and Overseas Policy Committee 158
Defence Policy and Global Strategy Paper (1952) 38–9

Defence White Papers
  1946 52, 58
  1947, 1948 52
  1955 99–100
  1957 (Sandys Doctrine) 89, 103–7, 111, 114, 130
  1965 140
  1966 140–2
  1967 155, 157
  1967 – Supplemental Defence White Paper 159–62, 163
de Gaulle, Charles 155, 191
Department of Economic Affairs 144, 154, 168
Devaluation, British
  1949 138
  1967 28, 148, 152, 156–7, 162–4, 165, 188
Diego Garcia 4, 148
Dockrill, Michael 18
Dominions Office 52, 53, 127
Douglas-Home, Sir Alec 135, 146
Dulles, John Foster 95

East of Suez debate 119, 132–5, 136, 142, 144, 150
East of Suez decision
  and British relative decline 18–21, 177–80
  significance for post-1945 Britain 10, 17, 174, 177
East of Suez role
  and Britain's 'world role' 5, 139
  assumption that bases are inherently valuable 5, 31–2, 129–32, 185
  significance for post-1945 Britain 1, 2–6, 10, 17, 174
East of Suez winning coalition
  and Cabinet politics 23–4, 27, 28, 29, 174–6, 180, 187
  and crises 22, 24–5, 26, 174–6, 178–80, 187–90
  and elite opinion: ministerial opinion 26, 32, 33, 181–2; mandarin opinion 26, 32, 33, 184–5; parliamentary opinion 26, 32, 33–4, 182–4, 187–8; articulate public opinion 26, 32, 34, 183–4
  and institutional change 25, 27, 35, 40, 185–7
  and patron-client diplomatic relationship 26, 29–30, 181
  and relative economic decline 15–16, 18–19, 22, 24–5, 26, 177–80, 181, 187, 189–90
  and strategic assumptions 25, 27, 31–2, 40, 41, 184–5, 187–8
  and B.M. Russett's triangular schema of executive pressures 23–7
Eden, Sir Anthony 66, 67, 73, 77–8, 90, 91, 93, 99, 108–9
Egypt 37, 68, 89, 90, 91, 94, 103, 105, 122, 129
Eisenhower, Dwight D. 90, 95, 103, 114
Eisenhower Doctrine 104–5
Elite theory 32
Epstein, Leon 94
European Economic Community (EEC) 118, 125, 151, 153–6, 162, 177
European integration 30, 85–6, 142, 146, 150, 164
Evangelista, Matthew 192

Falkland Islands 10
Far East 1, 3, 5, 13, 44, 50, 55, 58, 67, 68, 73, 103, 105, 113, 116, 134, 149, 158–60, 161, 164, 172
Foot, Michael 64, 75, 76, 78, 137
Foreign and Commonwealth Office 128
Foreign Office 12, 22, 45, 46, 52, 54, 60, 67, 72, 74, 83, 86, 93, 98, 101, 109, 113, 115, 116, 126, 127, 128, 138, 146, 158, 171–3, 185
Fowler, Joseph 156
France 8, 15, 21, 46, 84, 90, 95, 101, 177, 190–2
Franks, Sir Oliver 57

Gaitskell, Hugh 90
George, Alexander 39

Index

Germany, West 8, 15, 21, 46, 49, 72, 84, 85, 101, 110, 118, 134, 177
  as 'model' state 14–15
Gilpin, Robert 7, 20
Gorbachev, Mikhail 191–2
Greece 50, 52, 68, 70, 75, 79, 83, 179
Greenwood, David 160
Grimond, Joseph 144
Guns vs. butter debate 87, 100–2, 103

Harriman, W. Averell 83, 147–8
Harris, Kenneth 63
Hart, Sir Basil Liddell 68, 132, 183
Hartley, Keith 18
Head, Antony 93, 99–100
Healey, Denis 137, 143, 156, 157, 158, 164, 168, 171–2
Heath, Edward 145
Hennessy, Peter 57
Hermann, Charles 11
Hill, Charles 93
Historic causes 25, 41
Holland, Robert 47, 71, 129
Home Office 72, 93, 166
Hong Kong 4, 10, 101, 106, 170
Hooson, Emlyn 160
Horne, Alistair 104
Huntington, Samuel 123

Ikenberry, G. John 35
India 3–4, 36, 37, 43, 50, 54, 55, 56, 57, 58, 64, 68, 72, 80, 106, 119, 127, 179
Indian Army 3–4, 43, 55, 56, 57, 122
Indian Office 52, 53, 127
Indonesia 122, 136, 157
Iraq 5, 57, 104, 105, 117, 120
Iran 5, 46
Ireland 53
Ismay, Lord 125–6, 128
Israel 90
Italy 8, 14, 46, 67, 84

Jacob, General Sir Ian 125–6, 128
Japan 8, 14, 15, 19, 47, 120, 134, 177
  as 'model' state 14–15
Jenkins, Roy 142, 154, 158, 166–72, 174–5, 181, 182, 186
Johnson, Franklyn 126
Johnson, Lyndon B. 148, 153, 158, 173, 182
Joint Intelligence Committee 109, 112
Jordan 104, 105, 117, 120

Keep Left group 76, 78, 102
Kennan, George 83
Kennedy, John F. 139
Kennedy, Paul 6, 7, 18, 20, 192
Kenya 4, 68, 117, 121, 122
Keynes, John Maynard 48
Khrushchev, Nikita 114
Kilmuir, Lord 93
Kirkpatrick, Sir Ivone 101
Kitchener, Horatio 171
Korean War (1950–4) 55, 82, 84
Kupchan, Charles 13, 31
Kuwait 5, 10, 104, 130

Labour government(s) 1945–51
  and 'age of austerity' 83
  and Anglo-American relations 47–9, 50, 76, 82, 84
  and British press 78, 81
  and convertibility crisis of 1947 80, 179
  and devaluation 138
  and economy 43, 45, 49–50, 56–7, 71, 78–80, 83
  and election of 1945 67
  and European integration 85–6
  and popularity 79–80, 81
  cohesion of 61–3, 72–3
Labour government(s) 1964–70
  and Anglo-American relations 148–9, 150, 152, 172–3
  and Bevinites 137, 156, 158, 165, 168, 174–5, 181
  and British press 133, 145
  and devaluation 148, 152, 156–7, 162–4, 165, 169–70, 175
  and economy 140, 141, 150, 151–3, 162–4, 169

Labour government (*contd*)
  and east of Suez debate 119, 136, 142, 144
  and European integration 142, 150, 153–6, 161, 162, 164, 168
  and left-wing Cabinet members 143, 158, 168
  and loss of momentum 150, 153
  and parliamentary majority 136, 138, 151, 155
  and popularity 151, 153, 162
  and 1966 sterling crisis 151–3, 154, 156, 160, 161, 175
  and sterling's parity 138, 144, 148, 162–3
  and support for east of Suez role 119, 135–40, 142, 159–61, 181
  and 1966 election 151, 155
Labour movement 61, 63, 65, 73, 74–5, 77, 81, 136, 144, 156
Labour Party 45, 60, 61, 64, 65, 73, 75–7, 81, 86, 98, 102–3, 108, 110, 115, 124, 127, 137, 147, 149, 153, 156, 182
  and socialist foreign policy 44, 60, 74–5, 102
  left-wing of 62, 75–6, 137, 144
  see also Parliamentary Labour Party (PLP)
Latin America 7, 49
Leahy, Admiral William 47
Learning periods in post-1945 British foreign policy 36
Lebanon 105
Liberal Party 144, 160
Listowel, Lord 67
Lloyd, Selwyn 93
Longitudinal approach to foreign policy decision-making 39–41, 188–90
Louis, William Roger 58
Luce, Sir David 141

MacDonald, Ramsay 62
McMahon Act (1946) 48
McNamara, Robert 125, 157
Macmillan, Harold 52, 90, 91, 92, 98, 115, 135, 182
  and Anglo-American alliance 29, 95, 99
  and backbench support 94
  and Cabinet government 93–4, 96–7
  and defense cuts 96, 98–100, 103–7
  and defense of postwar consensus 96, 98
  and election of 1959 98
  and nuclear weapons 94–5, 99, 103–5
  and reorganization of defense apparatus 99, 109, 124–9
  and 'secret reviews' of Britain's global role 108–11, 114, 184
  see also Conservative Government(s) 1957–63
Malaya 50, 55
Malaysia 122, 147, 158–9, 164
Maldive Islands 4, 120
Marshall Plan 49, 81, 83–4
Matsu 106
Mayhew, Christopher 134, 141, 156
Meade, James 54
Mediterranean 44, 46, 50, 57, 58, 67, 69, 73, 83
Menzies, Robert 95
Middle East 5, 9, 13, 44, 48, 55, 56, 57, 58, 59, 66, 67, 68, 72, 75, 77, 78, 85, 86, 101, 103, 104, 105, 112, 113, 116, 120, 122, 134, 146, 158, 159, 174, 185
Mikardo, Ian 75
Ministry of Defence 18, 53, 99, 106, 109, 126, 158, 171–2, 174, 186
'Model' states 11, 14–15
Molotov, Vyacheslav 72
Monckton, Walter Sir 99
Monnet, Jean 85
Montgomery, Bernard, Viscount 9, 70
Morgan, Kenneth 61, 63, 81, 83
Morgan, Philip 17
Morrison, Herbert 62, 69, 81, 82
Mountbatten, Lord 124–6, 128
Mussolini, Benito 90

Index

National Economic Plan 140, 153, 165
Nationalism
  in east of Suez area 30, 41, 50, 88, 113, 117, 120–2, 133–4, 185
Neustadt, Richard 139
New Look program, Eisenhower administration 103
New Zealand 30, 52, 122, 127
Nigeria 163
North Atlantic Treaty Organization (NATO) 20, 82, 84, 181
Nuclear weapons 19, 44, 48, 66, 86, 98, 99, 102, 130, 133, 147, 148
  and post-1945 British defense strategy 5, 38, 51–2, 94–5, 103–5, 107, 130, 139–40

Official Committee on the Middle East 105
Oil
  importance of Middle Eastern 4, 56, 105, 134, 136, 146, 158, 163
Oman 104
Overextension, strategic
  and retrenchment 10, 12, 15–17
  British 7–9, 122–3, 134, 140
  causes 11–15
  consequences 6–7

Pakistan 80, 106
Palestine 50, 70, 79, 80, 84, 179
Paris Peace Conference (1946) 70, 71
Parliamentary Labour Party (PLP) 61, 64, 73, 81, 136, 153
  and Attlee government's foreign policy 75–6, 182
  and Macmillan government's foreign policy 102–3, 108, 110, 115, 127, 182, 183
  and Wilson government's foreign policy 137, 144, 147, 149, 152, 155–6, 157, 159, 161, 182
  changing character 76–7
  left-wing of 62, 75–6, 136, 137, 144, 182

  see also Labour Party *and* Labour movement
Persian Gulf 3, 30, 57, 69, 105, 116, 122, 142, 158, 159, 172, 177
Phillips, Morgan 77
Philippines 47
Pimlott, Ben 143, 149, 167
Plowden Report (1964) 127, 147, 186
Policy entrepreneur 169, 171
Pompidou, Georges 151
Port Said 89
Potsdam conference 45, 47, 63, 66, 67
Powell, Enoch 134, 144–6, 161, 183

Quemoy 106

Red Sea 3, 57
Retrenchment
  and overextension 10, 12, 15–7
  British, *see* East of Suez decision *and* East of Suez winning coalition
  defined 1, 10–11
Reynolds, David 91
Rhodesia 148
Rose, Richard 11
Rosecrance, Richard 14
Royal Institute of International Affairs 34, 109
Royal Air Force (RAF) 53, 100, 103, 127
Royal Navy 53, 55, 100, 106, 127, 141
Rusk, Dean 153, 157
Russett, Bruce 23–4, 192

Sampson, Anthony 95, 97
Sandys, Duncan 100, 103, 105–7, 111, 114, 124, 125, 130, 177, 185
Sargent, Orme Sir 60, 61
Saudi Arabia 5, 122
Second World War
  impact on Britain 8–9, 43, 48
'Secret' reviews of Britain's global role (1957–60) 89, 108–16, 129, 184
Seychelles 4

Shinwell, Emanuel 72, 82
Sinai Peninsula 89
Singapore 4, 30, 106, 122, 130, 147, 158–9, 164, 172, 177
Sked, Alan 137, 177
Skidelsky, Robert 114
South Africa 53, 127
Sterling crises of the late 1960s 36, 37, 41, 97, 180, 181, 183, 184, 188
  1966 151–2, 154, 156, 160, 161, 167, 175
  1967 163–4, 175
Stewart, Michael 137, 168, 171
Stinchcombe, Arthur 25, 40
Strang, Sir William 54
Strategic culture 11, 13–14, 31
Strategic assumptions
  defined 31
  see also east of Suez winning coalition, strategic assumptions
Soviet Union 4, 9, 13, 14, 15, 19, 37, 48, 58, 59, 60, 83, 95, 104, 105, 112, 114–15, 122, 138, 191–2
  British perceptions of 45–7, 49–50, 51, 66–72
Strachey, John 115
Suez military complex 4, 37, 56
Suez Canal 37, 44, 56, 88, 90, 108, 122
Suez crisis 19, 36, 41, 82, 84, 88, 89–92, 93, 95, 96, 98, 99, 100, 101, 102, 104, 106, 108, 109, 110, 114, 115, 116, 117, 118, 119, 120, 121, 124, 129, 147, 158, 163, 179, 181, 183, 184, 185, 186, 187
Suez rebels 94
Supplemental White Paper on Defence (1967), *see* Defence White Papers, 1967, Supplemental
Sweden 111
Switzerland 111

Tanganyika 56
Taylor, Peter 43
Thompson, William R. 7
Thomson, Sir George 147–8, 171

Thorneycroft, Peter 93, 96, 106, 125
Thornton, A.P. 121
Transport and General Workers Union 64, 151
Transport House 77
Treasury, HM 48, 62, 109, 110, 111–13, 115, 116, 144, 146, 166, 169, 174, 184
Trincomalee naval station 4, 117, 120
Truman, Harry S. 47, 48, 50, 83
Truman Doctrine 83
Turkey 46, 52, 79

United Nations 19, 66, 67, 68, 71, 79, 90, 91, 191
United States 8, 9, 14, 19, 21, 36, 50, 56, 66, 70, 75, 90, 96, 103, 110, 112, 114–15, 118, 125, 128, 133, 136, 138, 139, 141, 146, 153, 160, 164
  and Eisenhower Doctrine 104–5
  and special relationship with Britain 29–30, 47–9, 50, 76, 82, 84, 91, 95, 99–100, 113, 152
  post-1945 overseas military role 2, 7, 47, 104–6, 116, 192
  pressure on Britain to remain east of Suez 108, 147–9, 150, 156–7, 172–3, 180–1
  State Department 79, 105

Vietnam conflict 146, 147, 148, 156, 158, 160, 173, 181
Vital, David 23

Walker, Patrick Gordon 82, 137, 155, 157, 160, 161, 182, 188
Wallace, William 27, 115
Warbey, William 155
Waterhouse, Charles 94
Watkinson, Harold 107, 125
Watt, D.C. 36
Whitehall 12, 32, 33, 41, 44, 51, 54, 55, 67, 71, 84, 86, 87, 89, 101, 105, 108, 110, 115, 116, 122, 123, 157, 171, 183, 184, 185, 186
Wilkinson, Ellen 82

Index

Willson, F.M.G. 126
Wilson, General Sir Harry 8
Wilson, Harold 108, 119, 136, 145, 179, 183, 188
  and Anglo-American relations 148–9, 150, 152, 172–3
  and Cabinet government 137–9, 142–4, 165–9, 169–71, 172
  and 'crown princes' 143–4, 154, 166–8, 180
  and defense of sterling 28, 138, 144, 148, 152, 163–4
  and devaluation 28, 162–5
  and declining political capital 153, 165, 168, 169–70
  and European integration 154–6, 177
  and Parliamentary Labour Party 77, 144, 182
  and popularity 151, 153, 162
  and support for east of Suez role 137–40, 142, 144, 149, 152, 156, 157, 161
  see also Labour government(s) 1964–70
winning coalition
  defined 22
  see also East of Suez winning coalition

Yalta agreements 46
Yew, Lee Kuan 122, 158, 172
Younger, Kenneth 72

Zuk, Gary 7